COURAGE
ON THE JOURNEY OF HAPPINESS

12
Challenges
of Leaving the Comfort Zone
and Creating a Happy Life

ANITA FREIMANN, PhD

THE INSTITUTE
OF HAPPINESS

Osijek, 2020.

Title: Courage on the Journey of Happiness:
        12 Challenges of Leaving the Comfort Zone
        and Creating a Happy Life

Author: Anita Freimann

Editor: Anita Freimann

Translated from Croatian by Ksenija Vujčić

Copyeditor: Gabriela Kuštro

Cover photo: Igor Kelčec

Graphic Design, Prepress and Cover: Tihomir Ravlić

Published by: tredition GmbH
            Halenreie 40-44
            22359 Hamburg

To my dear son Matej,

who gave me his soul to write this book

TABLE OF CONTENTS

Introduction and Instructions for the Journey

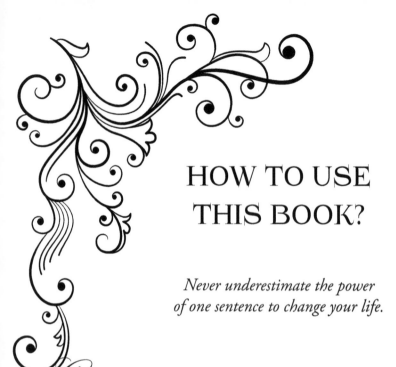

HOW TO USE
THIS BOOK?

*Never underestimate the power
of one sentence to change your life.*

*Courage on the Journey of Happiness: 12 Challenges of Leaving the
Comfort Zone and Creating a Happy Life* is conceived as a book that will
not discourage you by its' volume at first sight, but that can always be
at hand to help you face life's challenges. I would recommend that you
initially read the book one chapter at a time, and later you can go back
to the parts you are interested in. Some of the 12 challenges I deal with
in the book might already be behind you, some might be your current
issues, and others might yet emerge once you leave the comfort zone.
Other challenges might be reactivated as time goes by. This book does
not hold within "the recipe for happiness" that can quickly and effort-
lessly teach you how to be happy (because that is impossible), but what
it can do, is show you my path of happiness where you might find simi-
larities. In the end, the new knowledge and understanding might make
it easier for you to overcome certain challenges and create the life you
want to live.

The book contains numerous and various references (e.g. further reading recommendations, articles/books, video contents etc.). Even though
technology has its good and bad sides (and I will come to that later),
in this book I decided to use its advantages and equip the book with
interactive characteristics. All sources of information I used and that I
will refer to will namely be accessible in the margins in the form of QR

(Quick Response) codes, i.e. small icons containing pieces of information. For every external link a QR code was created; in the text you will find this marking ▣ meaning that the content is accessible via the QR code in the margins. The QR codes are consecutively numbered. If you own a smartphone with a camera and internet access, you just need to install an application for scanning and reading QR codes. Any application you choose will do the trick of decoding the two-dimensional code, so the choice of the app is really a matter of your preferences (there are many free ones). Simply run the app on your phone (or tablet) and scan the chosen QR code. The linked content will show immediately. Most QR code scanning applications will create a history of the links you opened and you will be able to keep everything in one place.

For all those who do not own a smartphone or are more inclined to read or watch the suggested content on the PC, at the end of each chapter there is a list of all sources mentioned together with the respective links. Given the speed at which contents on the World Wide Web are changing, it is better to have the contents accessible through different modes (if a topic at some point should no longer be accessible via the respective link, you will most likely be able to find it elsewhere by searching for the same title or keywords). Here are the symbols you will find at the end of each section entitled *Recommendations to inspire you on your journey of happiness*:

 video content

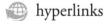 hyperlinks

 movies

books and articles

There you will find websites, YouTube channels, social media, books, articles and movies that helped me, inspired me and made my project of self-improvement possible, which led me to manifesting the life I want to live. The book mentions numerous persons who have had a great influence on my life, some of whom have become my friends in the process of growth. As you have probably noticed, the book does not have a formal acknowledgment at the beginning. This is because my acknowledgment goes to all people (and all the knowledge) that I mention in the book. To all of them who have really made an effort to make this world a better place for all of us, as well as those who have helped this book see the light of day. I simply felt the need to give back what they have given me and have done for me. I wanted to provide a quick access to concrete information and point you to verified and trusted people, who can help you, too (that does not mean that elsewhere in the world there are no other high quality people just as good in a certain field or line of work). I would also like to stress that of course there are similar contents to those I am sharing with you here, there are countless similar examples. In this book, however, you will find what helped me overcome the 12 challenges. Hence, here I mention those who have touched my life. You have the choice to follow that same path or find another one, or both.

I would warmly recommend that you watch some of the contents that attract you, or give you a certain *vibe*, because you never know where it can take you. Resolve to watch these contents, resolve to read, watch videos and keep educating yourself (regardless of your level of formal education), because the price of ignorance and dullness has always been and remains high. You must invest in yourself, because – as the saying (to some it is even a mantra for life) goes – you are either climbing or falling. Think about it, it really is true. If you come across something interesting that you consider worth sharing, let me know by e-mail (anita@myhappinessdoctor.com), via social media MyHappinessDoctor or using my website (here comes the first QR code and the opportunity to

QR 1

test how it works ▣ 1). The content that I find useful and meaningful might be included in some new editions of this book. ☺ Together we are stronger! Two heads are better than one - and many heads are even better. So, let us create synergistic effects together!

I have a priceless piece of advice for all of you who are reading this book, or books in general: take notes. I know this might seem trivial, if not banal, but I cannot emphasize enough the importance of doing it. For example, in order to write my thesis on happiness, I have read dozens of books that I found interesting, relevant and important. I would underline something in the text here and there (some books were borrowed so this was not an option), some I read on the computer and highlighted virtually, and most of them I read thinking *"this is so great, this is significant, this has relevance for life, I will definitely come back to this, once I've finished my thesis"*. Sounds familiar? By the end, having used over 300 sources for my thesis, for the most part I had forgotten what they said precisely or at the end of the process, I did not know where exactly to find a certain piece of information.

A few years ago, I have become aware of one (if not the only) way to effectively read books you wish to remember: taking your own notes (which you do not need if you have a photographic memory). The point is to underline parts in the book that are significant to you (especially if it's yours, your money - your book). But don't stop there! Take a notebook, a journal, an electronic notepad or something similar, that will serve as your book collection. Once you finish reading a book or a chapter (I prefer the first), go through the book again and write down notes in your notebook based on the underlined parts (some prefer taking notes while reading). I like taking notes by hand and editing them later, highlighting parts that are especially important to me. How many should there be? There are no rules. For some books you will need 3 lines, for others 30 pages. It all depends on what kind of a book you are reading, how useful it is to you, how deeply it has touched you and what meaning it carries for your future course of life. It also differs whether you are reading a book as a distraction, a reference book or one that you expect to change your life. In case of the latter, it is important to keep in mind, or keep written down, at least some crucial ideas, otherwise your reading efforts have been quite futile, because you will not witness the changes you wished for. That is why it is best to write it down. That way you will certainly remember it easier and learn faster. A Latin proverb says "Verba volant, scripta manent", i.e. literally "spoken words fly away, written words remain."

This technique of taking notes was not my invention (like most of the book content is not), which is why I suggest you check for yourself how the young popular millionaire Matt Morris reads books and benefits from it (◼ 2). The advantages of this kind of a reading strategy that includes highlighting and rewriting parts of the text that have significance to you, are multiple: in one of your "books" you will have many other books, you memorize the words that you write down much faster, and when you read the excerpts again, gradually the words become a part of you. You can always browse in your notebook and recall important passages. Several books later, you will have your own collection of knowledge, that you can be proud of, and that you can always carry with you. If necessary, you can always "ask" the original book "for help" (e. g. I write down a reminder like: "for more information about this and that check p. 44 in the book").

QR 2

Because of this piece of advice and this book reading technique, that has proved very effective and exactly right for me, I refrained from emphasizing certain sentences or parts by bold letters, italics or similar. Moreover, we are all tuned at a different wavelength, in different life's situations, having different experiences and quests. Sometimes certain things resonate with us more than others. What is important to one person might bear no meaning at all for another reader. Furthermore, what has a significance for us, changes as time goes by, so that after a while the same book/movie/video/song can convey (and often does) a completely different meaning, influence, sense and message. I remember a few books that my mom gave me, which I had found strange, incomprehensible, or uninteresting. Yet eventually, the day comes, when a book gains a completely new meaning for me and I wonder why it has been sitting on my shelf for 10 years. The time was simply not right for it. You, too, might find some of the concepts in the book strange, but this could change in a few months or after a year or several years (and it probably will). You will notice certain phrases or thoughts repeating in different chapters, which I did on purpose to help shape your path and remind you of the leitmotif, the central theme. So, grab your pen and smartphone, buckle up and we are really taking off. Where to? Beyond the comfort zone, where the magic of life happens and where true happiness resides.

Recommendations to inspire you on your journey of happiness ☺

- [▣ 2] How to Read a Book for Maximum Learning, Matt Morris:
  https://www.youtube.com/watch?v=_WCfaGarc4U

- [▣ 1] My Happiness Doctor Anita Freimann:
  https://myhappinessdoctor.com/

WHO ARE YOU AND WHAT'S IN HERE FOR YOU?

The mind is like a parachute – it only works when it is open.
Albert Einstein

Since you are reading this book, you are most likely one of the brave persons who have already stepped out of their certain comfort zone in active pursuit of happiness or you are ready to become that person very soon. In both cases you are on the right track and for that I commend you sincerely. Wise people said that every single journey begins with a first step. This book is supposed to serve you as a guide on the journey of happiness and help you overcome life's challenges that you encounter on the way. It is important to know and bear in mind the whole time that you are not alone on your journey of happiness and that you are by no means an isolated case (others might find you a little weird, but don't worry, that's a good sign ☺). All people were born with the desire to pursue happiness (more about that in the sections that follow). What I, as a happiness doctor (and having a PhD in happiness), can tell you, is that the emotional state of happiness really is achievable and that it is no utopia (regardless of what you've been taught and imposed to believe). My life and my story will testify to that, as will the stories and experiences of other people whom I will mention in the book. It is my hope that everything you read here and go on to research using this book will change your life at least a little bit, and encourage and motivate you to ask questions and keep questioning.

The fact that we really are the architects of our own fortune and that no matter how hard we tried true happiness can never ever be found in external circumstances might appear demotivating. But, since in the eyes of optimists the glass is always half full, this is a positive thing, I believe, because that actually means that we ourselves can (and must) create the life we consider worth living. Eureka! The challenging part for all of us is that sometimes, or often, we cannot remain indifferent to external circumstances. Instead, we mostly allow those circumstances to somehow grab hold of us and shape our lives, lives that we keep living out of habit. This mechanism keeps spinning in circles dragging us down deeper and deeper like a water vortex or quicksand.

But, my dear ones, there is a way out of this vicious circle regardless of your current age or state. What counts is that you are ready to change and willing to fill your years with life instead of just passively collecting and counting the years as they go by (restricted by the belief that change is not possible). Just remember that if only one person managed to succeed, that means you can too – maybe even better. If many others managed to exceed themselves, if I could, then you can too. I have also sought the help of others. This book came into being as a way to express my gratitude to precisely those people. Without those others (though we are all in a way actually one), I would not have succeeded, or at least not so quickly. We can all use some wind beneath our wings. Therefore, in this book you will find a handful of different examples, concepts and pieces of information that I have tested myself (people say one should not give advice to those who do not ask for it, but since you are holding the book in your hands – you have asked ☺). The book will describe my journey of happiness and make it possible for you, too, to embark on the journey of happiness in your life. Happiness really is a journey, not the goal or destination, as today's consumer society repeatedly keeps telling us. To begin with, it is important to express a clear intent and desire to improve, to tell yourself that you can do it and bravely move forward, one step at a time.

Do you know how many people reside within the comfort zone and do not want to admit it to themselves? How many people just rush, haste, do things out of habit, just so as not to stop and become aware of their actions? How many never pause to ask themselves a personal question, to question their choices and the meaning of life, to ask themselves if they are happy? I like to say that it takes a lot of courage to pause and look into the mirror, to honestly observe that reflection. If you defeat the "enemy" you see in the mirror, you have defeated all enemies (we could also ask ourselves who is the one looking at the mirror and who is the one truly seeing). If you cannot imagine how many people among us are like that (according to research results as much as 98%), take my word for it, because I work with them: they are numerous (of all ages, all kinds of professions, and yes, even materially wealthy ones are among them). In fact, there are many more people like those (for now), than there are people who are willing to make a change in life, finally taking their life into their own hands. Luckily, for the optimists among us, things are slowly but surely beginning to change, and on the whole, this process of transformation of the collective consciousness occurs at great speed. Therefore, be proud of yourself and keep in mind that you can live a happy life that is not just a myth or the last frame in a movie, the happy continuation of which directors leave open for you to imagine (as in "…And they lived happily ever after"), while you know such fortune can only happen on film. It is possible in real life too, I assure you! We have just been taught differently (and if we hear something frequently enough, after a while that becomes our truth, because the thoughts eventually shape our life).

In order to succeed in being happy, you need to break free from certain knowledge and understandings you have so far considered true. You will have to accept that in this book you will encounter numerous data and pieces of information that could seem odd, trivial, impossible, illogical, or that might appear like small revelations. These moments I call "Aha!", referring to the well-known Aha! moment or eureka effect which denotes a flash of instant knowledge or sudden understanding of information and/or contents of previously incomprehensible concepts. That is why it is necessary to open your mind while reading this book and prepare to experience the Aha! moments of inspiration that will give you better insight into a certain situation, enable you to look behind the scenes and widen your horizons.

Before writing this book, I promised myself not to censor any information, because that would be cheating and cheating both you and me is simply not an option. I would rather write down everything I feel is necessary and let you choose what is true for you and what is not, what you believe in and what you doubt. But before you judge – question and examine everything that has been written, "google" it, investigate, search, compare, seek and then draw conclusions: decide what is useless, what is not. Do not allow yourselves to be turned into sheeple (i.e. the sheep people). Don't be naïve, always doing and believing what you are told without using your brains and common sense. You could of course find all the information yourself, but it is wiser to learn from the experience and mistakes of others, because there is not enough time in life to experience everything yourself (even though in my reality there are no mistakes, only lessons from which we learn. I shall however call them mistakes, because that's the word we've been taught). In the book you will find a lot of content that you can look into in more detail according to your affinities. So, make use of my inquiring mind and learn from my experiences. Simply see this as an opportunity, because you are in a better starting position and you are more likely to come to certain knowledge faster and easier. That knowledge in turn will steer you on your road of happiness and unlock the possibilities of taking some new turns.

All people are facing challenges, day in, day out; nobody is an exception. As a professor at the Faculty of Economics I often tell my students how differently their peers behave after failing an exam: some smile, say "thank you" and go on about their business, while others cry over their faith (starting in my office already) for days or even weeks. This shows that everything is a matter of perception. There is a quote written on my bedroom wall, that I start every day with: "It's not what happens to you, but how you react to it that matters" (Epictetus). People say God will never give you more than you can handle. But remember, it is not that burden that breaks you, but the way you are carrying it. With this book, I will try to help you carry the burden. I will show you methods and ways of handling the load easier, or even how to be grateful for it (with a smile on your face nonetheless ☺).

Life's challenges are present and will not go away nor disappear if you ignore them and sweep them under the carpet. On the contrary, it even gets worse: often they grow when ignored until they completely consume you. The one you ignore grows and the one you face vanishes. The only right choice is to face everything life brings. For that reason, this book contains 12 most common challenges that we encounter when attempting to make changes (I mean the big life changes, incisions). They are divided into three areas: a healthy and cheerful spirit (life in the present moment), a healthy and serene mind (love for oneself and others) and a healthy and powerful body (love for oneself). Maybe not all 12 challenges described here will apply to your situation (all the better for you), and if they do not, you will see that they are not impossible to beat or at least reduce to a normal level (by the way, to live in peace in spite of a challenge is not the same as ignoring it). Some people may be challenged in only one of the three areas, but that challenge might appear so huge from their perspective that the burden they are carrying weighs much more, than that of a person challenged in multiple areas, but handling it better.

This book is for you if: you do not have enough time for yourself or none at all (or if that is presently your belief), if you wish to learn methods of deep relaxation and find out why that matters, if you are constantly waiting to become happy, if you are facing challenges with your family of origin (here I primarily mean with your parents), if you are challenged as a parent, if you have various challenging situations at work (work that you like or maybe not), if you have friends who are actually not your friends at all (and nobody is saying it out loud), if you have challenging relationships (girlfriend/boyfriend, wife/husband and all other combinations), if you weigh too much, or not enough, or if you are not entirely satisfied with your looks, not satisfied with your diet (or maybe you are but diseases are troubling you), if you wish to laugh more (out loud, heartily) and if you feel that life is more than what you are currently witnessing.

The concepts in this book do not stand for any *new age* movement, doctrine or anything similar. I am not trying to talk you into anything,

I am not selling anything, I do not wish to prove anything, I do not (re)present a political agenda, nor do you have to accept my way of thinking. With this book I intend to try and help those who are ready by presenting the understandings I have reached so far. I want to try to support those who are prepared to actually play the game of life. I wish to point you to some new or at least different considerations, present some new possibilities for you to reflect. Think of this book as a table laid out with lots of different food: it is up to you to decide whether you will try it, which one and how much of it. Surely you can at least have a look at what has been prepared, see what is there on the table. I wanted to share with you everything that has inspired me and brought me to the fullness of life that I am living and enjoying today.

The point is not to finish reading the book as soon as possible (since we have already established that happiness is a journey). Consider this book a sort of a guide and source of materials that can help you achieve the desired changes and find what you are looking for. When I was talking to a friend about me writing the book, he told me: "Just, please, don't write another book about somebody looking for peace, happiness and truth, then travelling the whole world just to come home and realize it can all be found within oneself. Enough of such books already!" That comment made me laugh. Of course, this will be no such book, because we already know – without having to travel – that everything really lies within ourselves, because happiness cannot be found elsewhere. ☺ To sum up, for starters, it is important that you accept happiness as your possible and desired state of mind that needs working on. You need to accept that on the journey of happiness you will encounter many challenges and that you should be open-minded about accepting "new" ideas and concepts (most of which have existed for ages, only nobody taught us or that was never in focus). Furthermore, you should – which is always the harder part – keep an open mind about correcting the beliefs you have been taught, which do not contribute to your growth as they should. Make the decision and start believing that it is possible to live differently.

WHO AM I AND WHY DID THIS BOOK COME INTO EXISTENCE?

It is not because things are difficult that we do not dare;
it is because we do not dare that they are difficult.
Seneca

When somebody gives me advice on a certain issue, the first thing I want to know is who that person is, so I check them (do they have experience, do I trust them etc.). Then I think about their competencies in the field they are providing the advice on. I think that the person consulting you is supposed to testify to the truth of the advice with the own life and example. For instance, I would not want to take advice on work from a person who is chronically unhappy with their work (if the advice was any good, they could probably solve their own situation first). It is wise to seek advice, but beware of those who give advice without having experience of their own. Would you really hire an overweight personal trainer? Do you want your diet to be prescribed by an ill nutritionist? Would you want your life coach to be grave, depressed and lacking interest? Having a "teacher" is important, but it is even more important to verify how good the teacher masters the teaching content. The outward appearance, a general notion of authority, oratorical skills or an excellent attitude are not necessarily criteria to be guided by. Think for yourself!

Since this book is quite likely to unsettle your assumptions of many issues and since it is offering advice on many areas of life, I think it is only fair and polite to shortly introduce myself. I have already told you that I have myself been through all the challenges laid out here, so talking about each challenge, I will be talking about myself, because the best and only way I can relate to you is from my personal experience. At the same time that is a method for my own growth and a way to raise my vibrations, because it is the rule of the universal law that by doing good for others, it comes back to me tenfold. If you are interested in my standard (professional) CV, have a quick glance at this QR code (■ 3). I was born in Osijek (Croatia, Europe) in 1983. I had a really happy childhood, many friends in my street (back in the days when children used to play catch, hide and seek, dodgeball and other games outside), an extraordinary family (I lived with my parents, grandparents and sometimes also my aunt) that always made sure I did not miss a thing. Moreover, my birthday parties were always different and special (as we like to recall even today); my parents took efforts to organize theme parties, prepare lots of special foods and cakes... they would do their best to succeed in all of this, for which I am infinitely grateful. I often heard my friends saying they wished they had parents like mine - joyful, kind, open-minded, always kidding and laughing, ready to listen - and that always made me proud. Everything we had, my parents built themselves with their own hands.

I was and have remained an only child. My parents wanted more children, but my mother's accident - she fell and broke her spine - resulted in her temporary disability that prolonged everything and in the end made it impossible. Those who know me, say that I am not conceited, being an only child, and I believe that credit goes to my parents and their reasonable upbringing, but also to the fact that I was always surrounded by friends, had a big clique, shared everything and was happiest with my peers around me. My grandmother, now 89 years old, also played a big role by taking care of me when my parents worked and infusing me with love for flowers (plants in general) and music.

In primary school I was an excellent student and always graduated with honors (I remember those class photos where I would sit upright with a red or pink ribbon in my hair). I sang in the school choir, sang and read at children's church services, participated in different extracurricular activities... I even founded a club in school, called the "Little Greenies", with an ecological agenda. In short, I was a cheerful child, interested in life, often ahead of my time. The only misfortune was that I was frequently ill (if somebody only sneezed with me around, I would end up with a tonsillitis for two weeks, a fever of 40 degrees Celsius and fainting). Cold sores were also a common occurrence.

Things went on in a similar fashion in high school with many activities, like singing, modelling for hairdressers at international contests, modelling at fashion shows, travelling the world, falling in love for the first time, organizing different social events... I often tutored others at home (I have obviously always loved the teaching profession). After graduating from grammar school, like most fellow students, I did not quite know what to do next (there were different ideas, from becoming a beautician to studying to be a dentist), but since I liked mathematics very much (I was the only one in my generation to write a graduation paper in maths), I took up mathematics and computer science studies. At that time I also found economics attractive – in a strange kind of way (destiny, probably), so I also enrolled in the Faculty of Economics as a part time study, on the side, so to speak. At the department of mathematics, which had been my first choice, the pace was crazy and the teaching style did not suit me at all, so I started taking lectures at the Faculty of Economics at the same time. There we were first welcomed by an English professor, with whom I instantly felt a positive vibe because of her irresistible simplicity and friendliness (She said something like "Hello! You are probably feeling quite confused right now, are you? So I am going to explain to you nice and simple how this all works."). That warmth radiating from her and her kind words of welcome had such a strong impression on me that I soon decided to study only economics. Besides, it was extremely stressful (and at times physically impossible) having to be at two locations at the same time; plus the professors were not really thrilled by my idea to acknowledge similar exams taken at another faculty. Though the following was to be read a few lines above, I will repeat it nonetheless: Never underestimate the power of one sentence to change your life. Years later, already as her colleague at the Faculty of Economics, I told that English professor about my experience of that situation and she was very glad to hear that, so now she often likes to tell that story of mine/ours. That is how life always steers you in the right direction, where you are supposed to be. What was that saying again? Man plans, God laughs (because God sees the whole picture, not only the small fraction that is visible to us). ☺

I graduated from the faculty within the designated time frame and one year after graduation I got employed there, which was my big wish because I have always felt that working with people is my vocation. And so, with 23 years of age I stepped into adult life. At the postgraduate studies I met my husband (then my future husband, now my ex) and two years full of work, fun and travels followed. We soon started living together; at that time I was finishing my master thesis and took up doctoral studies deciding to write a PhD thesis about happiness, that is about the economics of happiness (you probably haven't heard about that, but it really does exist), because I have always found happiness intriguing. While doing research for my thesis on happiness I started devouring books on positive psychology, so somewhere along the way I drove myself literally crazy with happiness. It had become my obsession. At that time I would interrogate all my friends and acquaintances: "Are you happy? On a scale from 1 to 5, how happy are you?" I spent every free moment studying happiness. Of course life itself was arranging circumstances for me back then and was sending certain people my way to serve as signposts on the road.

For instance, I remember one seminar that took place in 2010. It was entitled "The Positive Community" and held by a professor of positive psychology. She told us about happy people, about our goals, showed us different exercises, we filled out a questionnaire. It was a wonderful and inspiring day. I was fascinated by her as a person because she was so cheerful, smiling the whole day, in spite of some private problems (or challenges) that had occurred just at that time. She was absolutely present in the moment, which for me at that time seemed mission impossible. I talked to her in the break and within a few sentences she had really given me amazing support for writing my thesis on the economics of happiness. She was a signpost on the road that I needed at that time.

In the course of 2010 I did not feel very well. I felt pressured from all sides: be good at work, be a good girlfriend, be a good daughter, a good friend, people constantly asking "when will you get married and have children?" I felt scattered doing a lot at once, and me being a perfectionist by nature made it even more difficult. In short, I was constantly trying to make others happy while putting myself not only second, but at some position far behind, which in the end proved not that wise a strategy. Ironically, while I was struggling to make others around me happy, they would be complaining that I was always so self-centered (!?). Naturally, I felt even worse about that, so I kept spinning in a vicious circle of an unexplainable feeling of dissatisfaction that in the end culminated in the diagnosis CIN 1 and HPV, then CIN 2. Though most women probably know, here is the explanation for the male readers - these are premalignant cervical lesions, precancerous changes to the cervix. The main cause of this disease is stress. What I did not know back then, was that every disease of the body is in fact a disease of the mind and the body's cry for change.

I used to wake up in the morning without a drive for life, not even the will to get out of bed, because nothing made sense. These were probably some half-depressive states of mind given to me, so I could think about myself. And this was happening at a time when I was studying happiness! Whenever I would talk to my friends about this, it would appear as if I was making things up, and that anyhow everybody has their own problems (which to them seemed the biggest). I talked to my then partner (thank you, Damir ☺) and he understood some parts of what I was saying, but he did not burn with desire and the need for change as I did. I also talked to my parents (mostly to my mom), but it was really hard for me to explain what it was that was troubling me, and it was even more difficult for her trying to follow and understand. I need to pay tribute to my mother here, because as far as my memory reaches, we would always talk a lot and solve everything through dialogue. At one occasion, when I had explained to her in detail how I felt and thought, she told me I should be grateful for having such a wonderful family, full support, the job I wanted, a puppy that adores me, many friends, enough money, a car, an apartment, the person I live with and who supports me, travels every now and then, the PhD thesis I was writing, and so forth. The conclusion was that I was looking for better bread than is made of wheat: what would others only give to be in my place! You might even agree with that right now, but just try to understand that I did not feel satisfied with that situation. Though my mind was also telling me "It's true! You have all that. Stop fantasizing, you might invite trouble!", I felt that life must be something more, that I missed something, that something was not complete (though I did not diminish the value of all that I had and though I felt grateful for it all). Today I know that this was all a preparation for finally leaving the comfort zone (only back then I did not know that).

Eventually I succumbed to the general world-view that unremittingly crushes from all sides. I decided to stay in the comfort zone, attempted to sweep it all under the carpet and live like everybody else. I tried accepting that it was all just a phase, eat humble pie and continue like all other normal people. A wedding followed (more about partnerships in challenge no. 8) without special ceremonies. Everything was going according to my master plan. All that time I still had those same unsettling thoughts in my head, but I ignored them consciously and on purpose. People who know me, tell me today that they could not imagine what was going on behind my façade, because on the outside I always appeared happy. Today, I refer to that part of my life as *the theatre* because that's precisely what it was. Only when the curtain closes and you are left alone (eventually) do you realize that you are cheating on yourself. I was awarded the doctor's degree in economics on the topic of happiness in 2012. Shortly after that I became pregnant, my son Matej came into the world and one and a half months later my life started turning upside down. If in that September of 2013 somebody had told me what was awaiting me in the future and what challenges I will have to face, I would not have believed it. Luckily for mankind, we never know what the next day brings so we live hour by hour, day by day (and on the path of happiness we mostly live in the present moment, which is the most difficult, but at the same time the best way).

What happened? I decided that I was done sweeping things under the carpet and that I needed to literally step out of the comfort zone (regarding this topic, take a look at this short video by the excellent Steve Harvey ■ 4). At that period I reached most of the discoveries that were revolutionary for me and that I believe can help you, too. The messages and ideas from all those books and videos on happiness that I had read and seen were still spinning in my subconscious mind and now the time was ripe. I built up the courage to face the reflection in the mirror and get to grips with challenges. I finally realized that the following set phrase was true, or rather that it is not an empty phrase at all: If you want to change others, change yourself. Now, looking from this viewpoint, I can say that those years of my life were the happiest; that is when I changed myself from the roots (do not think it was easy). I will not tell you right now what those changes are, because that would diminish the allurement of the book and of the challenges; suffice it to say, that I refer to everything before as the old life, and everything after the new life and the new me.

QR 4

Today I live happier than ever and it shows on the outside. Not a day goes by that somebody does not tell me how different I look compared to before, or asks me what I did on myself. People comment how fresh I look, or that I seem really happy and that I am somehow "glowing". In the drab world we are living in, it shows instantly when a person is satisfied and smiling, which is why people often ask me about the magic formula. After numerous appearances in the media on the topic of happiness, after workshops and seminars I held, more and more people would come up to me asking different questions and seeking advice. In general, I try to have a positive effect on the young people in my lectures at the university, I wish to prompt them to act, to give them wings, encourage them, motivate by my example. Their numerous comments confirm that I also succeed in doing so. So little by little, the number of people whom I have helped became quite significant, and every single one of them told me I needed to systematize and expand this in some way. Now that I have finally arranged my life the way I want it, when I am daily manifesting that which serves for my highest good, when I am living happily, have overcome (or am controlling) all 12 challenges, I myself feel the need to expand it all, to help a larger number of people (who are ready) to be happy and joyful. That is how the idea of this book and of the project *My Happiness Doctor* was born.

Even though writing (academic writing, however) is an integral part of my job as a professor, this book has special emotional and spiritual value for me, and if it helps at least some of you, its purpose will be fulfilled. I know and I feel that precisely that is my calling: to share the collected knowledge and happiness with others. Finally, it is said that knowledge and love are the only things that multiply when divided. By my example and with my knowledge I wish to motivate you, too - of course only the ones among you who are ready and who will allow it. ☺ I do not expect everybody to like this book; that is impossible anyhow, because there are always those who do not like something, who are against something (even if for no real reason) and who have the need (and time) to share their attitudes with others. But I know, that when somebody comments on others, they are actually primarily talking about themselves. That does not make me halt on my path and I do not mind the barking dogs. Remember: every single attack is in fact a cry for help. So, when somebody attacks you, try not to engage, not to react but to send them love. On the other hand, there are many others who willingly accept the concepts mentioned in the book, who seek advice and help from me, search for solutions, ask questions, use methods, read, or engage in what we call "the mini-challenges". The inspiration for my work as *the Happiness Doctor* are precisely those people I have helped so far. The feeling that, because of me, somebody's life got at least a little better and happier, is invaluable to me and it is my highest motivation. Now that you know what is offered in this book (and you probably already feel/know why it came to you), what it will be about, what it is like reading it, who I am and why the book came into existence, it is time to tackle the challenges and the comfort zone. 3, 2, 1, go.

Recommendations to inspire you on your journey of happiness ☺

- [QR 3] CV, Anita Freimann:
  http://www.efos.unios.hr/afrajman/en/curriculum-vitae/

- [QR 4] You Gotta Jump To Be Successful!, Steve Harvey:
  https://www.youtube.com/watch?v=-PdjNJz7B1Q

HAPPINESS

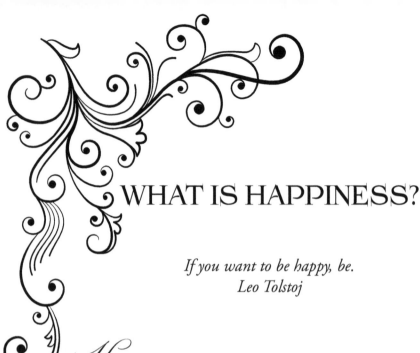

WHAT IS HAPPINESS?

If you want to be happy, be.
Leo Tolstoj

Happiness is an emotion we have deemed positive. Every person wants to be happy. Dalai Lama said that happiness is the goal in life. Indeed, happiness has been intriguing philosophers from antiquity and many books have been written about it, as it has never stopped and will never stop being priority topic. You can look at it from various sides: philosophical, religious, sociological, medicinal, psychological, artistic, economical etc. In recent decades, we have also seen rapid development of positive psychology, with happiness in its center (many years, the thing is, psychology has been researching only negative conditions and phenomena). As a result, many people, more or less known, have joined the path of happiness, and all of them have the same goal: to reach happiness, to discover the formula for happiness, to calculate happiness quotient etc. In 2012 United Nations have declared the 20th of March as the International Day of Happiness, and that was the exact date I chose for the first promotion of this book in 2017.

For me, what is most fascinating about happiness is this: although the wish to be happy is inherent to us, very few people ask themselves sincerely are they happy and what they can do about it. When we link all that with the story of comfort zone, it is clear how easy people lull themselves in everyday life without caring about how they feel. Consequently, their life just unfolds automatically. You can't imagine how many times I have heard something like this about myself: *don't mind her, she deals with happiness, she must have lots of time on her hands to be thinking about happiness; look how much actual work I have, where would I be if I read positive psychology books (often called self-help hand-books) and think about my happiness.* When I got divorced, there were particularly lovable comments: look at her – *she talks about happiness and she is divorced all the same.* Such comments really make me laugh. I am divorced precisely because I deal with happiness, but some people refuse to understand that. Why? Because they don't want to admit to themselves how they feel and whether they are happy. That is the step I have already mentioned: we should look ourselves in the mirror and face the truth. Not only that thinking about happiness isn't stupid, but it is necessary and serious for every one of us. Especially in today's world of 3in1, when more and more different forces hold us in comfort and fear zone with gravity strong grip.

Therefore, now is the time to look yourselves in the mirror (if you haven't already done that), and ask: am I happy? Do I live a life worth living? Do I look the way I want to? Do I feel great? Do I have energy, am I full of zest? What is the quality of my relationship with my family and surroundings? Am I eating healthily? Am I healthy? Do I feel purpose in life? Am I doing what I want? Am I laughing often enough? Are there any missed chances that I regret now? For parents among you: am I satisfied with the relationship I have with my child, or children?

Mini challenge:

Stop reading for a while. Answer these questions honestly, to yourselves.

If the answer is yes, put the book down. I congratulate you sincerely for you are already in the zone of magic in all segments of life and thank you for reading (you can give the book to someone ☺). If all answers, or some of them, are negative, keep on reading.

Mini challenge

What are your first thoughts when you say happiness? Try to answer this question without harassing your brain – just say out loud the first thing that pops in your mind when you hear the word happiness.

Throughout the world people link happiness mostly with health, family, money, love, freedom, weather conditions, success, holiday, friends… I suppose you aren't far from that either, because, according to the scientific studies, it is quite universal. Most of us think that happiness has everything to do with being healthy. It's only logical. There is a saying that healthy person has thousand wishes, but a sick one only has one – to get well. And yet, people on the "Titanic" may have had the health, but they lacked luck. ☺ Seriously, it isn't always black and white, but the fact is that today we spend health to gain money and then spend money to gain health. This is a paradox indeed.

Mini challenge

Are you spending your health to gain money? If the answer is yes, does it have to be like that? What can you do to preserve your health?

If happiness equaled health, every healthy person would be completely happy, and every sick person would be unhappy. However… It's not uncommon for people who have survived serious illness to say that their illness is actually a blessing as it has changed their life completely. The same applies to people with certain physical disabilities. Somewhat extreme example for that is Nick Vujičić, who says he is happy and he loves living even though he doesn't have arms and legs. Take a look at his speech, please (▣ 5). What do you think now? Are you speechless and on the verge of crying, as I was the first time I saw him? Naturally, everything depends on our perception, again (the same as with those students and their reactions to failing the exam). Life happiness depends less on what is going on, and more on the way you

QR 5

accept that. Honest truth. You have it the way you make it and the way you see it.

Furthermore, if happiness equaled money, wealthy people wouldn't be unhappy and they wouldn't seek happiness in all the wrong places. Famous and rich people often go to extremes trying to find happiness (e.g. Jimi Hendrix, Marilyn Monroe, Jim Morrison, Amy Winehouse, Janis Joplin, Michael Jackson, Anna Nicole Smith, Elvis Presley, Whitney Houston…). The list goes on; hundreds of celebrities died from overdose, and that's just one of the causes for their tragic destinies. Happiness, therefore, isn't equal to fame or money. Money makes everything easier, of course, but once you have your existential needs covered, additional money increase doesn't add to your happiness. If one could buy happiness, they would probably buy a size too large. There is something to it – to our vanity. We'll talk about money issue in chapter dedicated to job as a calling in challenge 10.

Be that as it may, we can conclude that every individual has his/her own definition of happiness (although the sense of its full realization is universal) which depends on perspective and life experience. The good news is scientists discovered that happiness is 50% influenced by genes, 10% by circumstances and 40% by decisions we make. That's very good; it means that our chances are as much as 40%. And if we take into consideration that life is 10% of what's going on (actual circumstances) and 90% of how we perceive it or react to it – the percentage could be even greater. Hence, happiness is in our hands. I believe that happiness shouldn't be sought after, and that the endeavor is pointless; happiness is always NOW. What makes it challenging is that our minds are "polluted" and we cannot comprehend it.

Analyzing happiness, I mustn't forget something I call the evolution of happiness. Let's ask ourselves has the notion of happiness evolved over time? Are the "things" and values that make modern people happy the same as the "things" and values from 200 years ago, or 1000 years ago, or BC? What do you give your children for birthdays or holidays? Our parents were happy with walnuts on Christmas tree, as you surely know (some of you may even witnessed to that). Not to mention those born between WWI and WWII. Everything was new – both radio and TV, which you could find in only one house per street (if at all). Today TV is often part of every room in house. My intention was to help you become aware of how fast we live today, how deeply the technology has robbed us and how we have become robots too (mind that some people already had chips build in their bodies). With every possible mitigating circumstance most of us live with (apartments/houses, washing machines, appliances of all sorts, cars, mobile phones, computers, TV sets…), the only logical conclusion would be that people today are much happier than previous generations. And you know what? It isn't so.

One of the fastest growing industries today is pharmaceutical industry, and one of the bestselling products are antidepressants. Thus, depression has become one of the most widespread modern illnesses. This means that something truly doesn't add up in equation of happiness; we have the things generations before us couldn't even imagine, and we are unhappier than they were. What's the catch? Well, there are many catches, and when it comes to medicine, it makes me furious when someone calls herbal teas and preparations, and work with energy – alternative medicine. Let's ask ourselves, is today's medicine really modern, and is everything else alternative? What with and how did people treat illnesses before? With pills, injections, surgeries? There weren't doctors, medicines, or hospitals; there were only medicine men that cured with what the nature had provided. And if that was first/before, isn't all this now (from injections to pills and so forth) actually alternative? I am not against conventional medicine; I just don't think it's fair for something that is here forever to be called alternative, and something that is younger to be considered conventional, normal. I believe that conventional medicine treats the result rather than the cause of illness; alternative medicine, on the other hand, offers help through prevention, diagnostics and treatment, and it deals with causes. Today we have more than 200 alternative techniques, i.e. methods, including those that, in some countries, are recognized by the conventional medicine as well.

We want happiness, but we are not ready to work for it. We often live as if we will never die, and then we die as if we have never lived. People often think they would be better off if only they didn't have to work, if they had more free time, more money, if they lived in some other country, if they were younger… but those are just some of the myths related to happiness. Have you recognized yourselves in some of them? Those really are myths; not one of them will, therefore, make you happy in long term. In short term they might (it's called affective happiness), but in long term they aren't effective (cognitive happiness). Happiness is, in general, related to short term condition, i.e. it is a feeling of positive emotions; in long term we talk about life satisfaction (but in this book we talk about happiness, and we all know what we mean by that). It's the same with thinking like: *I will be happy when I get well, when I move to another apartment/house, when I find love, when I buy an apartment, sell my car, buy a dog, pass exam, get a job, get married, get kids, see my kids through school, get retired, go traveling, lose weight…* The list goes on. Achieving those goals won't make you completely happy; it can only be for the moment. One Croatian author said that he finds peculiar how little we need to be happy, and even more peculiar how often we miss exactly that little bit.

Have you ever tried to figure out what's on the other side of happiness? Misfortune? Renowned author Timothy Ferriss somewhat provocatively said that on the other side of happiness is boredom. I agree with him. Even though it sometimes seems that there is nothing going on, the fact is Earth rotates faster than 62,000 miles per hour, and nature changes constantly (from the seasons to phenomena such as photosynthesis), as are we humans (blood runs through our veins, we are changing, getting old). Happiness therefore surely isn't in doing nothing (which is impossible anyway). Every person who has, or has had a job probably knows about the holiday phenomenon: we can't wait for it to start, and after few days most of us feel bored. It's the same with life. Boredom lives in comfort zone.

I have already said that the key in life is to ask questions, and the question that initiates all human progress is "Why?" The difference between us and other mammals is that we are able to think and we have consciousness. According to Aristotle, the beginning of philosophy is question, expression of human curiosity about everything, attempt to create a meaning about life. Nick Vujičić, as you have seen in his video, asked three provocative questions as well: Who are you and what is your value? What is your purpose in life? What is your destiny after this life on Earth? Therefore, ask yourselves questions repeatedly, do it every day as it is the only way to steer your lives in wanted direction. The goal of this book is precisely to shake you a bit and make you think. And since we are taking about raising questions, maybe it's appropriate to finish this chapter with a questionnaire, about happiness of course. It is taken from the book by Croatian authors Dubravka Miljković and Majda Rijavec, and the explanations are based on the research by Martin Seligman and his book *Authentic Happiness*.

Mini challenge

Answer the questionnaire.

Read the following statements and answer how much they relate to you, on the scale 1 to 5.

    1 – It doesn't relate to me at all,
    2 – It mostly doesn't relate to me,
    3 – It somewhat relates to me,
    4 – It mostly relates to me,
    5 – It completely relates to me.

1. Whatever I do, time just flies. 1 2 3 4 5

2. My life has a higher purpose. 1 2 3 4 5

3. Life is too short for postponing pleasures it can give us. 1 2 3 4 5

4. I seek situations that challenge my skills and abilities. 1 2 3 4 5

5. When I choose what to do, I always consider whether it would benefit other people too. 1 2 3 4 5

6. Whether I am at work or I am having fun, I am usually very focused I am not aware of myself. 1 2 3 4 5

7. I am always very dedicated to whatever I do. 1 2 3 4 5

8. I am willing to do a lot in order to become euphoric. 1 2 3 4 5

9. While considering what to do next, I always make sure it is something that will completely occupy my mind. 1 2 3 4 5

10. While working, I am rarely distracted by the things around me. 1 2 3 4 5

11. It is my responsibility to make the world a better place. 1 2 3 4 5

12. My life has a permanent meaning. 1 2 3 4 5

13. While considering what to do next, I always make sure it is something pleasurable. 1 2 3 4 5

14. The work I do is important to the society I live in. 1 2 3 4 5

15. I agree with the statement *Life is short – eat the dessert first!* 1 2 3 4 5

16. I like doing things that arouse my senses. 1 2 3 4 5

17. I spend a lot of time thinking about the meaning of life and my role in the world. 1 2 3 4 5

18. The good life for me is the life full of pleasures and satisfaction. 1 2 3 4 5

Results: Write your answers (1-5) next to question numbers and add together at the end of each line.

Pleasant life: 3.____, 8.____, 13.____, 15.____, 16.____, 18.____= Sum ____

Good life: 1.____, 4.____, 6.____, 7.____, 9.____, 10.____= Sum ____

Meaningful life: 2.____, 5.____, 11.____, 12.____, 14.____, 17.____= Sum ____

In what line did you get the highest sum? Now you know which of the three paths to happiness you follow. Here is a short explanation. Pleasant life (the first line), just like the word itself, means that for your happiness is attained through earthly pleasures, and your goal is to have as many as you can (happiness = sum of pleasant moments). It is somewhat hedonistic and rather widespread view on happiness. However, satisfying desires isn't always positive (e.g. alcohol, drugs); think of the list of celebrities that died of overdose. In other words, although there is nothing wrong with pleasures, happiness isn't (exclusively) in indulging, i.e. satisfying desires won't bring you permanent happiness by itself.

Good (or engaged) life (second line) is life in which you use your abilities and skills daily and without a special goal, just for the fun of it. Psychologist Mihaly Csikszentmihalyi described an important phenomenon related to this – which he called flow. It's a state of ecstasy, i.e. complete focus on whatever you do and enjoy regardless of reward and benefits (as I have felt while writing this book ☺). Motivation for such activities is extremely positive feeling we get while engaging in those activities. What can cause flow? Lots of things, for example enjoying in: body (physical activities: walking, cycling, sport, yoga, sex...), thinking (brain teasers, learning to control mind – daydreaming), work (challenging!) and free time, solitude, but company as well. It's those situations when you do something and literally forget about time and physiological needs. It is important to mention that flow requires combination of high challenges and high skills, because when our skills and challenges are low, we are in a state of apathy (numbness, depression, indifference). Low skills and high challenges lead to anxiety (agitation, fear), and boredom is a result of low challenges and high skills. I recommend you to take a look at Csikszentmihalyi's book *Flow* and watch the video *Mihaly Csikszentmihalyi: Flow – The Secret to Happiness* (■ 6).

QR 6

Mini challenge

Think of activities which make you feel the flow, i.e. cause you to be completely in the moment and forget about time.

For those of you that had the biggest sum in the last line, let's explain meaningful life. You strive to contribute to something bigger than you, to love other people, to serve and help them. Such persons are Mother Theresa, Mahatma Gandhi etc. They believed they were here to become better and wiser so that mankind can evolve spiritually, to seek truth and knowledge (fight for truth), to contribute positively to society we live in and to spiritual evolution of mankind, and to leave the world a better place than it had been. I have found myself in this, which explains my need to type this book, to motivate and to transfer knowledge. In the end, it's not hard to see that good and meaningful lives bring the greatest amount of happiness, and that full life consists of all three paths.

We should keep in mind that happiness is never outside of us. I too had a hard time to understand and accept that, but that doesn't make it incorrect. That's exactly why I want to awake you to your challenges and to show you that they are not insurmountable. When there is a will, there is a way, and everything else is just an excuse.

We will complete this part with little more deliberation and your personal analysis.

Mini challenge

Write your answers, i.e. finish the sentences below. Do it honestly and without much thinking.

Life is ....

Wisdom is ....

Happiness is ....

Courage is ....

Persistence is ....

Love is ....

Freedom is ....

We will get back to these associations at the end of the book, where you will see my answers as well. In the next chapter I will present you the economics of happiness, the one that should have you citizens at its center of interest. Is it utopia?

⅋ Recommendations to inspire you on your journey of happiness ☺

- [QR 5] Nick Vujičić – Never give up:
    https://www.youtube.com/watch?v=Q6HnFuzSJdQ
- [QR 6] Mihaly Csikszentmihalyi: Flow, the secret to happiness
    https://www.youtube.com/watch?v=fXIeFJCqsPs

- Timothy Ferriss: The 4-Hour Workweek, 2011.
- Dubravka Miljkovic & Maja Rijavec: Tri puta do otoka sreće (Three roads to the happiness island), 2008.
- Martin Seligman: Authentic Happiness, 2002.
- Mihaly Csikszentmihalyi: Flow, 2006.

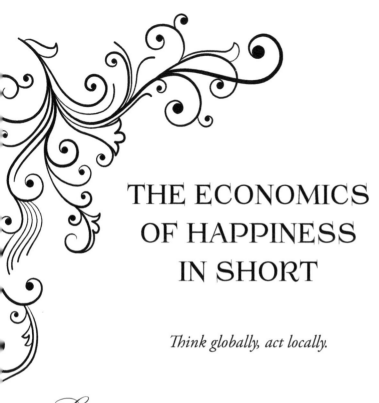

THE ECONOMICS
OF HAPPINESS
IN SHORT

Think globally, act locally.

Slowly, but firmly happiness is entering many sciences, including economics. I am very glad to have started researching happiness as nothing else could engage and fulfill me more. Even today, when I tell somebody what I do, they usually say (even my fellow economists, say, at some conference): "Ha-ha, seriously, what do you do?" Although the economics of happiness is officially present for about 40 years, it isn't generally accepted in every country.

Economics of happiness is not when you are being bombarded with offers of happiness in marketing purposes. If you buy this and that, you will be younger and happier; this will make you skinnier and happier, that will provide happy dreams; during happy hour in cafés and restaurants the prices are lower… Think about it and try to see what is behind all that's being marketed today. Happiness has been packed in every product and service, and it is precisely happiness that's selling them (on conscious or unconscious levels). And it's OK, there is nothing wrong with it (every commodity has its buyer; if they dupe us into buying something we don't need, it is our own fault), but it's wise to be aware of it and to try to read between the lines when it comes to marketing intrusions into our lives.

What the economics of happiness is all about, then? It has been discovered that, in a long term, economic growth (i.e. increase in ubiquitous GDP, which politicians emphasize, favor and lean on when leading and decision making) doesn't necessarily lead to increase in happiness, i.e. something called subjective well-being (OK, they are not the exact synonyms, but let's not complicate). It was Richard Easterlin who came to that conclusion back in 1974. He has formulated Easterlin Paradox, which states that individual happiness doesn't increase with the increase of income. And if everybody just runs to reach as high as possible GDP, and this economic growth means little or nothing to common people when it comes to happiness – why such an approach then? Even if life conditions are excellent, it's of little use if people didn't perceive them as such.

As an economic measure, GDP is extremely flawed and often misused. It can be increased by, say, fires, floods, wars, flu season etc. It seems unbelievable, doesn't it? Yes, but it's true. This materially oriented economics have led to (economic) crisis, (global) warming and dangerous destruction of natural and other resources – that's why recently there's more and more talk about circular economics, which relies on recycling, reuse, repair, and which is based in natural processes and nature without the waste as a category, where waste ends up being resource again. Numerous eminent economists and people have talked about it (including Amartya Sen, and even Nicolas Sarkozy, former president of France, for example), and lots of actions have been undertaken to change that and bypass GDP.

This GDP inefficiency in measuring well-being induced occurrence of hundreds alternative indicators for assessing state of society and progress. For example, there is a happy planet index, world happiness base, world book of happiness, gross national happiness, various prosperity and well-being indexes, and more. They are based on serious and methodologically strong studies aimed to discover what people of certain regions consider important when it comes to happiness, and how politics can help them lead happier, high-quality life. In other words, national and local governments have to lead country in such a way to enable increase of happiness for its citizens as much as possible. I know it sounds as utopia in some countries (e.g. in my Croatia). Some mayors in United States conduct research of their citizens' happiness/life quality once a year in order to present and disseminate results in brochures, and to create local politics together (at least to some point) based on the results. Citizens are mostly thrilled by the fact that someone (often for the first time) asks them how they feel and think, so this is a frequent political pre-elections toll for some. Well-being of people is exactly the thing politicians should be striving for, isn't it? Especially local ones.

Some of them went a step further. Bhutan, for example. Then young king of this small Himalayan country thought of a concept of gross national happiness, and introduced it to schools – making people's happiness a primary economic goal. Back then it was a new concept in world economic scene, but now more and more countries try to achieve the same. A lot has been done in Canada and United Kingdom. Bhutan, as well as United Arab Emirates, Venezuela, Ecuador and Madhya Pradesh (second largest state in India) have their departments of happiness (can't wait for one in Croatia as well) in order to implement various projects and ensure that policies don't disrupt the quality of living. The goal is, therefore, satisfaction of people, i.e. smile on people's faces. This has just reminded me of the fact that Thailand (the country near those pioneers of happiness promotion) has been promoting itself as a "land of (thousand) smiles".

It's a matter of time when studies of happiness and satisfaction will become a legal obligation. By then, we'll have to manage with the actions of scientists, proactive politicians and various organizations. Such organizations are especially active in promoting other dimension of economics of happiness – localization. One of them, Local Futures, led by Helena Norberg-Hodge has created the whole movement for promoting economics of happiness. The movie called *The Economics of Happiness*, which has received several awards, shows how globalization has brought us very little good, and how localization of economic actions (i.e. saw, eat, work, create, live locally) is the first essential step towards the economics of happiness. In addition, these organizations

QR 7

QR 8

have been implementing numerous projects in local communities around the world in order to make them self-sufficient as much as possible. I am not saying we should ban international trade completely; it is OK to import what you don't produce, but you should produce everything you can. Take a look at the website (■ 7) or watch a part of the movie very few people will find unmoving (■ 8).

Of course, life conditions are different in different places, and that has an effect on both cities' and countries' competitiveness. Hence we have all sorts of studies in order to rank cities by attractiveness, life quality, sustainability. For example, life in my hometown Osijek is quite different than life in Vienna, Austria (the city that is often at the top of the list of the most desirable cities) as the quality of life is almost incomparable. However, it's important to remember that moving to Vienna alone won't make you happy, maybe not even happier than you already are. There are numerous studies ranking countries by happiness, and one of the countries that are always at the top of the list is Denmark (with other Scandinavian countries). Director of Copenhagen Happiness Research Institute Meik Wiking said the reason for it is *hygge* (take a peek at his book about hygge, ■ 9). Be as it may, until your country launches general campaign for national (economics of) happiness, let us work on ourselves and happiness that lies within.

QR 9

❧ Recommendations to inspire you on your journey of happiness ☺

• [QR 8] The Economics of Happiness (abridged version):
https://www.youtube.com/watch?v=pyQaUDLW6ts&t=1s

• [QR 7] Local Futures: http://www.localfutures.org/

• [QR 9] Meik Wiking: The Little Book of Hygge: Danish Secrets to Happy Living, 2016.

LIFE JOURNEY

THE FAMOUS COMFORT ZONE

A ship in harbor is safe, but that is not what ships are built for.
John A. Shedd

You must have heard of the famous comfort zone, sometimes referred to as the zone of security, comfortableness, gratification. The comfort zone is a psychological concept related to a state of mind characterized by routine actions and behavior, i.e. actions with predictable pattern. The Cambridge English Dictionary defines the comfort zone as a place in which someone's ability or determination are not being tested. The comfort zone can be related to your life in general (which is the most common case), or to some parts/dimensions of life (e.g. family, work, kids, relationships, physical body...) where you have created conditions with no growth or progress. I believe the most logical illustration of the comfort zone is a shape of drop (*Image 1*).

questions

COMFORT ZONE (inertness)

Image 1: The Comfort Zone

The comfort zone has a misleading name and connotation as it denotes that you are well (gratified), when in fact it is a zone of inertness (you could even say boredom). Simply put, the comfort zone is when you sit in your favorite chair, turn on the TV and watch the movie of your life, playing the passive observer. It's where you feel secure, where you are equipped with everything you need (and accustomed to getting by within the limits), where you are isolated from external influences and comfortable, where life goes on habitually and routinely. As you passively follow the movie of your life pretending that you are not its leading role and writer, you often blame government, legal order, politicians, authorities, establishment, bosses, people that surround you or someone else for a poor life or certain situation. They are not to blame! Life is nothing but the choices you have made by now, even if you don't want to admit that.

People trapped in the comfort zone never even try to ask themselves whether it's possible to make different decisions and actions or to live differently. They take life as it is, they are completely inert and, in that state, they will probably spend the rest of their life. This doesn't mean they lack challenges in life; on the contrary, they encounter many challenges, but they repeatedly ignore them and don't want to bother with them. Even if you try to make them acknowledge a certain challenge (e.g. tell them they have a health problem), they will ignore its existence rather than accept it. Or they could be in a dysfunctional marriage but decide not to think about it – they "got it over with" and swept it under the rug. Basically, they don't question their life, they live routinely by the model "I am what I am, I can't and won't change". This zone holds security, everything already seen and familiar, everything more or less predictable (habitual), and there aren't many oscillations. Life just goes on, and people go with it "suffering" as everyone around them; life is everything but beautiful (except in rare, exceptional moments); it's hard, but it will be even worse; everyone has problems, nobody has it easy in life… In the comfort zone everything has its course: from birth to death. People are born, go to kindergarten, go to school (the longer the better), get a job, get married, have children, work, buy/rent a roof over their heads (by taking a loan), raise their children, get retired and then just kill time as they are in their old age and life is already behind them. They have enabled their comfort zone to become the general comfort trap; they are the victims of life and circumstances. And what entrapped them is the great amount of fear of change. The comfort zone, therefore, is characterized by total inertness regarding changes and asking questions about existence; people just vegetate at the lower state of consciousness and categorically refuse to think that anything can and should be different. They refuse to hear.

It's easy to constantly blame others for our own state and situation – whether it's people, circumstances or institutions. And that is exactly what most people do, for two reasons: firstly because it's easier that way – to at least seemingly/temporarily transfer responsibility to someone else; and secondly because they are accustomed to it – they live by life-long programs adopted from ancestors. However, it doesn't mean it has to be like that. The comfort zone gives you the sense of gratification and security, and that is the reason you bind yourself to it and never question certain dimension of life. People are somewhat naturally programmed to be in the comfort zone, i.e. neutral state where everything goes by the plan and the risk is minimal or non-existent. In the comfort zone, therefore, the rule is: no risk, but no gain either. Think of the time when you were kids and when it was normal and fun to constantly try something new. Children are naturally open-minded, curious, they constantly research, experiment – and trying something new all the time makes them more creative. At a certain age, when children become mature and serious adults ("as it should be"), they start to lose those traits and their lives start to follow habits in the comfort zone. The comfort zone at some point, therefore, becomes natural human desire, and every leap in the unknown feels like an unnecessary risk. We are not designed to do things we consider unpleasant, hard or frightening. Our brains are designed to protect us from everything that can harm us because they are trying to keep us alive. The comfort zone, hence, may be comfortable, but it certainly prevents us from growing.

The natural desire of every person is to feel the urge to grow and progress at some point, and to think that they can and should get more from life. Growth is the meaning of existence because life is dynamic in every sense. Think about it: everything constantly moves and evolves; the nature we live in is in constant change. Nothing stands still, and neither should we. Standing still isn't the purpose of our journey on Earth. You are not made to limit your life journey on the comfort zone (although many of us make that a conscious choice; I hope not in a long term). You can't expect to grow and evolve in various life domains if all you do is sticking to habits and routines. For different results you need different choices.

The key for recognizing and consequently leaving the comfort zone is this: you have to think independently and raise the right questions continually. That is why the comfort zone illustrated in Image 1 isn't closed, but has questions at the top instead. You are probably among those who ask questions, and that is precisely why you are reading this book. I can't emphasize enough how important is to continually ask (the right) questions and to have a mind of your own, without the influence from others. That is the precondition for leaving the comfort zone. The happiest people question themselves constantly and try to become better, while unhappy people evaluate others and judge them. People frequently neglect raising questions because they believe they already know all the answers; that is surely true, but within their current comprehension. Therefore,

when people ask themselves could something in their lives be different and when they start to feel the need for change, the right moment for this book has arrived. When they reach this phase, people start asking questions, they become angry at the usual course of life, which does not suite them, and from time to time they ask themselves whether something could be different. Questioning life and raising questions transfers them from the comfort zone to the fear zone (*Image 2*).

Image 2: The Comfort Zone and the Fear Zone

Talking to people, I often encourage them to question their lives from the foundations: where are they going, why have they chosen that path, what frightens them, what are they doing and why, what would they like to do, what could be different, what would they do if they were sure it would turn out well etc. At the beginning most of them have the same opinion: "As long as it's not worse…" But after having dug deeper and opened up a little, everybody admits the same: they work, hurry, rush, live their own definition of "life as usual", everything so as not to stop. Because when they stop, it's over – the moment of comprehension, of facing oneself has arrived. They consequently approach the mirror that awaits tirelessly for a close look and an honest talk with the person on the other side. That's the moment of truth. And it's an excellent moment as it holds great potential for change. Some of them seize it, some don't. Most people under all sorts of external influences (and expectations) quickly forget these questions and get back to the old ways, i.e. continue living the way they used to (they go back to the comfort zone, as it is always open). They doubt their abilities and let the obstacles paralyze them, rather than challenge themselves regularly and turn dreams into reality.

Unlike the comfort zone, the fear zone makes people admit their challenges from time to time and apprehend them as well as feel the need for change, but they aren't ready to face their fears – and that prevents them from moving on. For instance, they are aware that their job doesn't satisfy them, but the fear of existence and everything new that another job would bring prevents them from taking a specific action to change anything; or they face health challenges but neglect to seek help or change anything if they have; they aren't satisfied with their parenting, but they lack courage and will to change anything etc. The fear zone, therefore, is characterized by relative awareness of the existence of challenges (apprehension and acknowledgement of challenges), and by the lack of determination to face them (concealed with different excuses). Being in this zone means to hear, but not act.

Living in the fear zone, thus, is characterized by procrastination, i.e. postponing obligations. This behavior consists of tendency to leave unwanted task for later, if possible never. According to behavioral science, two of the most common causes of procrastination are: anticipation of negative outcome (fear of failure makes a person repeatedly postpone some action, and it is often linked with absence of self-confidence, skills and knowledge) and lack of order, i.e. structure, plan or "bigger picture" (not understanding the importance of certain job or task and not having clear sense of priorities). People don't like unknown and change in general, often to that extent that they find something bad better than the unknown. They don't want to alter their current situation because of the eternal fear of failure (or sometimes success), while the comfort zone gives them the sense of security, stability and gratification. Fear is the biggest ally of the comfort zone. Rather than run away from the fears that have entrapped you and spend your life energy trying to think of a way to avoid them, it would be wiser to use those fears as guidelines, whereas they can often point to the areas of your lives that are not how they should be and that need additional effort. The worst thing to do is to deny fear and push it deeper and deeper within, while recognizing its existence is the first step towards the exit from the procrastination phase.

Procrastination is denoted by delegating unpleasant responsibilities, ignoring calls or messages we believe would require certain changes from us, making excuses constantly etc. Some of the excuses which prevent us to transition from this phase are: I don't have to do it now, I can start tomorrow – now is not the best time, I will start after I have gained more of this and that, this is the last time I put off things, today I will have fun and tomorrow I can focus on my goals, I don't know how, I am too young, I am too old, I am worried about what others might say… Hence it is crucial to keep in mind the benefit expected from the action we plan to take, as it will motivate us. In addition, in the fear zone it is important to try to change attitudes such as "I won't, I can't and I don't have to" into "I will, I can and I want". Of course, perfectionism and waiting for ideal circumstances go together with putting things off. John Assaraf, bestselling author whom I had a chance of meeting in person on a cruise, told me during one private conversation: "Anita, remember: done is better than perfect". And he was absolutely right. It's better to face fear and act, even if the result isn't perfect, than do nothing and stagnate.

You will never be completely ready and you will never feel the urge to exit the fear zone, hence don't wait for the magical moment when your life will get off the autopilot by itself – as it will never happen. You have to create that moment of readiness and determination to face challenges that will enable you to become the best version of yourself and to live your own life instead the lives of others, to live authentically rather than mechanically. Once you apprehend your fears and really become determined to face them, you will start to exit the fear zone through the top of the drop, armed with courage and determination. That auspicious moment is called inspirational action, and it lasts few seconds only. If, therefore, an idea that requires different action crosses your mind, you have few seconds to act before your brain prevents you from action. Sporty "three, two, one, go" is of help to me. Those few critical moments are what sets you apart from action, and if you don't seize them, you will stay in the fear zone. How many times have you wanted to say something, but moments later, after you had started thinking, your brain has discouraged you? You wanted to act differently, you were in the moment of inspirational action, but seconds later you thought you will end up being ridiculous, stupid or whatever – and you didn't do it at the end. The moment of inspiration is great, but the challenge is that it lasts for a very short period of time, and if you fail to jump on that wave of inspiration, just seconds later the window of opportunity will close and you will remain in the fear zone. Next time try to use the "one, two, three, go" method and observe the wonderful effects these actions will have on your life.

For example, medical report and the fact they have started to develop diabetes might trigger obese people to be determined, really determined in desire for change, despite fear. They decide they want to live and they are willing to do whatever it takes to normalize their condition, they face fears and start acting. Instead of daydreaming about change and thinking about what they want, they know precisely what they want, they are committed and determined to do whatever it takes. That's the difference. This difference between being interested and being committed, that John Assaraf explained during his lecture I have attended, has etched in my memory in particular. This is, therefore, the right moment to watch his excellent video "Are You Interested or Are You Committed?" (▣ 10).

QR 10

The key emotion you need as an additional equipment for leaving the fear zone is courage (hence the top position on the drop representing the fear zone). But, mind that courage here isn't the opposite of fear and isn't the lack of fear! Courage means you have decided to do the thing that frightens you despite the fear. Courage is the ability to do the things that are uncertain. And that is precisely why the word "courage" is in the title of this book. Without the courage you are not likely to leave the fear zone; you will need courage as a companion to transform the knowledge into action. Knowledge alone would keep you in the fear zone, with lots of unfulfilled desires and potentials.

That moment of exiting the fear zone, overcoming the procrastination and mustering courage is the key. Thus, we shall pay more attention to this moment, analyzing its critical obstacle: fear. According to the evolutionary psychology, fear (of the unknown) protects us in moments of crisis and it enabled the survival of human species throughout history. It certainly isn't wise to stand barehanded in front of the bear and face the fear – as this fear is justified (genuine) and it can help us to save our skin. On the other hand, most of the fears we experience today, which keep us within the comfort zone, are irrational by their nature (false) and they limit our growth and development (because in most of the populated areas there are no bears these days). Fears immobilize you in a way, because facing them leads to uncertainty. Apart from that, in time those false fears will become permanent tenants of your mind; they will be transformed into chronic fears and will cause numerous stress reactions, consequently compromising your health. You are all well aware that the cause and catalyst of numerous diseases we are witnessing today is precisely stress. Therefore, trying to create a quality, fulfilled life outside the comfort zone truly isn't the question of luxury for those with time to spare; rather it is a matter of developing the healthy attitude towards life and mustering courage for living a healthy, happy life to the fullest.

They say that everything we do, we do out of either fear or love. Even though this seems trivial at first glance, when we reconsider, we will find it very much true. Everything but the unconditional love is actually fear (short overview and comparison of fear and love you can find at ▣ 11).

QR 11

In fact, you should be asking yourself in every occasion whether you are acting out of fear or love. As you can imagine, most actions (about 95%) are fear-driven. Now take a look at this excellent motivational video about love and fear (■ 12) and make a decision to improve your own and other people's lives continuously. Since ancient times fear is highly efficient crowd manipulation tool as well; the world today is based on fear, there is a want for keeping people in state of worry. That isn't particularly difficult because the idea of worry has been planted in our minds for generations and from young age; as a result, we have developed a habit of worrying about this and that. And just worrying, about anything anywhere, really, truly doesn't make sense. Have you ever helped anybody or solved a challenging situation by worrying alone? Specific action might have helped, but worry certainly hasn't, as it isn't of use to anybody (nor to the person worrying nor to the one he/she worries about); indeed, it is harmful for everybody involved as it literally steals energy.

QR 12

For a moment think about this statement: today is the tomorrow I was worried about yesterday. Haven't you been worried hundreds of times, but the world just kept on turning no matter what was going on in your life? Haven't you experienced how a situation that got you so worried started to feel insignificant after a while, and you were even able to laugh at yourself for worrying about such banality? For me, discovering the sheer pointlessness of worry was a true aha-moment, which helped me in life (every parent will know exactly what I mean). Whether you worry yourself or you have paid someone to do it for you, worrying has the same effect regarding solution to your source of worry: none. Hence, if it makes it easier for you, pay someone a certain amount of money to worry instead of you; this will leave you more time for other things and it will preserve your health. Or you can place an ad saying you will worry someone else's worries for 100 dollars per hour. ☺ This is a joke, of course, but I hope you have come to realize the pointlessness of worry in general. Worry creates incorrect images in your brain, and brain doesn't differentiate those images from reality, making your life complicated and hard. If you think it will make things easier, you could hand over your worries to God (the aspect you believe in). You can make or just imagine a lovely box called SFGTDB or Something for God to Do Box. Instead of carrying it inside, worrying and polluting your body and mind – every worry you have you should just put in the box and hand it to God, while promising yourself that you won't be thinking about it anymore. This tool works, provenly.

Paradoxically, worry and fear – permanent tenants of people's minds – make people more aware of what they don't want from life then what they do (and they always concentrate on the things they don't want, attracting them consequentially in their lives as experiences). As though they are afraid to say to themselves (especially out loud) what they want; very often they have actually forgotten or suppressed it deep within, because their whole life they have been doing what is expected of them. Or, to be more precise, what others expected of them. If you don't work on your dreams, someone will come along to make you work on theirs, keeping you in the fear zone. There's a great inspirational video about regret, which will make you rethink your missed opportunities and find out what you can learn from that in order to follow your dreams and reduce the number of missed opportunities in future (■ 13). Notice how people mostly regret things they failed to do. That's the way it is, near the end of their lives, people regret the things they didn't do more than the things they did. Let's face it, we will all die someday, but the point is to really live while we are still alive, instead of just wasting our time. Don't let your past define you, but find a way to live your new present. Take a look at another excellent motivational video about that (■ 14). Consider this: when have you accepted the general point of view that you are too old for this or that, who made you stop dreaming, not to engage in something you have been given – your life? Who is to say you shouldn't change your career even in your sixties? Who is to say it doesn't make sense to give birth at the age of 50 or remarry at 80? Who is to say it isn't normal to choose career over motherhood, or to be a mother of five instead of career woman? Why any of this should be considered unnatural? Who defines normal anyway? Don't let others determine for you what is normal and clip your wings, especially if your existence doesn't depend on them. You are born to fly, to be successful, to use the talents you've got

QR 13

QR 14

and all your potentials; you aren't born to spend your life in mice hole at the bottom of the comfort zone.

At one congress on healthy life I have met an 83-year-old man. After my motivational speech on the comfort zone, he approached me, slowly with his walking stick, saying he wanted to meet me and share with me what he was currently researching. I was glad to meet an older person who still possessed the will and desire to live. During our conversation, the man told me he was just writing his PhD, believe it or not. Everybody has been asking him why so late, he added, and he usually replied that he had been collecting experience so far; now he was writing and it is never too late. I will remember this encounter for the rest of my life, as he was the one to inspire me. When I think that I can't do something, that it isn't the right moment, that I am too much this or that (excuses), I think of him and his story and positive spirit. We're back to that old one: where there is will, there is a way. This is the honest truth; everything else, I mean EVERYTHING, are just excuses we make to stay in the comfort or fear zone.

The comfort zone wasn't made over night, and consequently leaving it and passing through the fear zone won't be instantaneous, but for leaving the fear zone you will need an instant decision. An excellent TED Talk on this subject was given by Mel Robbins, and you can watch it by scanning this code: ◼ 15. It's important to understand that exiting the comfort zone isn't a matter of gift or talent that possess merely chosen; it is a skill powerful enough to transform the life in general.

QR 15

However, nothing evolves without hard work and effort; neither relationships, human, flower nor muscles. It's a long-term process which requires you to improve and evolve because the moment you exit the comfort zone, you will be given undreamed-of possibilities for growth and development, and the quality of life as well. This book will help you ask the right questions, apprehend challenges and muster courage for action, for leaving various comfort zones. Next, we will consider what happens when you succeed, i.e. what's beyond the comfort zone.

❧ Recommendations to inspire you on your journey of happiness ☺

- [QR 10] Are You Interested or Are You Committed? - John Assaraf:
  https://www.youtube.com/watch?v=Nrl0YLC-KtM
- [QR 12] Love or Fear:
  https://www.youtube.com/watch?v=5Qz3DVX7GjQ
- [QR 13] 70 People Ages 5-75 Answer: What Do You Regret?
  https://www.youtube.com/watch?v=N8i6rUL4UIY
- [QR 14] Everybody Dies, but Not Everybody Lives,
  https://www.youtube.com/watch?v=_YIwPUQ2ftM
- [QR 15] How to Stop Screwing Yourself over | Mel Robbins |
  TEDxSF:
  https://www.youtube.com/watch?v=Lp7E973zozc

- [QR 11] Love versus Fear:
  https://tinybuddha.com/blog/love-versus-fear/

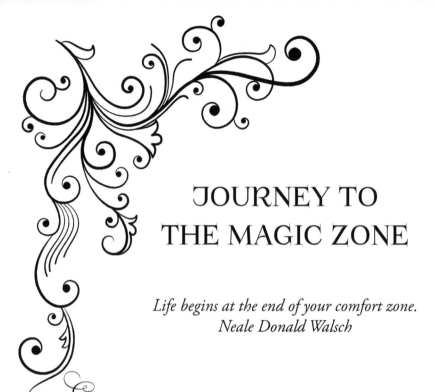

JOURNEY TO
THE MAGIC ZONE

Life begins at the end of your comfort zone.
Neale Donald Walsch

Exit from the fear zone is going to bring you things you couldn't even imagine to exist, and people usually say it's at least 10 times better than they have expected. You will probably get to know and see yourself in a totaly different way, discovering multitude of skills you have already possessed but kept muffled by routine patterns and automated actions. This will increase your self-confidence and give you additional stength and zest for other life challenges. So far I haven't met a person who regrets taking responsibility for his/her life and leting go the patterns of control. After you have exited your comfort and fear zones, things that were once unknown and frightening become nothing but new and normal for you. Your consciousness is widening as well, and now you are functioning in the action zone (we could also call it the learning zone). Here is an illustration of the journey from the comfort zone via the fear zone to the action zone *(Image 3)*.

Even though from time to time it would seem to you that the action zone has made you lose your ground, you will actually grow, climb and, most importantly, you will not stagnate. You will experiment, widen your horizons, overcome challenges and develop your skills. By overcoming challenge after challenge, you will be keener to face the next one, and the fear will consequently diminish. This doesn't mean that the ultimate goal is to eliminate fear completely, as life without adrenaline isn't entirely welcomed. Facing challenges in the action zone implies exactly that: taking specific action. That in turn means to be open for changes, which in time become the way of life and something that wants to be continual.

Image 3: The Comfort Zone, the Fear Zone and the Action Zone

When you succeed in facing your fear and exiting the fear zone, in the action zone you might experience something like this: you will start to grow incredibly fast (personal growth), you will come to like setting challenges to yourself, you will realize that your fears are mostly unreal (fictional), you will replace regret with excitement, you will laugh to your old self, you will find out more about your strength and weaknesses, you will increase your self-respect, you will create a new source of incredible satisfaction, you will realize the only way to success is through discomfort, you will start to inspire people around you... When you take risks, when you face challenges and do things outside norms and usual way of thinking, your brain starts to function differently, your neurons wire differently. This certainly doesn't mean you should drive at 125 miles per hour at the highway, start acting like a delinquent or anything like that. It's about overcoming personal, often completely imaginary boundaries we have in our heads. The action zone, therefore, is all about acknowledging challenges and possessing determination for facing them. Thus this zone is often called the growth zone or the learning zone (◼ 16).

QR 16

Let's reconsider the example of someone with unsatisfactory job living in the fear zone, i.e. procrastination. Once that someone has truly acknowledged their fears, made a clear and firm decision they had enough and were ready to change, once they've mustered courage and left the fear zone – they are in the zone of action. Inhere they will move past their everyday life, start looking for a new job, try to give the best at the present job, go to work with joy knowing that there is something better around the corner, learn new things, take new courses, decide to surround themselves with inspiring people who can help them grow, discover multiple opportunities, open their minds towards new possibilities, talk with joy about their life, try some of the reprogramming techniques. In short, they will do everything they can to change what they don't like – job in this particular case – and they will act. They won't stop at thinking; they will act because they have made a decision to work daily for their prosperity and solving challenges. You may have asked yourselves two questions now: Firstly, how long will this someone be in the action zone, i.e. when will they enter the magic zone? And secondly, could they return to the fear zone? The answer to your first question is that the duration of the action zone is individual; it depends on the size of the challenge the person is facing, on the speed the person is learning and adopting new habits and on the time dedicated to solving the challenge, i.e. commitment. The answer to your second question is: yes, it is possible to fall back, all the way to the comfort zone.

In order to stay in the action zone rather than go back to the fear and comfort zone, it's necessary not to focus on the fear, but on all the fun aspects of the process of change, i.e. of the action zone. Focus on the goal you are trying to achieve and think of your motifs often in order to shake the fear that is pulling you back to familiar, and decline. Tony

Robbins's video on training your brain and staying focused might help you with that (■ 17). The purpose of leaving the fear zone isn't to instantly change yourself profoundly. As much as it isn't good to live in the zone of comfort and fear, it isn't wise to spread beyond potential and make radical changes in the action zone in several areas of life at the same time; facing many challenges parallel will make us tired very soon. Moreover, by feeling pressured to progress, enhance efficiency and face fears, i.e. being engaged in the action zone in several areas at the same time – we could end up in a state of panic, feeling exhausted and less productive. When you are in a state of panic, you feel tense, tired, frustrated, anxious, exhausted etc. If your expectations are too high and your goals unrealistic, your efficiency is more likely to decrease and you are more likely to fall back to previous habits and familiar. If your new challenges are too big, you are more likely to be even more frightened and the chances are you will go back to your comfort zone. The idea is, therefore, to turn to your new choices step by step, to widen your horizons, to make your decisions more spontaneously.

QR 17

You don't want to go through life lulled, but straining too much isn't the point either – that way you will increase the odds for failure because excessive fear isn't good for your body. It's wise to respect your limits and make good foundations. In life, balance is always the key and it is good to have everything in moderation. I believe the best way to function in the action zone is to set everyday, small and achievable goals in order to push limits. This is what I call mini challenges. When you accomplish your goal, you realize you can do it, you feel satisfied because you have outdone yourself. You know how children are sometimes reluctant to do something out of fear, for example they refuse to go down the slide, but when they muster courage and overcome themselves, you can't take them away. It's the same with the adults; we are just like kids, there is a kid in every one of us, we have just forgotten it along the way. Certain successful people have started with very simple challenges – say, showering in the cold water; you have to start somewhere. Being consistent in this mini challenges is the key, because when challenges become your lifestyle, you will reach the next level.

Defeat the imaginary limitations that you have set for yourself, step away from the routine of life or your typical day. Go to your destination taking different route, spend time with strangers, smile at anyone you meet on a certain day, get up five minutes earlier, go to the night stroll, try some new and unusual dish… anything. You might find it funny, but you have to start somewhere, and take it step by step. When you do that, you push your brain to create new neuronal paths and that will make you a whole new person. Once you have made the first step, you will find out it's not that hard and frightening as you thought. Limitations define your current circumstances, and this in turn reflects on your life quality. Limitations sprout in your mind and mold your perception and, consequentially, your reality (watch the video on brain limitations ◼ 18). The reality of life is important, of course, but for your success and fulfilled life, the way you look at it is far more important.

QR 18

You can (and should!) experiment with mini challenges by yourself (make a list of new things and do one every day). In addition, in every chapter that deals with the 12 challenges you will find my suggestions of mini challenges. Accept at least some of them and you will see how soon it will become your way of life. Besides, you will feel better and better, and there is no better motivation than the one coming from within (intrinsic) and based on our own experience. Not to mention that mini challenges will make your day distinct and memorable.

What were you doing this time last year? This month last year? Most of us can't recall that because our lives unfold routinely. We recall only the big events (graduation, marriage, giving birth, divorce, deaths of our loved ones…) and those distinct days that have disrupted our daily routine (e.g. flights, boat trips, crazy parties with friends), both in a positive or negative way. Hence, the idea is to fill your days with as much memorable things as you can; those things will therefore be unusual, and this would mean you have broken certain habit/routine, you have mustered courage to become aware of fear and face the challenge. Life is too short to spend it vegetating.

I have already explained the concept of worry and we have concluded that worry doesn't bring us anything positive and that it's wiser to concentrate on dealing with challenges and facing fear. The positive side is that the braver you and your actions become, the more you think outside the box, the more you deflect from your usual norms and habits, the more you face your fears – the more alive, free and eventually happy you will feel. The happier you become, the more energy and courage you will have for facing fears, i.e. overcoming obstacles. There is this sequence: courage -> happiness -> courage and so on (fortune truly smiles upon the brave ☺). Therefore, the keener you are to face your fears and challenges in one area of life (e.g. relationships), the more likely you are to awake and start to grow in the other areas of life (e.g. work). Because every new achievement, every growth, every progress will slowly transform you in a new person, it will create new neuronal connections in your brain – and you will start to think and live differently.

This wonderful process will reduce the likelihood of falling to the lower zones, as every new success will motivate you for the next courageous moves. If you keep overcoming your challenges persistently, this will make you transition from the action zone to the magic zone (Image 4). The magic zone is the place where you have solved most of the challenges in certain area of life and where you simply flow with your life. You are attuned with the Universe, there is no life control; but there is full acceptance of whatever life brings, there is a clear understanding of the beginning and the end of your responsibilities. You live your dreams, you live your purpose and life is beautiful. Light. Spontaneous. Fulfilled. Joyful. Happy. Relaxed. Magical. The ultimate goal of life journey is reaching the magic zone, i.e. living as much of your lives and as much of your days in that state. Of course you will fall from time to time, of course you will sometimes go back to the action zone, or to the fear zone, depending on an area of life and the seriousness of challenge. The important thing is not to let the life routine and habits to take you down, but to be awake. To observe and take actions. To make effort to change, to stay in the action zone and to keep pushing your limits. True happiness isn't in the comfort zone; the bursts of true happiness start in the procrastination phase, and the happiness grows with the progress.

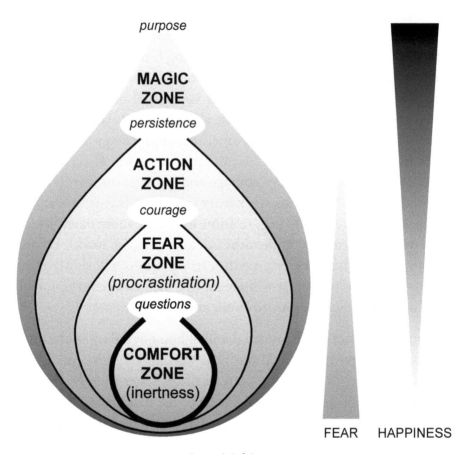

Image 4: Life Journey

It's important to clarify that it is impossible to position one's life exclusively in the comfort, fear, action or magic zone – there are different areas of life (e.g. family, relationships, work, parenthood, physical body etc.) and for every area we can draw a different picture regarding life journey *(Image 4)*. Let me illustrate: someone can live in a marriage full of violence and disrespect believing it is supposed to be like that, never even considering different life and change because of their upbringing. When it comes to relationships, that someone is trapped in the comfort zone denying the challenge. But that same someone may have changed several jobs in order to grow and progress, knowing their quality and refusing to work for employer which hasn't been able to value them as it should. They have been analyzing the situation at work and, when they sensed that they are stagnating and are unable to express their potential, they faced the challenge and set out to work for another job. Therefore, they aren't at the comfort zone regarding work; rather, they are in the action zone. This is just an illustration; throughout the book and the 12 comfort zones I will discuss, every one of you will discover in which phase you are regarding different areas of life.

Mini challenge

Try to figure out in which zones certain aspects of your life are at the moment. Find out are you in the zone of comfort, fear, action or magic when it comes to parenthood, relationship with parents, work, relationships, friendship, your physical body (looks), your state of mind, health…

I wish you all a happy journey to the magic zone in as many areas of life as possible, and lots of fun and new discoveries along the way.

❧ Recommendations to inspire you on your journey of happiness ☺

▶

- [QR 16] If You're Not Outside Your Comfort Zone, You Won't Learn Anything:
  https://www.youtube.com/watch?v=UsnIp1jRq30
- [QR 17] Tony Robbins Helps You Train Your Brain to Stay Focused:
  https://www.youtube.com/watch?v=-eCeLdY-wpg
- [QR 18] Limitations of the Brain:
  https://www.youtube.com/watch?v=9BdzhWdVaX0

CONNECTING DOTS AND PERSISTENCE

Motivation is what gets you started. Habit is what keeps you going.
Jim Rohn

We all need motivation, as it is that kind of urge, i.e. stimulus that makes us want to achieve certain behaviors, results and goals that make us satisfied. Every life coach has their coach, persons whose work and actions they follow, persons who lift, motivate and inspire them. That's great as it enables us to choose who we are going to watch/listen and who will affect us. For example, if someone doesn't speak some foreign language, he can choose someone who does to transfer him/her a message. I believe we all serve as trainers to one another, and every new situation is an opportunity to learn.

The key is to start concentrating on ourselves, not others. It is believed that the ones to succeed are those that are willing to change, and that is indeed so, because changes aren't residing in the comfort zone. By changing ourselves, we change the world (and that's actually the only way). Rewinding my life, I have realized that I constantly had the need to change and control others, and that led to my divorce, broken friendships, all sorts of things. However, I have no regrets; I am 100% certain everything is exactly as it should be and everything has happened for a reason. That's the only conclusion we get when we connect dots looking backwards. That was the exact thing famous Steve Jobs (Apple cofounder) said to graduates of the prestigious Stanford University;

he has told them only three stories that stuck with me (◼ 19). I warmly recommend you to watch that speech, one of the most inspiring I have ever seen. Especially exciting is his first story about connecting dots; I am sure you too, looking back, many things see differently. In any case, watch the whole commencement speech and share with others, because it's worth of watching.

QR 19

- Steve Jobs wasn't the only one with an unusual life story. Read the next lines for inspiration. Have you known that:
- Albert Einstein learn to speak at the age of four, learn to read at the age of seven, and was being ridiculed at school because he was a slow learner and everybody thought he was mentally ill;
- Michael Jordan was expelled from the basketball team in high school;
- Marilyn Monroe was advised by the modeling agencies to give up modeling career and start working as a secretary:
- Stephen King's first book was rejected as much as 30 times; his wife convinced him to try one more time;
- Steven Spielberg failed to get in as much as three universities;
- Elvis Presley was fired after his first performance; he was told to go back to driving trucks;
- Henry Ford had several unsuccessful projects; he kept started over and have bankrupted two times;
- Walt Disney was fired because he allegedly lacked imagination and good ideas;
- Shakira was expelled from the school quire in her sophomore year because her voice was "too deep";
- Oprah Winfrey got fired as a journalist and reporter because she was "unable to share emotions from her story"; she was also raped at nine and pregnant at 14;
- Thomas Edison was told he was too stupid to lean anything; he was also fired from two previous jobs as he wasn't productive enough;
- Cindy Crawford was often criticized because of her physical imperfection – birthmark over her upper lip;

- Gisele Bűndchen was rejected by as much as 42 modeling agents;
- Jim Carrey has left high school, started to work and lived in a van, because of his father and poverty;
- Charlie Chaplin was rejected by Hollywood studio managers, because they thought he wasn't profitable;
- Vincent Van Gogh has sold only one painting during his life, to his friend for peanuts?

I have already said you are not alone in your pursuit for happiness. You are also not alone in your fears and challenges. As you could see in those videos, others had challenges in life as well, even the famous and (now) rich (materially). Those challenges were often incredibly big; life wasn't easy on them, but they didn't hide in their comfort zone. Instead, they mustered their courage, decided to face challenges and they were persistent. That differentiates them from those who have given up.

I particularly remember a part of a great book by Dr. S. Johnson *Who Moved My Cheese?* This book carries deep life messages, and you can read it from cover to cover in an hour. There is also a short animated movie based on the book (▣ 20); it is a metaphor of the thngs you

QR 20

want from life – good job, love relationship, goods, health or peace within. At the beginning of the book there is a quote by A. J. Cronin that says: „Life is no straight and every corridor along which we travel free and unhampered, but a maze of passages, through which we must seek our way, lost and confused, now and again checked in a blind alley. But always, if we have faith, God will open a door for us, Not perhaps one that we ourselves would ever have thought of, but one that will ultimately prove good for us.“

Mini challenge

Remember the times your ideas/wishes didn't come true and things didn't go as you wished them to, but nevertheless, in time you have realized that everything was exactly as it should have been and if you have had it your way – it wouldn't have turned out well.

During my seminars I often share an unusual story related to the first Croatian edition of this book. I had just finished the book and had everything sorted out with the publisher, the book was supposed to go to print and I had the book promotion arranged in two weeks' time – when things unexpectedly got complicated. I returned home from a meeting and started to doubt myself and the whole project (I had fallen back in the phase of procrastination). Then in a video about success I heard that 95% of people give up on the last step, just before the finish line. I promised myself then that I wouldn't give up, that the book would be promoted as it had been planned; I made a decision. That way I encouraged myself and started to act (in the action zone). I decided to publish the book myself and to start my own company (even though I knew nothing about publishing at the time). This is how Happiness Institute, the company that I had always wanted to have, came to life. Everything went smoothly, doors kept opening for me, I published the book by myself, called of sponsors and paid for everything myself – and the book was released as planned. The book promotion was at 7 p.m., and copies had arrived from printing house at 6.30 p.m. (still warm ☺). Don't think that was easy; those were two of the craziest weeks of my life. But it was worth it at the end. Therefore, when I sometimes catch myself thinking about giving up certain ideas, I remember the challenge with the book and tell myself: I can do it.

As soon as the book hit the shelves, it started to sell fast. Eventually it was sold out and the project in general had bigger success than expected. I especially cherish hundreds of letters and messages of support from the people the book has touched, who had found themselves in my story, who had been inspired by my words to take some new, bold actions and choices. It's priceless to know that someone is living at least slightly better life because of you and your actions; I feel the best when I serve and when my work has a higher purpose. This English edition of my book is a new project for me as well, a new challenge that I have readily faced. Even though I cannot know what will happen and how, I do everything with lots of love and completely relaxed because I am certain it will go the best possible way. Hence, when life gives you lemons, say thank you and make a lemonade (or a raw lemon cake like me ☺).

Therefore, nobody says your happiness journey towards the magic of life will be easy, only that it would be worth the effort. You should always keep that in mind.

Mini challenge

For the end of this chapter watch this short motivational video Dream (▣ 21).

QR 21

Recommendations to inspire you on your journey of happiness ☺

- [QR 19] Steve Jobs' 2005 Stanford Commencement Address:
    https://www.youtube.com/watch?v=UF8uR6Z6KLc
- [QR 20] Who Moved My Cheese?:
    https://www.youtube.com/watch?v=jOUeHPS8A8g
- [QR 21] Dream - motivational video:
    https://www.youtube.com/watch?v=g-jwWYX7Jlo

Spencer Johnson: Who Moved My Cheese?, 2000.

* * * * *

The goal of the first part of the book was to familiarize you with some of the concept this book deals with. The next part is dedicated to your spirit, mind and body, in which the challenges are woven into. There are 12 of them, but don't worry, take it slowly, let them come to you one by one. I have tried to organize them in a logical way, although they are actually intertwined and inseparable in reality. The first part deals with healthy and cheerful spirit, with emphasis on the importance of being in the present moment and taking time for ourselves. This, of course, doesn't mean that healthy and strong body, for example, excludes present moment or that healthy and cheerful spirit excludes loving ourselves. Ready, steady, go. ☺

HEALTHY AND CHEERFUL SPIRIT - LIVING IN THE PRESENT

CHALLENGE 1:
HEALTHY SELFISHNESS
AND THE PRESENT MOMENT

Before you help others, you must help yourself.

Every culture has its own values and norms that we have to accept up to a point, whether we like it or not, in order to function in this world. In collectivist cultures people are accustomed to put interests/benefits of a group/community in front of their own. In other words, collective attitudes and behaviors – which emphasize the significance of a group rather than the significance of an individual – are more welcomed. On the other hand, there are individualist cultures (it is often the case with Scandinavian countries), where individuals prioritize their own goals rather than the goals of a group. I am telling you this so you could think about the society you live in and about the ways that has shaped you and affected your life and decisions.

Have you ever been told by the people close to you how selfish you are? How you think only about yourself? How you care only about your own goals? How you don't care for others? I've heard that many times so far, and it always made me feel torn. I've wondered how can it be that even though I often put the needs of others, of people dear to me, in front of my own needs – I was being accused of selfishness by those same people!? We live in times when selfishness is often defined as flaw, and that surely has a significant role in our perception of selfishness.

When it comes to this subject, I had an aha-moment during one flight to London, while flight attendants were showing us the standard procedure in case of emergency. We were explained that in case of significant pressure drop in cabin, masks with oxygen will automatically fall. Flight attendants showed us where they will fall and how to use them, and then came this sentence: "Parents with children, put the masks to your mouths first!" Even though I had flown many times before, I somehow always missed that part (hence the proof we hear as much as our circle of comprehension allows us to and as much as we are ready to hear). Yes, parents, put the masks on your mouths first. It's only logical, you can't expect your child to take care of himself and of you!? Dear readers, I can write until tomorrow explaining how logical it is to put yourself first at certain situations. Because, if you aren't well, you can't do good to people around you either. On the other hand, when you are well, you attract good things to your life; people around you will see that, and they will start to change. This is especially the case with your loved ones and the people closest to you, whom you spend most of your time with.

Therefore, if you value good relationships with your children, partner, family and people around you in general, you have to put yourself first. This doesn't mean you are selfish (as you were probably taught); on the contrary, it means you are responsible (to yourself and to others). And the difference between being selfish and being responsible is enormous. Selfishness is actually a virtue because you should take care of yourself and not let anybody use you. It took me a long time to realize that. Children, for example, sense everything, they are very sensitive and intuitive (especially those we call indigo, crystal or rainbow children). Every external and internal mood we experience – is reflected on them; if you are angry, they won't be crazy about having you around, for sure. Every parent among you will know what I am talking about. The same applies to other relationships as well. If you aren't well, you can't be good to other people. While you are young (say until 18-20 years of age) and/or while you're living with your parents, you still need limits in a way, but later – you live your own life. This sentence often pops in my mind: When we accept the thing we didn't want, we actually give up the thing we've wanted. You decide for yourself how you will act: will you be doing things others want you to do, or the things that make you feel fulfilled. I remember well how during the time prior to my decision to get a divorce I wasn't very fun to be around, and my child noticed that of course. You know the feeling: you feel like a burden to yourself, and you've had enough of everything and everybody, you would prefer to disappear for a while. How could I be a good mom in that condition? I couldn't. And a friend? I couldn't. Daughter? I couldn't. Employee? I couldn't. In times like that we are trapped in various negative thinking about ourselves, about the things that bother us – in other words, we are slaves of our thoughts and we certainly aren't in the present moment.

Being responsible to yourself in that matter and putting yourself first doesn't mean you should neglect the needs of others. Besides loving yourself, you can love others as well, you can take care of them, give them your time; i.e. you are capable of loving yourself and others at the same time. Run from the people who are constantly crying over everything (mostly because of their destiny, or yours), people who choose to be victims, who "give everything, but get nothing in return", who blackmail you emotionally (if you do this or that, I will be sad etc.), people who deny you your happiness (how can you be happy when I am unhappy) and make you think you are responsible for their life and happiness (this is often the case with parents, who do that unconsciously). Those were the examples of true selfishness, often called unhealthy selfishness.

Mini challenge

Think about the following: Have you ever experienced moments of emotional blackmail from the people close to you? How that made you feel? Do you still have those people around? Why? What's preventing you to love yourself more?

On the other hand, being selfish is desirable. Not only that, it's essential for our health. Now may be a good time to mention famous Louise L. Hay. When I read her book *You Can Heal Your Life*, not many people, at least in my country, knew who she was. However, lately we hear her name more and more often, and words "affirmation" and "meditation" slowly lose negative connotation they have had for years. The best way to invite you to study her work is to tell you that she is still one of the best known and influential authors of self-help who advocate self-healing. She has made a step forward and told us we are the true cause of our illnesses and the key for everything is to love ourselves. What do you say about healthy selfishness now? Do you think she is wrong? Do you think her success in many countries throughout the world and the fact her books were translated to many languages – is accidental? She has cured herself from cancer with the help of affirmations, visualization, body cleansing and psychotherapy. The book *You Can Heal Your Life* was published in 1984 and sold in more than 50 million copies, Hay's Facebook page (▣ 22) has more than 2,620,000 fans, and she has got numerous letters from people who have successfully used her methods of healing. She has written many books. If you haven't discovered her work yet, I warmly recommend you to do that now. Even though she has recently passed away, her work and teachings continue through her team, and everything she has done, changed lives of lots of people.

QR 22

With this I've wanted to emphasize once more that it is crucial to take care of ourselves first; only then we can take cake of everyone else. I hope you have absorbed this idea, or at least you are about to by the end of the book. You shouldn't resent anybody; they have taught you the best they could and within their comprehension. If your parents hadn't loved themselves, hadn't been happy, cheerful and smiling, hadn't loved life and hadn't lived in the zones of action and magic – they couldn't have taught you to be like that. But never mind that, you create your life, you are at the crossroads right now, you are ready for change and now you can start a whole new life. Remember that past has a power over you only if you let it. As Albert Einstein put it: "It's crazy to do the same thing over and over again and expect different results." Therefore, turn a new leaf and put yourself first, as every change begins with loving yourself.

Mini challenge

Apprehend the things you always do the same, even though you aren't satisfied by the results. Apprehension itself will trigger a change.

It's common today, if not popular, to constantly repeat how we don't have time. The fact is, it is merely an excuse for being in the fear and procrastination zone, remember the picture? The same is with smile. It's lame to be happy, you are strange if you are smiling (maybe you are even high on drugs, one never knows). It's lame to have time, you are strange if you have time, you instantly worth less. It's not cool to say we have time because than we're not *in* and we aren't participating in general fuss about the lack of time. How pointless that looks to me! Think about it: every day lasts for 24 hours, there is always time. The question is how you decide to use it, i.e. for whom and when we take the time. So, you have time – the only question is for whom and what; let's be honest to ourselves and others. A friend of mine once pointed out that out of 24 hours, we spend eight hours sleeping and eight hours working – so we still have another eight to do with as we pleased. The problem is most people don't know what they want as they never or rarely think about it. We often say we are happy just to say it, and because we have been raised in a "be humble, don't overdo it, don't stand out, don't be too smart" culture, we often don't even dare to wish for a better luck. Because, who knows what kind of problems we could than attract (we may even have a lemon dropped to our heads ☺). Besides, it's "selfish" and ungrateful as well (plus – we may have to repay it multiple times).

In any case, you and only you know what suits you; what you will do, how and when. Nobody else can take responsibility for your life (even if they want to). You are responsible for your actions and doings; you reap what you sow. You are not obligated to do something just because it is sociably desirable, especially not on other people's terms. Do not seek approval for your values and actions in other people's eyes. Remember when I said how I had it all and yet felt sad, anxious and a bit depressed, how I felt that life has to be something more? Well, that's it. I have been doing what other people thought I should, what was normal, common and acceptable. But to whom? In what culture? Was it the same around the world? One status from a friend made me laugh recently: "I don't have to do anything, I had my share of *have tos*." The gospel truth. By doing something out of sense of duty, you won't help anybody. We all sense when somebody is truly present, just like we know when they are there only in the flesh, but not in spirit, as we like to say. It's a real blessing to free ourselves from the things that "imperatively and necessarily" have to be done (contrary to our wishes). Let them talk, truly let them (they always will, anyway, no matter what you do) – and do it your way. If that means to dye your hair the way you have always wanted, so be it. If that means to stop eating meat, so be it. If that means to spend a day drinking beer with the guys, so be it. If that means to make time for beauty treatments, so be it. Get up earlier every morning and use the spare time for yourself. Otherwise you will constantly feel dissatisfied, and end up being frustrated. Live your life authentically, instead of distinguishing other people's fires and living in a robot mode.

Mini challenge

Think of the things you really want to do, but keep postponing because you don't have time for them. Choose one that is objectively doable and do it tomorrow.

In order to say yes to your needs and your life in general, you have to say no to other people, things and unnecessary duties. It's logical, isn't it? The time of our journey here on earth is limited and it's wise to be well aware when we give it, to whom and why. Today it's popular to make to do lists. They are, of course, useful, and I will come to that later, but right now I want you to apprehend that those lists have no end. Every new day creates new responsibilities, and they just pile up next to those you already have, without a doubt. The lists consequentially keep getting longer, and due to limited time and the pace of life – we often aren't able to do them all, which leads to stress and frustration. My advice is to prioritize to do lists, as your duties aren't equally urgent. We often say "yes" to wrong things, but "no" we say rarely if ever.

It's even wiser to make not to do list, and really avoid doing things on that list. The key is to than use the spare time this has given you to do the things you really want. Creating not to do list is part of the self-discipline and responsibility you have to yourself. Learn how to say no to situations, duties, people. Again, this doesn't mean you should become irresponsible to others and neglect responsibilities that are and should be integral part of your life. This merely means you will seriously consider everything you do and see clearly what can wait, or needn't be done at all. Think about the things you can say no to in order to say yes to yourself and your life. Numerous books have been written about this issue, because this small two-letter word – no – has great power and potential for improving the quality of your life. Now is the time to use it. In order to live your purpose, you should be doing more of the things that benefit that purpose, and this inevitably means learning to say no. Easier said than done, though, because people are generally afraid to utter this brave word. They think what others will say or think, what consequences will that have. Fear has an important role, again, as it keeps us trapped and immobile in the position where we fulfill other people's dreams (and that leads us back to the comfort zone). However, the first no is the hardest. When you learn that you have gained far more than you have lost, every other no will be easier. Warren Buffet said: "The difference between successful people and really successful people is that really successful people say 'no' to almost everything." You can say no to life in the comfort zone, to procrastination, to social pressure, fear, negative thinking, setting too many goals, perfectionism, people who control you and lie to you, media consumption (which will be our next challenge). You have the right to say no to everything you don't like, to everything that hurts you, to everything that doesn't serve you, to everything you don't truly believe in, to everything that doesn't make your heart beats faster. Before your next mini challenge, watch the video The Art of Saying No and listen to Kenny Nguyen, who will explain to you how we are taught from early on that "no" means rejection, even though we should use the power of that word for growth (■ 23).

QR 23

Mini challenge

Make your own not to do list; write a few words on it, and regularly update it by adding things to the list.

It's not easy to know how to say no, when and why, but it's important to initiate this process. Slowly you will come to realize what the healthy selfishness is. It's a thin line between healthy and unhealthy selfishness, but I believe you will eventually find it, each of you in your own time. With this I wanted to show you that many people often give their personal power, joy and life energy to others, which means they neglect to live their own lives and purpose. They suppress their wishes and potential – which in turn frustrates them and often makes them ill. That's why throughout the book I invite you to thoroughly shake up and analyze your lives. And in order to find out what you want, you must first recognize what you don't want. That's why creating healthy selfishness is a good foundation for leaving the comfort zone. It's also tightly connected with the concept of living in the present moment.

To be in the present moment is to feel ultimate gratitude for everything in life and to have full confidence and faith that everything, I mean everything, happens for our greater good. Only in the present moment there is no time; now is the connection between past and future which is always here (and where the flow I've mentioned earlier resides). To that fragile moment we dedicate too little time, and that's where all the secrets and all the happiness and joy in life are. Many books have been written about the present moment, and I especially recall a movie that can be the introduction of the importance of the present moment, where the main character learns to be in now and here (Peaceful Warrior, ■ 24). One of the simplest methods for apprehending the present moment is to pay attention to breathing (more on that in challenges 5 and 11). Actually, we all live in the present moment all the time, we just don't realize that, and therefore we don't use the potential that lies in that realization. I remember well my "bad" period, and now, from the distance, I can say that I was constantly ei-

QR 24

ther in the past or in the future. How? With my thoughts. Given that I was a perfectionist back then, I planned everything very carefully (today I don't make plans for more that few months ahead, because every day is a new adventure). I've had my little notebook, i.e. planner, and I have been writing down all my to dos in it. Sometimes I would wake up in the middle of the night wondering whether I've finished all of my tasks (some of them I was supposed to do in a day or to, but some of them I had already finished). This was a clear proof I wasn't in the now, so it's only logical I wasn't happy or satisfied.

The author who talked the most about the importance and power of the present moment is probably the famous Eckhart Tolle. He claims many people aren't aware of the present moment at all, and they aren't recognizing it because they are too focused on the next moment, which they consider more important. Consequently, they live in the future, which is nothing but the next present moment. The future exists only in the form of thought, just like the past, of which you contemplate in the present moment as well. The reality of life is always now. That's why it is wrong to put the happiness in the future, to seek happiness, to search for a way towards happiness. Happiness is the journey itself, not the destination. It has to be now. Once you realize that, it will change your perspective forever. Tolle's book The Power of Now quickly became bestseller, so I warmly recommend it. And now watch his video about the present moment (■ 25).

QR 25

Mini challenge

Set an alarm titled The Present Moment on your cell phone; when it goes off, you will simply say: "I am now, and I am here", and you will take a deep breath and exhale several times.

But in order to overcome the first challenge – to be healthy selfish and in the present moment as much as possible – we must first admit we don't lead the life we want. Then we have to think about what we want and finally we have to find time for it, because after we make a decision, we will enter the action zone and act – do different things. Since you have this book in your hands, we could say you have found a time and you are climbing. Talking about books, you will rarely have time for them, and in those rare moments you will maybe think about doing something else. So, it's best to have the book you want to read (and a pen, of course) with you all the time. That way you could read few pages whenever it's possible: in the morning while you are still in bed, in the evening before sleep, while you are waiting for washing machine to finish, while you are waiting for someone to call, at work while you are on a break, while you are commuting… basically in every situation. Why? Firstly, because you will rarely have time for reading only, and secondly, because books are composed from limited amount of pages, and every page you have read means you are one page nearer to the end of the book. You shouldn't worry about the number of pages read; if you read merely 2-3 a day, in two months it will be the whole book. If you commit to read 15 minutes per day, in a year you will have read approximately 25 average-size books – and in a lifetime you will have a small library implemented in your heads. Imagine how many new knowledge you will gain, as if you have finished several universities. Try to make those 15 minutes and let me know whether you have succeeded. From my personal experience, I can promise you that it works. You just have to find time by yourself. Some books you will like instantly, and you will even bring them to the toilet with you. ☺ Not to mention that today you can find audiobooks as well, which could easily be with you at any time. Therefore, many a little makes a mickle. In other words, page after page – book.

Mini challenge
Make time for reading a book 15 minutes a day. An alarm called Book on your cell phone can help you stick to the plan.

Let's conclude this first challenge: you have to help yourself first in order to be able to help others. Be selfish in a healthy way and put yourself first in order to be content, and then share your good spirit and motivation with others. While doing that, tackle the issue of postponing your duties, and start acting. Change yourself. Try to apprehend the present moment is all you've got, you always have only now.

There is a presentation I often show to my students in order to shake them up a bit and make them think, so I will complete this first challenge of healthy selfishness and life in the present moment with those encouraging sentences. I believe it will be a good summary of everything I have said so far and it will show you how wrong it is to live in the future and wait for a better moment to arrive – because it will never come.

We convince ourselves that life will be better when we finish school, when we go to university, when we finish university, when we get a job, when we get married, when we get a child, another child… Soon after that we are frustrated because the children are small, so we wait for them to grow up a bit and get better. Then we complain about our adolescent children saying it's hard to handle them. We will surely be happier when they outgrow that phase. We say to ourselves we will be happier when we have more money, when we get well, when we find a partner, when we buy a car, when we go to holiday, when we buy this or that, when we have more energy, more support, when people respect us, when family support us, when we retire… The truth is, there is no better time to be happy than this time, right now. When if not now? We shouldn't postpone happiness. For a long time, you have been waiting for your life to start. True life. But there were always some obstacles you should overcome, mess you should take care of, tasks that needed to be finished, bills that needed to be paid. As soon as you took care of it, you were thinking, true life would start for sure. At the end of the road, you might realize those obstacles were in fact life. Therefore, life will always be full of challenges. It's better to accept that and decide to be happy – not because of that, but despite that. You should understand there is no right path to happiness; happiness *is* the path. Therefore – enjoy every moment. Stop waiting to finish school, to start at the university, to go back to university, to lose 10 pounds, to gain 10 pounds, to start working, to marry, to buy a car; stop waiting for Friday to come, for spring and warmer days to come, for winter to be over, for 15th, 30th or 60th birthday, for your song on the radio; stop waiting to earn more money, to get well, to die… – before you decide to be happy. Happiness is not a destination or a race. There is no better time to be happy than NOW! Live and enjoy the moment the way you think is right. Don't wait for anything; waiting moves us away from the present moment and pulls us back to the comfort zone. Present moment is everything you've got – therefore, it is wise to use it.

🐾 Recommendations to inspire you on your journey of happiness ☺

- [QR 23] The Art of Saying No: Kenny Nguyen at TEDxLSU,
        https://www.youtube.com/watch?v=FtPRrn5nwAo
- [QR 24] Peaceful Warrior - Official Trailer:
        https://www.youtube.com/watch?v=gegNMYvY_yg
- [QR 25] Oprah & Eckhart Tolle - Living in the Present Moment:
        https://www.youtube.com/watch?v=KmCjR1_N14E

- [QR 22] Facebook page Louise L. Hay:
        https://www.facebook.com/louiselhay/?fref=ts

- You Can Heal Your Life, Louise L. Hay, 1984.
- Echkart Tolle: The Power of Now: A Guide to Spiritual Enlighten-ment, 2003.

CHALLENGE 2:
SCREEN AND MEDIA DIET

In order to hear our internal voice, we have to silence all others.

If you still think there is no time and you couldn't find time for yourself during the day (which is *conditio sine qua non* for any change in life whatsoever and for leaving the comfort zone), think of the time you daily spend in front of the three screens (TV, computer and cell phone) and (non)electronic media (newspapers, magazines, web portals, social networks etc.).

Mini challenge

Try to calculate how much time overall you exactly spent in front of the three screens every day. Is it an hour, two, five or more? Be honest and calculate the hours as realistic as possible.

Most people believe they aren't addicted to screens and media, but when they solve a test or two created for measuring that kind of addiction, they are surprised to find out they actually are addicted, at least slightly. This is the topic of utmost importance because screens consume enormous amount of our time. I will, therefore, analyze every one of them in more detail. In fact, they are so important that reducing them is special and essential challenge I have called screen and media diet – because it is exactly them that have an enormous power to trap people deep in the comfort zone. We witness a great crisis of information today – but the problem is not that we lack information, but rather we are overwhelmed by them. I've read somewhere that in just one day we absorb the same amount of information people of the 16th century absorbed during their entire lives. In today's civilization media has become ubiquitous and the most important factor of information and communication. It's time you reconsider the information you let in your cortex. Think about why you do it and what consequences that has. Let's start from the beginning.

First, we'll discuss television – our dear, colorful box. Or these days – flat screen, as thin as possible and as big as possible, we are prepared to give a pile of money for. And do it several times, for that matter. Firstly, because newer, bigger and thinner models constantly hit the shops, and secondly, because our houses/apartments usually have more than one room, and every room deserve to have at least one specimen of this powerful device. Do you know how many hours per day children spend in front of the TV on average? As much as three hours; at the same time, they talk to their parents merely 30 minutes. Elementary school kids on average watch four movies every weekend. Astounding, isn't it? We adults spend more than few hours a day watching television. Many people watch TV even while they eat. In more than 60% of households, TV is on the whole day, and the number of children with TV in their rooms is constantly increasing. During the 75-year-long life, an average person spends as much as 12 years in front of the TV! Is it really so easy to control us, is there really nothing else we would rather do than be the slaves of information and content others serve us? Have you ever wondered how people used to live before television, how they managed without it? Maybe some of you still remember that time, not so long ago.

Those questions led me to reduce watching television drastically for a year, and to eventually abstain from it completely for five years (which left me with enough time to absorb new knowledge). I know this is shocking for some of you, but I assure you that many people in my immediate surroundings don't watch TV as well (and some of them actually work on television). Those people say it was one of the best decisions in their lives; they stopped watching, and started living. I used to be one of those people who watch TV regularly and I didn't wonder whether I could live without television, should I try it and why. I would simply turn it on by habit and watch (I even know some people who couldn't study and/or sleep without it; though I wasn't one of them). Television was an integral part of my life. I remember how 10 years ago a colleague from work told me she and her family have a deal not to watch TV during the Lent. I clearly remember how shocking that was for me. To renounce chocolate – I would understand that; but TV? I couldn't grasp the purpose of it or what they could gain from it and how could that be even feasible. I remember I used to talk about that with others astonished: "Imagine, my colleague and her family renounce TV for as much as 40 days!" I couldn't comprehend that for a long time, but then I've started to come across different studies and information that have changed my opinion. First, I've started to wonder what would I be doing if I wasn't watching television at the moment? Then I've started to replace TV-watching with other activities (playing with my child, socializing with friends, walking, reading, studying, relaxing, researching the topics I was interested in). And the ratio began to turn in favor of the later. As my level of consciousness rose, TV became more and more secondary in my life.

Don't get me wrong, I am not advocating radical cuts, nor I think that you have to renounce TV completely in order to live happily. But if you habitually turn on the TV and dully switch channels (inevitably concluding how "there's nothing on" despite 300+ channels), you certainly and verifiably won't become happier. TV content shapes our thoughts, serves us with chosen and sought for information, making us addicted to it. Media are truly the creators of reality, and they actually commercialize our unattainable wishes. They encourage us to wish for things we otherwise wouldn't wish for, or even wouldn't know they exist. Very advisedly and targeted they serve us certain contents, some of it in order to lower our vibrations and keep us "down", under the radar of real things. You know the proverb: dogs bark, but the caravan goes on. Media decide what's important, and what's not. When was the last time you've watched only positive news on TV? That kind of content is rare if it exists at all – as it doesn't sell well (with rare exceptions). Television is entirely one-way communication through which viewers only receive information, i.e. dictated content – without being forced to.

There is nothing wrong in watching content you've selected from the TV program (e.g. some people like to watch news, others like documentaries, or movies, or sports matches…), but remember to turn off the TV after the program ends! Don't let other content (going on endlessly) attract your attention. You will be shocked with the amount of spare time you'll have once you reduce watching TV and with the things you can accomplish in that time. Television doesn't kill us, but it makes us passive – because it's not interactive, it limits creativity, it transforms us into perfect clay which is (too) easy to control. It's as seductive as opium, it's infinitely more efficient in shaping our thoughts and opinions than politics and religion. That is why television is considered the most powerful weapon of psychological warfare. The relevance of the information TV provides, you can estimate with a simple test: follow the news on national and several commercial television channels, and focus on the difference between them. Journalist and editorial freedom aside, the differences in conveying information and news are still huge – every television channel emphasizes whatever suits its purposes, for variety of reasons. Despite that, and considering the fact we live in the age of consumerism, as consumers we often adjust our lives, habits and behaviors according to what we see on television. Television, therefore, transmits consumerist messages and offers a life model of sorts for people to follow and wish for. It's implied you cannot be happy if you don't own certain product, if you don't look like certain celebrities, if you don't drink certain beverage, if you don't follow certain lifestyle. As much as nine out of ten women in the Western world aren't satisfied with their looks, because the media defined how we should look. The sole purpose of advertising often is to open your emotional weaknesses and to make you feel you are flawed if you lack certain product. In truth, most of those products you don't need at all, and they certainly aren't related to your happiness. Or, to be precise, it can bring you short-term happiness, but we have already discussed the connection between happiness and money – and concluded that more money and more possessions lead to new aspirations and wishes, but with the same level of happiness.

An excellent book about television is *Remotely Controlled: How Television is Damaging Our Lives*, by American doctor and psychologist Aric Sigman. By scanning the ◼ 26 you will be able to read several pages from the beginning of the book. You will see, the book is full of literally shocking information and scientific proofs on damaging effect of television. It says television even destroys our health: it slows down metabolism, stops the development of children's brains, increases the odds for violence and crime, and it is the leading cause of depression. There you have it, one of the key ways to decrease depression is to turn off the TV sometimes! And that isn't as hard as it seems. I warmly recommend the book, especially to the parents among you. You are responsible for your children, especially in the early childhood. Your children imitate you, thus you should be the role model for them, act the way you want them to act. In addition, you are the ones to decide when and for how long will your children watch television. It isn't wise to put TV in children's room early on, because it's harder to control the consummation that way. I will discuss the issue of children as consumers – who are one of the main interests of modern business and marketing – in challenge 7 (inspiring parenting).

Next screen we will discuss is cell phone. Their overall use is the most natural thing in today's world. Many kids get their first mobile phone at the beginning of elementary school (in order to be able to call their parents); three-year-old children of my friends often know how to use smartphone (and that makes the parents proud, of course). With smartphones we wake up, we go to sleep, we spend the day. Without them we feel as though we miss the part of ourselves. With the arrival of 3G network and smartphones, mobile devices have become close to us almost as the members of our families. There is a saying we live in the age of smart phones and stupid people. Cell phones are now true palm computers and they are so much more than phones (even mobile ones) of yesterday. When was the last time you have divided two numbers without calculator? What about decimal numbers? How many telephone numbers do you know by heart? As a child, I remember I knew phone numbers (landline, of course) of all my friends; now I have them memorized in my phone, so I don't bother remembering them.

QR 26

Mini challenge

Install an app for mobile phone usage analysis and analyze your weekly data (how many hours you use your phone, on what content mostly etc.).

Have you ever considered not to be available on your phone 24/7? Do you have to confirm a meeting at 5 p.m. five times and then at 4.55 call to say you will be three minutes late? Do you have to have your mobile phone constantly at hand? Are you afraid you are going to miss something important? Have you ever considered how our parents managed to meet and date before cell phones (with occasional landline at hand)? Well, they arranged, for example, to meet at the same place at a certain time the next day. And they didn't exchange million messages, calls and everything else in the meantime. If someone happened to miss the meeting the next day, after a while life would show what to do and how. Once, I was traveling by train to Ljubljana to attend my doctoral studies and I had forgotten my mobile phone at home in Osijek. When I realized I hadn't brought my phone, I felt as though a part of my body was missing. I couldn't imagine what it would be like, how I would call home when I arrived; I worried what if this or that person called me – after all, four days was a lot. But, as you can see, I have survived. I contacted whomever I needed to, minimally, via email. Not only I have survived, I felt somewhat liberated.

3G, 4G, 5G – technology is constantly evolving, with both positive and negative effects. Today electronic devices emit electromagnetic radiation in our homes more than ever and that has an effect on our bodies and health without a doubt. Numerous studies have shown radiation has different consequences on human body. Unless we plan to move to some isolated country where technology hasn't arrived fully yet, all we could do, unfortunately, is to protect ourselves as much as we can, i.e. minimize the effect of radiation. I suggest, therefore, not to keep mobile phones in pants' pockets (especially if you are male), to spend part of the day without your mobile phone, to keep the phone at least three feet away from you whenever you can, to talk through ear set instead directly through phone speakers. Cell phones add to hearing and sight damage, they can increase number of traffic accidents and lead to attention disorders or decrease of concentration, they can trigger depression and lead to poor psycho-physical condition or other health challenges.

For example, even if you use Bluetooth technology in your car (ear set or integrated), the talking itself will distract you just as much and decrease your concentration and presence. Studies show texting during the drive is six time more likely to cause an accident than driving under the influence of alcohol. More than 25% of all traffic accidents in

QR 27

U.S. is caused by cell phone usage! Don't let the message you write while driving be the last you'll ever write. Watch a short video on this subject (■ 27).

QR 28

Try not to use mobile phone one hour before sleep, as looking at screen can lead to insomnia – photons tell the brain to stay awake. Watch dr. Daniel Siegel, Mindsight Institute director, talk about the influence cell phones have on sleep (■ 28). In addition, you shouldn't keep mobile phone beside you at least during the night, and you should turn it off completely from time to time. The world will not disappear or stop turning in those few hours, while you will feel totally different and, what's most important, you'll get time to work on yourself.

Mini challenge

Don't sleep with mobile phone beside you; take it away from your bedroom at night.

Combined with the third type of screens – computers (most working people can't do without) and tablets, the arena for developing all kinds of habits and addictions widens beyond belief. Those addictions aren't different from drug or alcohol addictions at all. There are, for example, SMS addiction, Internet addiction, computer games addiction, social networks addiction or online gambling addiction. The number of addicts is a growing problem in South Korea (around 20% of population has a risk of developing Internet addiction); one of the first clinics for treating internet, technology and videogame addiction, called Save Brain Clinic, was established in South Korea. The most addicts are adolescents, but there are adult addicts as well. Internet addiction came under the loupe after World Health Organization added gaming disorder to the International Classification of Diseases 2018, 10 years after China first recognized it as a public health threat. The biggest challenge – the same as with every other addiction – is to recognize and admit it. And the treatment is based on medication, i.e. antidepressants, because the key to the problem is serious depression and anxiety.

It's horrible, but the trend of opening hospitals around the world reflects the seriousness of the "lost on the internet" issue. Apparently, there are more technology than alcohol addicts. I've read on a news portal how at special risk are anxious and depressed persons who live in constant stress, whose social life is poor and who already have an addiction. Internet addicts are persons with compulsive and addictive potential and they usually don't recognize their problem, even though they suffer from various symptoms – they are preoccupied with internet, they lose track of time, they are isolated from their families and friends, they tend to get euphoric when using the internet and they aren't able to distinct real from the virtual world. And there are physical symptoms as well – headache, neck pain and vision problems.

In fact, if we stop for a second and take a look at ourselves and people around us, we'll realize that we have all become addicted to technology to some extent. I have a colleague who constantly complains about her husband playing videogames at night (and whenever he can, basically), and the extent of it has become disastrous for him and his relationships, especially with his wife. Today, many people are being treated for that, gaming addiction; some deprive themselves of sleep completely in order not to lose score/points in the game, and even forget to satisfy their physiological needs – hence, there are records of death in front of the screen. Can you believe that? More than 1.15 million people in Japan suffer from *hikikomori*, condition in which a person decides to withdraw from society and spend time in their room with nothing but technology for more than six months, and experts suggest the numbers can be even higher, maybe as much as 10 million people. No wonder, as in the virtual world you can be anybody (even MickeyMouse55), you can have superpowers of your choice, you can be hero, the best and fastest – regardless of your real condition. It's easy to enter that world, but it's much harder to find a way out. Finally, when the game is over, we face the truth that can be bitter. Not to mention people stay in the game mode an hour after playing (especially violent games), and they are more prone to act that way in the real world as well, they generally become antisocial and aggressive.

Today brain ages faster than the body as it is less and less activated by the right contents. If you have a habit of playing online games, at least try to make them somewhat beneficial to your brain. Do crosswords, word games, games that increase concentration and memory, games that activate both cerebral hemispheres. You can try popular Sudoku and similar games that stimulate your brain to think. Look for games/contents that develop intelligence (IQ building games), such as memory games, math games, puzzles, brain teasers.

Mini challenge

Talk to at least one person that is close to you and knows your habits, and ask him/her to tell you how much you use screens and media.

Even if you aren't an addict and you use screens moderately, other dangers lurk from virtual, cyber world 24/7. To mention some: hacker attacks, identity thefts, credit card abuse, viruses, uncritical adoption of other people's opinions (suggestibility), electronic violence regulated by the law – threats, extortions, blackmails, insults, slander, displaying of personal or family situations, child pornography… The worst is probably the fact that media promote the picture of an ideal life – people with perfect physic, looks, without wrinkles – implanting into our subconscious the notion that consumerism is a solution to all our problems. Enter newspapers and magazines. Watch the video The Ugly Truth behind Beauty Magazines (■ 29). What do you say now? Adds, adds, adds and made-up models younger than 21, sexual messages, bombastic covers. Have you noticed how the news from the crime section often end up at the front page of newspapers? When did it happen; not so long ago it was just another section of papers? Other times, other manners – I don't blame journalists for writing like that or editors for their newspaper politics. We consumers should be conscious, or at least conscious enough to understand that our every – I mean every – purchase and choice is actually a vote. If we ask for more positive news, they will have to provide. If you read newspaper, you should focus on the content you are truly interested in, and you will always find the things you are interested in and that you like to focus on (both privately and professionally).

QR 29

If so far I haven't encouraged you to think about the noxiousness of screens, to be more rational when you use it and to go on a screen diet, the next term related to that topic might: subliminal messages. It's something that is being researched for a long time, but only recently (in 1950's) it has become, let's say, public. Subliminal messages are the messages that lie at the threshold of consciousness, and they represent a sophisticated way of planting wishes and taboos into the subconscious of an individual, with the ultimate goal: to influence someone's decisions and to implant certain mental patterns. There are, basically, five types of "mind games" related to subconscious manipulation: subliminal messages, reversible messages, symbols, optical illusions and hidden messages.

Propaganda, or marketing is the extreme way to send subliminal messages. Even though such messages can appear in different types of media, let's concentrate on those in images. Given that one frame rate (the frequency at which consecutive images appear on a display; every image is a photograph that in quick succession makes an illusion of movement, i.e. animation) has 24 images per second, our eye won't notice if someone deliberately insert one additional, 25th image, with the desired content. That can significantly increase the probability of purchase of a certain product or it can direct an individual towards desired behavior. As expected, sex and death are the most intimate urges in our thoughts. No wander such messages are most common. Who cares, you can say. Maybe we should care, as such messages are often planted into cartoons (yes, and Disney cartoons, to make things worse). Watch the video with lots of examples from cartoons (■ 30), but a simple search on the internet will lead you to numerous other examples, because subliminal messages are ubiquitous. And they can also be found in music, below the audible level, or they can be combined.

QR 30

The question isn't whether subliminal messages exist (no one denies it, not even their creators), but what effect they actually have on people. We shouldn't live in fear because of those messages, but we should think for ourselves and abandon our usual life. Therefore, look, search, research, and draw your own conclusion and your own truth with 5% of your consciousness (because science confirms that 95% of our actions and conclusions is based on subconscious). Solution is very simple and at hand, but apprehending the need for change of certain habits and their noxiousness is something completely different.

The message of this challenge is to stop molesting yourself with screens and to put yourself on a screen and media diet, purposely and with dedication. This doesn't mean you should abstain from all screens and without exception (that isn't even possible, just like being on a diet doesn't mean you shouldn't eat at all, but rather to be careful about what you eat and drink, how, how much and when). Rather, it means you should use screens as much as necessary. Therefore, use screens wisely. You've got to do what you've got to do (and today in the context of cell phones and computers there is too much of it); for everything else think 10 times. This will give you more time to do whatever you like, to be happier and more optimistic, to empty your head from negative news and images. Remember: to hear your inner voice, you have to turn off every other voice.

> **Mini challenge**
>
> *For the next 10 days, go on the screen diet (do only what is necessary). Write your expectations, and I recommend you to write a journal of sorts – write down in short what you did, how you felt, whether you have missed the screens etc.*

I don't think technology is bad per se, and the same is with social networks, television, computers (after all, this book isn't written on the typewriter), media, or cell phones. But it's wrong to let technology control your lives, it's wrong not to understand what it does to you and how harmful it can be: it's wrong that there are so many people who don't even want to know because they feel great "as it is" in their comfort zone. However, with the huge amount of time we spend on the three or four screens, we have to wonder why and were it will take us. Technology is like a knife, which saves lives in the hands of a surgeon, but kills in the hands of a murderer. So that object is neutral until it is engaged in certain action, just like television and other media. For a moment imagine a different world, world in which media increase our vibrations and want to make us grateful and happy, to serve us and promote only good and edifying stories. You know what, even though they are in minority, it doesn't mean such stories don't exist, and your job is to focus exactly on them.

Therefore, the story about screens has a happy ending after all, because their use and presence in our lives is 100% under our control. We are the ones to create our social networks profiles, we are the ones to decide for what content we will press "like", we are the ones to choose our background images, we are the ones to decide what portals we will follow and read, we are the ones to choose which radio station we will listen, we are the ones to turn on the TV and pick a channel, we are the ones to buy newspapers… Hence, we could lie to ourselves that we live in different times and that this or that is impossible, but the truth is everything is still under our control – the same as with using the knife. If you refuse to become sheep, or sheeple as someone put it, technology can really be of great help to you, it can make your lives easier and enable you to find information quickly.

Let me share my example with you. For some time now, my screensaver shows two hands touching (one from heaven, the other from earth), and this reminds me of my spiritual path every time I turn on computer. The case of my cell phone says "Live the life you love". When I turn the cell phone on, the pink image with the message by Louise Hay pops up: "I feel glorious, dynamic energy, I am active and alive." On my planner, which I pick up several times every day, this year there is a line "Believe in miracles". Because my job requires following daily and economics news, I read the news on the internet – but only when I want to, as much as I want to and what I want to. Social networks I have organized in such a way to feed me mostly positive content from the areas I consider interesting and inspiring.

Mini challenge
Start to follow at least one positive web site or person on social networks.

The time is actually always here, we just have to take it in order to put ourselves first in a healthy way and to start making positive steps towards the magic zone. It is challenging, of course, because some of our behaviors have become our habits after so many iterations. But this is exactly why this is challenge in the first place. If your goal is to adopt a certain knowledge, then don't neglect it in order to indulge yourselves with something you would rather do at the moment (e.g. your goal is a firm body, but in this moment you give priority to sitting in front of the TV). Abandon this lifestyle and the comfort zone in which you "don't have time", while you probably waste a lot of it on screens. To sum up, in order to be good to others, you have to be good to yourselves first. And in order to do that, you have to make time for yourselves – don't lie to yourselves that you don't have time, as this holds you in the comfort zone. You have to eliminate, at least partially, screens and media or two from your lives, i.e. put yourselves on a screen diet, and you will have plenty of time. You could also make a habit of getting up earlier. Or you could follow my example and do both. As Mahatma Gandhi said: "Watch your habits, for they become character; watch your character, for it becomes your destiny." What kind of destiny you want for yourselves? I wish you peace, for everything else will follow naturally. And how to achieve it? By practicing spirituality – let's make new step out of the comfort zone. Through the door number 3. There is a saying you will change a habit most successfully by replacing it with another. Therefore, replace the habit of watching screens with some other daily practice from our next challenge.

₰ Recommendations to inspire you on your journey of happiness ☺

- [QR 27] Wait for It... This Could Save Your Life,
    https://www.youtube.com/watch?v=E9swS1Vl6Ok
- [QR 28] Dr. Daniel Siegel: How Smartphones Affect Your Sleep,
    https://www.youtube.com/watch?v=_1V0rDSTC9I
- [QR 29] The Ugly Truth behind Beauty Magazines,
    https://www.facebook.com/watch/?v=2510756312280746
- [QR 30] Disney Illuminati Satanism & Sex Symbols Exposed:
    https://www.youtube.com/watch?v=fGvIkc0tdpI

- [QR 26] Remotely Controlled: How Television is Damaging Our Lives, Aric Sigman, 2010.,
    https://www.amazon.co.uk/Remotely-Controlled-television-damaging-lives/dp/0091906903

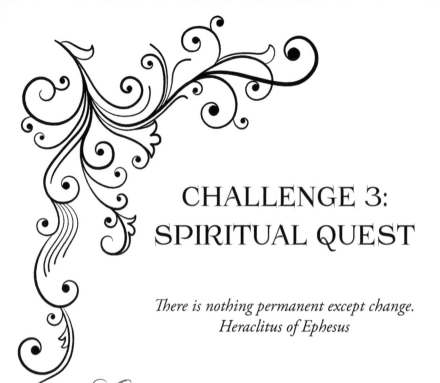

CHALLENGE 3:
SPIRITUAL QUEST

There is nothing permanent except change.
Heraclitus of Ephesus

After you have made time for yourselves and gone on media and screen diet, it is time for the next challenge: spiritual quest. The goal of this chapter isn't to persuade you to become more or less religious, or to change your opinions, but to encourage you to think, to analyze your life and ask the right question – just as the rest of this book. According to 2019 data, dominant world religion is still Christianity (with around 33% of believers), but the number of atheists/agnostics is rising (currently about 12%). I am Christian myself – I have even taught catechism in my parish for a while, I have sung in church quire for more than 20 years, I have read Holy Scripture during the mass, helped in parish office etc. It is not my intention to write against this or that religion and well-established system, I just want to share my experiences and observations with you.

The thing is, throughout my religious path I struggled with several question, and they became more frequent and louder as I grew up. For example, I've never liked the selection of songs for youth-focused mass (and that eventually spurred my decision to stop singing in church after more than 20 years). Whenever we sang merrier and more zestful songs, we were merrier and more zestful ourselves – and we would convey that energy to others. People would praise our singing and they would be somehow happier after the mass. I wandered why we weren't allowed to sing this or that song, when it was allowed in another church. It all depended on priests. After some masses my heart just wasn't as full as it should have been. Moreover, after one confession I cried for two days because the priest literally predicted me a terrible future due to my "sins", that were really just small misbehaviors. I generally couldn't understand why was I obliged to confess my sins to the priest when he is sinful too? If God is in all of us, why did I need an intermediary? At last, why did I have to say "…I firmly resolve to sin no more…" when both priest and I knew I would sin again?! I really didn't like that because I felt as if I was lying to myself, to the priest and to God. In addition, some masses lasted for an hour and a half; and after we'd complained about it, we've been told the liturgy is holy and it has no duration. So, I've started to attend mass at other churches and I've realized, to my great surprise, that what was the rule in one church, didn't have to be in another at all. That has planted numerous questions in my subconscious, and the answers have started to come slowly, with time. Less and less young people visit certain churches, and that doesn't surprise me at all. Priests and others who are responsible should ask themselves about the direction they are going, they should try to find ways to collectively modernize church and bring it closer to young people – within what is possible and in accordance to their rules.

One of the breakthroughs in my understanding of this topic was my honeymoon in Thailand in 2011. In every temple there, I could witness how deeply religious Buddhists actually are. In their temples and sacred places, you could feel a certain peace, everybody was taking their shoes off at the entrance, and they had numerous rituals (from pouring the oil in little vessels and burning the scent sticks to attaching real gold leaves to statues and beating the belfries…). I asked a friend born in Bangkok how she knew what to do, when and how long she prayed, and to which of the hundreds of Buddha statues in temple, what were their rituals like. She replied: "It's complicated, but in short – everything is up to you." I would get the same answer every time: as you wish, however you feel, it's up to you, there are no strict rules. After 15 days, I started to answer the questions myself: yes, yes, I know, everything is the way I decide and choose. Well, why is it so different from my religion, which is full of rules and limitations? When I later talked about it with my colleague from church quire, she told me that this was all fine, but our God was the only true God, much more correct than Buddha, and all those people that didn't believe in Christ were mistaken. Our God was the God. Well, to me that sounded like children's statements – *my Barbie is prettier than yours*, or *my dad is stronger than yours*. I guess the following is clear to everyone: If I had been born in Bangkok, I would most probably have been Buddhist or Hinduist. And what would that mean? That I am religiously mistaken and that I worth less? My colleague aside, but lot of people have this kind of, at the very least, unusual attitude.

Mini challenge

Think for a moment about how you think of God.

I remember the time I asked my grandmother why she did this or that in church, and she didn't have specific answers to my questions. She said it was simply the way things were done, and she even got a bit angry with me for asking so many "stupid" questions and bothering her with it. However, how many Christians today truly live Christian lives? How many of them really understand the depths of Ten Commandments? How many of them have read the Bible? When I talked about this with my mom, I was very surprised to find out she actually supported and understood me fully. She just didn't want to exit the comfort zone. She said she was used to live in faith, it was easier for her that way and she was taking the best of everything anyway. And that is fine, I respect that. It's funny, though, if not paradoxical, how certain quite indoctrinated Catholics looked at me in wonder when I had said to them I truly, completely believed in angels. They wanted to call me crazy and declare my statement a sacrilege of a kind, but then I stopped them with question: "And you don't believe in angels? Isn't our Church preaching about different angels, aren't we praying Guardian Angel Prayer before going to sleep every night? Just a minute, you want to say you are actually praying to something/someone you don't truly believe in?" It's paradoxical, isn't it?

To make it short, eventually I've come to understand the difference between religion and spirituality, and the fact that they are not synonyms, not even close. The role of religions of the world (Christianity, Islam, Hinduism, Buddhism and all others) is to connect people with God, to serve as intermediaries. Religion is a set of beliefs and rites established to lead us into correct relationship with God. It is, therefore, some kind of institutionalization of God, i.e. church is institution. As such, it has its rules and a great power of influence on masses. Some will say that through different fears it cultivates (of sins, hell, death…), this institution has a powerful tool for manipulation. In fact, every religion claims it is the one, true religion and the only correct story (although each respects other religions more or less).

On the other hand, spirituality doesn't work through intermediary, i.e. you have direct, so to speak, connection with God. Focus is on the spiritual stuff and spiritual world, rather than on the physical/earthly things. Spirituality denotes notion that we are more than just body, that we are also a soul with endless potential and possibilities. That is why people often impart a mystical tone to spirituality. Given that there are no strict rules, nor following particular ideology or fear cultivating, spirituality allows you to follow the inner voice of God. The reward is peace within, feeling of satisfaction and happiness. Spirituality accepts all religions, reminds us there are no divisions and we are one. In other words, according to one of the influential people, doctor who advocates alternative medicine, writer and speaker Deepak Chopra: "Religion is belief in someone else's experience. Spirituality is having your own experience." For more information on this topic, watch an interesting lecture on difference between being religious and spiritual (■ 31). QR 31

Mini challenge

Are you a religious or spiritual person? Think about it for a while. What do you want to be? Is there something that you have been drawn to throughout your life, but you didn't have the courage for it until now? Just say it aloud and apprehend it.

I was brought up as a religious person. Everything we are today, everything we know and do is defined by past: by our upbringing, culture, origin, by patterns our parents followed. Everything we've been given by birth we can picture as a foundation upon which we weave the fabric of our lives. As always, the key is in understanding that the fabric is in our hands (responsibility, remember?) and in learning to weave as beautiful and as rich fabric of our authentic lives as possible. It isn't something you can finish in a day or two, it is a task that lasts as long as we live. That's why I chose the quote at a beginning of this chapter, saying there is nothing permanent except change. After we have realized we are capable and obligated to weave our fabric, it is important to understand we can do it in any way we want. We can use completely different materials and colors than before, we can change certain threads, we can create completely different picture from the one we had at the beginning.

That is why the name of this challenge is spiritual quest. Because in the sea of possibilities and beliefs, you have to find your own place. You have to, as I have underlined at the beginning of this book, ask questions and search for answers, and create your own reality. It's easier, of course, to follow formal and well-established patterns, but that's not authentic; it will lead you back into the comfort zone, and it will not bring you closer to true happiness and the magic zone. Next, I will talk about some of the cognitions that answered several questions for me and that are a part of my spiritual practice. You might have heard about some of them, all of them, or neither of them. So let's be open-minded.

Firstly, we must accept that everything around us is energy. I mean everything. We live in a vibrating world. Therefore, it is unbelievable how all of us know there are thermal energy (something or someone obviously makes our lunch cooked), energy of the sun (we really can get sun burns), energy of the wind (something powers the windmills), energy of gravity (we walk firmly on ground, instead of hoovering)… All of us believe in that. Why? Because we were taught about it in schools, because we have heard it so many times it has become our belief, our truth and our reality. But if we say something about "general" energy as a concept, it will still make some people's hair curl. The fact is, energy is this book you are reading, and the furniture supporting your body at this moment, and the food you eat, and the water you drink, and your thoughts, and stone, and sun, and animals – everything. It wasn't me to realize this (luckily), but Einstein within his theory of relativity. He wrote, long time ago, one of the most famous equations $E=mc^2$, where E is energy, m mass, and c speed of light, which is constant, 670 616 629 miles per hour in vacuum (with that speed, flash of light from Earth will reach the sun in eight minutes). Given that c is a constant, if we disregard it, we will get $E=m$, i.e. energy is equal to mass. In other words, everything that has a mass (no matter how small or big), I mean everything, all matter – is energy. From the equation, we can also conclude that energy and mass can transform from one to another. Thanks to Einstein, modern physics got closer to the ancient spiritual teachings of Far East and admitted that everything is energy.

I have watched many videos about this topic, but one really made me think, so I will translate the introductory text for you. It is called Physics of Manifestation. *Believe it or not, our every-day and usual perspective on the world and universe is a reflection of scientific cognitions from ancient 1687! Belief in "objective" reality and one, singular universe – which obeys clear, precise laws of physics like some kind of mechanical device – is based on Newton's physics, which is… well… somewhat obsolete. It was replaced firstly by relativistic, and then quantum physics, but we still act as small, pathetic, helpless observers within gigantic, cruel and indifferent universe, to us at least. Nothing is further from the truth! If you really want to understand how the creation functions on its basic level, or what is our role in the story, if you want to appease the rational part of your mind with formally stricter and scientifically more acceptable explanation of the fact (among other things) that by positive thinking we attract positive experiences and move to the parallel realities whose circumstances sustain our inner frequency – this lecture is for you! This topic will blow your mind. As Mark Twain said: "The truth is stranger than fiction, because fiction has to have sense."*

Everything around us vibrates constantly. We vibrate constantly. And vibrations are motions that repeat regularly. The number of motions' repetitions within one second is called vibration frequency. One cycle in one second we denote with herz, Hz. Bees' wings vibrate 150 times per second; therefore, the frequency of that motion we hear as buzzing is 150 Hz. Our brain is electro-chemical organ, and its electricity is measured by brain waves. There are four categories of brain waves, from faster to slower ones (■ 32). It's interesting that the fastest brain waves correspond to lower frequency consciousness, while the slowest brain waves correspond to higher frequency consciousness, i.e. widened consciousness. Beta waves from 13 to 40 Hz (or cycles per second) are the fastest brain waves related to the state of alertness, when brain is involved in activities. For example, while we are reading in the evening, we are probably in low beta state. The more intensive activity – say, fear, anger, hunger or surprise – faster the frequency. Alfa state from 8 to 13 Hz is the state we are more relaxed in, but not drowsy. It is the state of daydreaming, meditation, creative visualization, artistic and intuitive processes, state we are in when we spend time in nature, or when we are relaxing or exercising. Theta state from 4 to 8 Hz is the state of slower brain waves and it is related to imagination, intuition, first phase of sleeping and mystic states. Theta state is similar to trance, to those moments when we lose the sense of time. Delta brain waves from half to 4 Hz are very slow, we can find them in deep sleep, and they are related with sleep walking or talking, with deep trance and self-healing processes. Body relaxation and deep breathing are the key to increasing our personal vibration. Unhealthy habits block our souls and contaminate our lives. Those habits are dwelling in the victim's position, blaming others for our troubles, judging, postponing, being envious, imagining the worst-case scenarios of future, using negations, gossiping, mocking and many other things. So what should we do? Radiate. A part of us that isn't stopped by lamentations and bad habits, really radiates. We should ask ourselves what part of us is radiating, and bring light to places of fear, sorrow, and pain. The miracle will happen immediately. Because, we cannot turn off the dark, but we can turn on the light. Personal transformation has a global effect. Where we are going, the world is going too, because the world – that's us. Our personal revolution will turn the world upside down.

QR 32

I have learned the most about states of consciousness and brain waves by following the work of Dr. Joe Dispenza and attending his course. I will tell you more about him later (in challenge 5), but now, when we are talking about God, I would like to share some of Dispenza's data aimed to make people aware of the existence of intelligence bigger than us, but present in all of us. We are magnificent creatures. There is an intelligence that gives us life, and that same intelligence organizes our bodily functions such as heartbeat. Heart pumps around 7.5 liters of blood per minute, more than 378 liters per hour, more than 100,000 times per day through more than 59,962 miles of blood vessels, and cardiovascular system takes up merely 3% of your body weight. Every second we lose and create 25 million cells, and each cell of the body has from roughly 100,000 to 6 trillion functions per second. We have to multiply that with 50-70 trillion cells in our bodies, and acknowledge the fact that this communication is faster than the speed of light. Besides, every day we breathe in 2 million liters of air, and it is transferred to each cell within few seconds. It is obvious we cannot follow and control these processes by ourselves. Our bodies are a collection of atoms, and they are made of 99.9999999% of nothing – which is energy, information. Only 0.0000001% of atom is a particle that exists, and only temporarily, for that matter. We go in and out of quantum field eight times per second. If we took one cell from the body, and stretched its DNA, it would be two meters long. If we took all DNA material from the body and stretched it, it would go to the sun and back 150 times. If we took the DNA from all 7 billion people on Earth and squeezed it together, it would fit into the grain of rice. No matter how you define God or whether you believe in it or not, after hearing this, the majority of you undoubtedly have realized there must be some higher intelligence to make all those processes in our bodies even possible.

Dr. David R. Hawkins developed and presented the scale of consciousness or scale of frequencies of (emotional) vibrations in his book *Power vs. Force*. You can check it out by scanning the QR code (■ 33). Values vary from 20 to 1000, and the scale is divided into several parts ranging from suffering to enlightenment (700 – 1000). At the bottom of the scale are hatred and guilt, with the level of con-

QR 33

sciousness from 20 to 30; they are destructive and the basis for all kinds of diseases. According to Dr. Hawkins, two of these levels enable great spiritual growth: first at 200 and second at 500. Everything under 200 is very exhausting for humans in the sense of energy. Level of 200 is the level of courage (enters strength and power) and that is why this book is called *Courage on the Path to Happiness*. It is the magical boundary we have to cross in order to exit the fear zone and enter into the action zone.

According to research, 85% of human race dwells under the critical level of 200. Overall average level of human consciousness currently is at 207. The good news is that one person vibrating at the level 500 compensate for 750,000 people at the levels less than 200, i.e. bigger group of people vibrating at the frequencies of love and peace in theory can affect the whole world. We should aim for 500 or more, i.e. the goal of personal development is to reach as high frequencies as possible in order to change the emotional state. We all vibrate at different levels, depending on our prevailing emotions.

Mini challenge

Test yourselves – tell yourselves how you feel (name few emotions, e.g. joy, sorrow, content, fear, and suffering), try to understand what's prevailing and then figure out where you are at the scale of frequencies. Analyze your body – are you full of zest (high vibrations) or are you sick and sluggish (low vibrations). Note down your results.

In addition, it is important not to ignore moments that give us the goose bumps. Some people interpret those moments as a near death experiences (?!), but I believe those are the moments when we are connected to a higher consciousness, i.e. the moments when the events are resonating with our souls and when we are in truth. Try to observe it. Next time you get the goose bumps, analyze what you were doing, thinking or watching at that moment, i.e. ask yourselves what you are resonating with. Very soon, you will realize how fun, and useful, that is; it will somehow make your life journey easier.

Everything around us has a certain vibration: our thoughts, words, actions, values, behaviors, goals, businesses, relationships, beliefs – everything. Given that vibrations have a much stronger influence on subconscious level, it is clear how important is to take this seriously. The goal is to make a connection between our mind, subconscious and creation (Universe, God, or whatever you believe in). If we interact with positive people, it affects us in a positive way, i.e. it increases our frequency. Negative emotions hold us at the lower levels of scale, affect our health in a negative way and attract negative experiences into our everyday lives. In order to increase the frequencies of our vibrations consciously and purposely, we can meditate, visualize or practice other spiritual techniques (more about that in the next challenge) – all in order to change our energy fields. Besides, it is important what we eat and drink, i.e. what kind of diet we have; where we reside, whether we spend time outdoors, what kind of electric devices we use, whether we exercise regularly, what kind of relationships we have, what is the state of our sexuality, etc. If you check the content pages of this book now, you will understand how and why these exact challenges have been chosen. Actually, our final goal is to have the vibrations to work for us, i.e. to balance our energy fields and to achieve inner peace and synchronization with everything there is, and to live in complete gratitude.

It is what the law of attraction is all about – what you radiate, you attract. When I talk about the law of attraction, people often ask me whether I have watched documentary *The Secret* (■ 34). Yes I have, several years ago, and that marked the beginning of my spiritual journey. There is a book with the same title, and the movie has a sequel, *Beyond the Secret* (■ 35). To those of you who haven't heard about the law of attraction, I recommend to stop reading for a while and to watch *The Secret*. Look for some videos on this topic, there are a lot of them, really. In addition, I recommend the books *Ask and It Is Given* and *The Law of Attraction* by Esther and Jerry Hicks. Similarly great read is the book *Jack Canfield's Key to Living the Law of Attraction* by Jack Canfield and D. D. Watkins.

QR 34

QR 35

Why is this important? Because the law of attraction is the law, i.e. tool that works for everybody and all the time, whether we like it or not. According to it, we are just magnets, attracting the things we mostly think about. Thoughts attract similar thoughts: thoughts about disease attract disease, thoughts about happiness attract happiness. The point of the law of attraction is this: what we think and what we believe in is what we will get, sooner or later. Just like the saying: you reap what you sow. Indeed, the things we resist grow, and the things we face disappear. The key is, therefore, to focus on the things we want, instead on the things we don't wont. You are the only ones capable of creating your reality. That is the concept accepted in most religions too, and they had interwoven it with their teachings (with more or less subtleties). To all our wishes and thoughts, the universe reply: "Let it be." Um, what thoughts and actions does that provoke? It reminded me of a 2003 movie *Bruce Almighty* (■ 36), where Bruce as "God" gets over-whelmed by the prayers from people, so he marks them all and replies: "Yes." At first, he feels relief because he got the job done,

QR 36 and he doesn't see the downside. However, soon he realizes that with this move he has made quite a mess, and caused many problems. Each team in a competition wants to win, and it's impossible to have them all as winners. Nevertheless, you understand that this applies mostly to trivial, if not bizarre wishes. And here we talk about true, life-long wishes. The wishes that, combined with pure heart and complete confidence in our Creator, always result with what is best for us. And that often isn't what we believe is best for us – because we can't see the whole picture.

As long as we are talking about books and movies, I'd like to share with you the movie that had a deep impact on me and my spiritual quest. It is called *Conversations with God* (■ 37). Long after watching the movie, I have read the book with the same title by Neale Donald Walsch. As it is often the case, watching the movie and reading the

QR 37 book were somewhat different experiences. Perhaps you will find my recommendations of this or that a bit annoying, but this is how this book was meant to be. Some things had a great significance to my life, and I think it would be pity not to share that with others – especially

when I am aware how much good the right information or sentence at the right moment can bring. *Conversations with God* (with its sequels) is one of my favorite books, and one of those after which your life cannot be the same. What can I say, it is allowed in some churches, and "forbidden" in others. It's best you read it and decided for yourself.

Mini challenge
Read the book Conversations with God, regardless of your religious commitments.

Walsch is, by the way, often on Watkins' list of world's most influential spiritual persons, and that was the case for 2019 as well. Take a peek at this list by scanning the QR code (◼ 38) because it could be a very good starting point for your spiritual quest. At the list, you will find many other, very popular names such as Dalai Lama, Eckhart Tolle, Deepak Chopra, Paulo Coelho, Oprah Winfrey, Louise L. Hay, Ester Hicks, Mooji, etc. Their names, you've noticed, are woven into this book as well. Challenge 3 (spiritual quest) is something you should work on your entire life, so it is fortunate that on that list you can find 100 persons. Of course, this doesn't mean you should avoid the work of people that aren't on the list; the key is to simply be open-minded and search for your own truth, and the way is going to steer you to the place where your soul want you to be, sooner or later. You will know you are on the right track if you are more and more interested in some topic, if you dedicate your every free moment to it, if it serves you in a way that your life has more meaning, if you are happier, more relaxed. When you do something because you should, because it is the right thing to do, even though you don't think much about it – you aren't on the right path.

QR 38

Normally, I believe there is no book or movie that can alienate you from your true belief and something you resonate with. If you are converted, it can't be because of a book or a movie alone, as nobody changes beliefs and faith every few days. Actually, people change very rarely. I remember the time the movie *The Da Vinci Code* was released. It stirred up public interest and caused numerous debates. Without going into the content and topics of the movie – and its accuracy, as it is not within my competences – I find it funny to forbid any movie because it alienates people from this or that. Every person can decide for himself/herself what he or she want or don't want to read or watch, remember? Apparently, we live in a free world, and we are free to make our own decisions. If we take into consideration how many lies can be found in media today, how many "dangers" lurk from the virtual world, it's a bit absurd to make such a fuss about just one movie or to forbid certain content. Are you an adult? Yes, great. You are than responsible for your thoughts, words, actions and behaviors. A book or a movie merely have the ability to come to you in the right time and resonate with you, they can ignite your interest, trigger the change, or understanding. In other words, throughout life we collect (spiritual) experiences and every day shapes us a bit more. One book can't make a revolution in your life, unless you are ready for it. And if the book is right, it will merely open Pandora's Box for you, and the questions from the box will guide you further, and further, and further.

One of the questions that often pop up on a spiritual journey is a question of life and death, i.e. whether reincarnation exists. I believe it would be very unfair to have just one life considering the fact that there are people among us who live in truly hard life conditions, who have been given somewhat poorer fabric to start with. If we truly have just one life, then someone has planned it very unfairly. I cannot answer the question of reincarnation because I don't have specific recollections of life other than this one, but many people claim they had one. One of those people (mentioned on the list I have told you about) is my namesake and popular author Anita Moorjani. Her story was narrated in the book called *Dying to Be Me: My Journey from Cancer, to Near Death, to True Healing*. This bestseller recounts Moorjani's experience in 2006, when, as she claims, she had a near death experience (you can watch her interview by scanning the code ■ 39). In my opinion, this much references and experiences from people around the world must mean there is something in life after life (by the way, the book

QR 39

with this title watched me from the shelf throughout my childhood). Where there is smoke, there is fire too. Nevertheless, all we have is now, so let's enjoy in what we have and concentrate on that. ☺

To my child the story of faith and God I present differently, through the concept of 100% love (more on that in the challenge of inspirational parenting). I go to church from time to time, when I am passing by or when I feel the need. I love empty churches, I enjoy the peace and quiet, and oneness with God. I believe God is pure and unconditional love, devoid of fear, and I somehow follow the equation: Human - ego = God. In my opinion, there is nothing wrong in being born and brought up in a religion, in living in a religion for a while; but it can be wrong to die in it without answering all the questions.

For the end of this challenge, I therefore recommend you to watch your vibration and try to be high on the scale. ☺ In challenge 4 I will present you some of the spiritual techniques that can help you with that. It's on you to decide if they "vibrate" to you and which one. Stay on a spiritual journey, follow your path; every one of them is correct. But be prepared for all kinds of discoveries along the way. Remember one of the well-known scenes from the movie *Matrix* (◼ 40), where Neo has to decide whether to take the blue or the red pill. Morpheus tells him: "This is your last chance. After this, there is no turning back. You take the blue pill – the story ends, you wake up in your bed and believe whatever you want to believe. You take the red pill – you stay in Wonderland, and I show you how deep the rabbit hole goes." Some people simply choose to live a lie, to believe in whatever the society impose on them, to let others steer their focus and create their reality encouraging them to stay in the comfort or fear zone. The choice is yours: blue or red?

QR 40

Recommendations to inspire you on your journey of happiness ☺

- [QR 31] Religiosity and Spirituality – Zac Poonen:
     https://www.youtube.com/watch?v=_7_vhBlyGBw
- [QR 32] Types of Brain Waves and Their Functions:
     https://www.youtube.com/watch?v=h5LT9b-L9_Y
- [QR 39] Anita Moorjani – Dying to Be Me:
     https://www.youtube.com/watch?v=7jFN9XQeEn4

- [QR 34] The Secret:
     https://www.youtube.com/watch?v=mjmK8aJu5Qg
- [QR 35] Beyond „The Secret":
     https://www.youtube.com/watch?v=lwPIlZ4cpIw
- [QR 36] Bruce Almighty:
     https://www.youtube.com/watch?v=fe-luzrqWSk
- [QR 37] Conversations with God:
     https://www.youtube.com/watch?v=Ip8iHSRZ8R8
- [QR 40] Matrix,
     https://www.youtube.com/watch?v=vKQi3bBA1y8

- [QR 33] Hawkins Scale of Consciousness:
     https://positivedirection.com.au/hawkins-scale-of-con-
     sciousness/
- [QR 38] Watkins' Spiritual 100 List for 2019:
     https://www.watkinsmagazine.com/watkins-spiritual-
     100-list-for-2019

📖

- Power vs. Force, dr. David R. Hawkins, 1994
- Ask and It is Given, Esther and Jerry Hicks, 2007
- The Law of Attraction, Esther and Jerry Hicks, 2008

- The Key to Living the Law of Attraction: The Secret to Creating the Life of Your Dreams, J. Canfield and D. D. Watkins, 2009
- Conversations with God, Neale Donald Walsch, 2011
- Life after Life, Raymond Moody, 2005
- Dying to Be Me: My Journey from Cancer, to Near Death, to True Healing, Anita Moorjani, 2014

CHALLENGE 4:
PRACTICE OF SPIRITUAL TECHNIQUES - RAISING VIBRATIONS

If someone can do it, everybody can.

Before I recommend you some of the techniques I use, I owe you the story of my beginning. I sometimes wonder where I got all the cognitions I have today, and how and when my circle of knowledge on spirituality and life formed. My mom played an important role in all that. She is, as I would put it today, one very "connected" lady. The house of my parents is filled with flowers, and we sometimes joked that we live in botanical garden. I remember my mom used to often water all those plants (and they were really thriving) talking to them: "Hi, how are you today? Good morning – oh, look, you will have a flower! The leaf has fallen – what is it, don't you like this position" etc. My dad and I used to mock her because of that, but she claimed plants are alive so you have to talk to them constantly, and that is why ours were so incredibly beautiful. Apparently, there are plants with "bad radiation", so we never had those in our house. Under every bed, we kept wreath of wild chestnuts, because they supposedly protect from Earth's natural radiation, i.e. neutralize it (you know, underground water veins, Hartmann and Curry lines etc.).

My mom made for me positive messages, and she kept them for years over the desk I used to study at. She kept encouraging me to repeat that I can do it, that I want to do it (for the things already in motion), and she constantly talked about the power of positive thinking (actually, sometimes it was a bit annoying). During my exams, my mom sometimes sat at home in peace, sending me positive energy. She repeatedly advised me to think about what I was saying because brain remembers everything, especially the things we have last said/thought (e.g. I shouldn't say I would surely flank the exam today, but I would surely today pass – this last word was positive, and my brain would remember it). On the shelves in our home, there were books on emotional intelligence, power of subconscious, power of positive thinking, food healing etc. Today, when you can see these positive topics everywhere, it may not seem so odd, but 20-some years ago it was different.

Mom also regularly knew what had happened to me (e.g. as soon as I got home, she knew if I had passed or failed the exam), and with great probability she knew exactly how I felt without me telling her (the same is today). When I told her that she would become grandmother, she said she already knew, because my eyes shone differently for the past few days (um, she knew before I did). My father and I didn't object to all that, but I haven't seen deeper meaning in it either. Mom didn't bother us with it, she wasn't obsessed; she just did what she felt was right and what she thought she should. It was and still is something normal, ordinary to her. She often predicted certain events; she knew what was going to happen or what just happened before she was told about it, and sometimes she dreamed about it. Therefore, if my mom says, "I've dreamed about you, be careful on the road", you should better have your eyes and ears wide open. The woman has a very good intuition, you can say. When I was four years old, my mom broke her spine in front of our house and she was told she would never walk again. After two months of staying brutally 100% immobile (at home, at her own request – without doctors' consent), she began to build a "new life". With the incredible power of will (imagine how strong and persistent you have to be for that) she succeeded and started to function normally. Mom, I know you prefer when people express their love with deeds rather than with words, but words are vibrations too, so here is one big thank you for leading me – probably completely unconsciously – towards spirituality my whole life. Without you, I would not be everything I am today; the pieces of the mosaic would be different, and so would the whole picture. Who knows, maybe this book wouldn't come to life either. So, that is one more evidence that everything happens for a reason and in the right moment. There are no coincidences.

In the meantime, let me tell you about one particularly thought-provoking moment from my high school days. Psychology teacher draw an iceberg and waterline over it. She said that above the sea level you could usually see only 10% of the whole iceberg, as its biggest part is under the surface. She then marked the tip and said, "See, this tip is your conscious, and everything below the waterline is your subconscious." It got me thinking then, but it took me almost 10 years to start researching this Sigmund Freud's idea more profoundly and to think about questions of conscious, subconscious and superconscious. Subconscious mind makes up for 95% of our "self" – it causes the occurrence of habits and behaviors. Given the fact that subconscious is like a garden – whatever you saw, grows – it's worth to focus on it. That brings us to the second part of my voyage, i.e. to the PhD thesis phase. It was about happiness, and to write it I was devouring books on positive psychology and researching everything that was related to happiness. At that time, I have watched the movie *Secret*, I have discovered the work of L. L. Hay, and I have watched the movie *Conversations with God*. Besides, it was a time I wasn't feeling very well (mostly with myself).

The third phase (or the beginning of part three), during which pieces of mosaic that I had collected for 30 years started to fall into place with great speed, started in September 2013. It was my son Matej who triggered that process. He was just one and a half month old, and he was one of those babies with terrible colic that started as early as two weeks after his birth. My husband and I were going mad day and night. You know, the baby cries, you cry, and you have no idea what to give him or what to do to make things better. I was being careful about what I ate because of breastfeeding, I was listening to every advice I heard, but to no avail. Then one day my mom suggested we should check the underground water veins in our apartment. After few more days of unbelievable crying, my husband agreed we should do it because we would go mad, both him and me, and our son (you know those moment when you would do everything, absolutely everything, in order to solve the problem). Through a bioenergist we got the number of a man who "deals" with underground water veins. Soon after that, Kristijan came into our apartment with two copper dowsing rods, sat down and started to talk. I remember how I said to him then, "I have been waiting for you my entire life." We spoke for more than two hours, and for me it was the conversation of my life because Kristijan understood everything I was talking about; because he was at the same frequency as me; because he knew the answers to all my questions; because he knew of all the books and movies I was telling him about; because he also went through an unusual life story that his child steered him through. At the end, he checked our apartment with that primitive dowsing method – compared to today's devices – and detected the veins. He then sat and cleaned our apartment with his thoughts. After that everything was fine, the rods weren't crossing anymore (I tried it with my own hands, and it wasn't fake). At the end he said dowsing wasn't something he did regularly; he just did that from time to time, if someone asked him to. So, why this bioenergist recommended him of all people to clean the place from underground veins? Well, Kristijan had to come to me somehow, hadn't he? ☺

During that first visit, Kristijan mentioned spiritual – or, we could say, energy – technique, i.e. ancient Hawaiian art of solving problems with an unusual name Ho'oponopono (I too was struggling with the name for a while, before I remembered it and learned to pronounce it). For more information on the subject, he recommended the book *Zero Limits* by Joe Vitale and Ihaleakala Hew Len. Some of you may have heard of the technique, made famous by Mabel Katz and her book *The Easiest Way*. Katz holds seminars all over the world talking about the technique that made her well too. With Dr. Len, she flooded the world, and the topic was covered by CNN, Oprah Show and many others.

I was thrilled by the technique and I still practice it today (as soon as I open my eyes in the morning, and during the day as well, whenever my mind starts to wander; when I prepare a meal, walk, shower etc.). I believe the fact that this was the first spiritual technique I came across wasn't a coincidence – because it is very simple and it has been resonating with me from the first moment. As I have already mentioned, change may happen in a certain aha-moment, but it is actually a sum of all our previous experiences and cognitions. While I was reading *Zero Limits*, hardly ever putting it down, I wasn't responsible to myself or to the others. It was that period of my life when I had it all (even a child), but something just did not add up. *Zero Limits* talks about going back to zero state where there are no thoughts, words or deeds; where nothing really exists, but everything is possible. The book describes the case of psychologist and therapist Dr. Len, who helped cure all mentally ill criminals in a state hospital (on a dangerous and unpleasant ward, where staff was changing constantly) – without meeting any one of them. To do that, he used Ho'oponopono method, i.e. the process of getting rid of toxic energies within us in order to get rid of the influence from thoughts, words, deeds or actions.

The technique's key is to take 100% responsibility for our lives. Dr. Len took full responsibility for the lives of his clients, he leafed through their files and, while analyzing them, he worked on himself. In time, the patients started to get well, the tied-upped ones were allowed to walk freely, the staff started to return to work. He explains this outcome by the concept of total responsibility for our lives, which encompasses everything because this everything *is* in our lives. Problem, therefore, is never in others, but in us. In order to change others, we have to change ourselves. Although this concept is not easy to accept, let alone live, the technique itself is, fortunately, one of the easiest to practice. In fact, all you need to do is say: "I am sorry, please forgive me, I love you, thank you", as often as possible. It was this simplicity that attracted me. I didn't think that those universally beautiful words (that reminded me on those four important little phrases we had all learned and sung as kids: please, thank you, here you are, sorry) could ever disturb religious part of me. I didn't think that by repeating them I was doing anything against this or that God. The process of repeating the words is actually called "cleaning".

Dr. Len explains that Ho'oponopono is about searching for remnants, mistakes and blockades in our conscious minds, which reproduces them as judgements, falls and other similar problems. He underlines that we are perfect; imperfect is only the data in our subconscious minds, and that is what we should work on. The world lies within us and by changing this world – we change everything else! I told my mom about the book and the technique, and she came up with the music for the words "I love you" and "thank you" and sang them to my son when she was putting him to sleep. What do you think about this technique? Can you look yourselves in the mirror and say that you love yourselves? Now you know why I mentioned that as one of the very important things at the beginning of this book. For those of you that want to dig deeper into the subject, I recommend the series of nine videos Zero Limits (■ 41). There you will definitely find all the answers.

QR 41

Mini challenge

Try to practice Ho'oponopono technique. For start, you can repeat mentally or aloud: "I love you, thank you", whenever your thoughts start to wander back in past or towards future.

In later meetings with Kristijan and his then partner, we have worked on cleaning my life using the wake-up method. Kristijan had finished and practiced many different methods before he channelized wake-up method. It is based on, as you can guess by the name, keeping people awake, mainly by eliminating different distracting factors. Characteristic of the method is that it eliminates causes of certain conditions by entering into previous lives, where those conditions originate, and by reprograming basic lessons. In addition, this method enables installation of protective energy grid that needs to be cleaned every day. During those meetings, I especially liked that Kristijan never spoke from the position of superiority; instead, he said everybody could do what he did, they just had to work on it and have a firm belief in God or the Energy of Creation. That always intrigued me and gave me a sense of verifiability and confidentiality. I would pay top dollar, every time, for somebody to fix my life the way he did. I have recommended Kristijan to many of my friends, and all of them praise him, grateful for leading better lives now. If you want to try this method yourselves, you can contact Kristijan by scanning this QR code (▣ 42).

QR 42

One part of his work is based on Theta healing of sorts. What is Theta healing? The technique was named after low frequency theta brain waves (4-7 Hz), detected by devices during deep meditation. Those slow waves are responsible for our behavior, tendencies and beliefs, and they lead us to a state of deep relaxation by letting us function below the level of conscious mind. Theta healing is meditative process and brings physical, emotional, mental and spiritual healing. It is done by the levels of existence (four out of seven are used: basic, genetic, historic and the level of soul) and by the muscle test – that way our subconscious gives us answers. We are connected to the energy of all existence, our healing takes place, our DNA is activated, it is possible to contact angels, to clean the body and aura from everything negative, to manifest what we want from life, etc. As you can see, it is a deep, comprehensive and complex technique, which is very precise and methodologically concrete. Two important aspects of Theta healing are – working on our beliefs and dealing with our feelings.

By the way, you can try the muscle test by yourself, because they say body never lies. Muscle test is a form of applied kinesiology (▣ 43), and by using it, we get the information on physical, emotional and mental levels. Given the fact that lies weaken the body, while truth strengthen it – every positive answer ("yes") causes muscles to contract. There are several ways to practice this method; for example,

QR 43

you can stand facing north, with arms down, and say your name (e.g., I am Anita) – your body will react by leaning forward. Everything that isn't true makes the body lean backwards. In addition, you can do it with your arm lifted in front of you shoulder high; you can do it by making a circle with your thumb and forefinger, i.e. use the muscles of your hand (miostatic ring or O test), etc. It all really comes down to the same thing, no matter what group of muscles you use for testing (given that your body is hydrated). Analyzing and practicing this method, which is in use ever since Hippocrates (and standard in some hospitals), can be beneficial to those of you at the beginning of your spiritual growth because it will allow you to apprehend yourselves better and find out what is under the surface. It will work even if you ask the question in your head, and even if the person who tests you does that. Your body, i.e. your subconscious will give you the yes/no answer nevertheless. Interesting, isn't it? As you grow spiritually, the circles of your apprehension will grow as well, discovering new dimensions for you.

Mini challenge

By using the muscle test, ask your subconscious the questions of your choice.

One such new dimension for me was chromotherapy, or healing with colors. We often marginalize the importance of colors, even though they are all around us (just look at the nature). Colors actually trigger different emotional reactions and we all have certain colors that attract or repel us (look at the colors of your clothes, the way you have decorated your home – and you will probably find out that one color or several of them are dominant). This technique can give you the idea why you love certain colors, and dislike others, i.e. what areas of your life are in disbalance. In modern wellness centers, you can often find rooms with color therapy, along with music therapy. Every color affects certain centers in body (■ 44) in order to restore energy balance and solve problems. Color therapy actually affects aura – energy field that encloses body, i.e. our energy mantle. You can chose whether you will believe or not in the existence of this radiating cloud around our bodies, but today it is possible to record aura – i.e. we can find out certain things about our energy field (its color, size and shape – even though it changes with time). We emanate energy, which has a different color and intensity in different parts of body (depending on health, and emotional and spiritual traits/features/characteristics).

QR 44

Aura usually stretches about one meter from our physical bodies. Some people say it can't be science fiction because everybody, truly everybody can see it after some practicing, especially children, who see aura much easier (and some people are born with the talent to see it in more detail than others). Aura is a subject of interest of bioenergists and other alternative healers, who often use cameras for recording aura (before and after treatments) as a helpful tool.

At a consultation recently, a man asked me, "How will I know that I am on the right track?" I thought it was charming, as the answer is very simple: along the way, you will come across signs you would not be able to ignore. The same was with my spiritual journey; when I was on the right path, I constantly received confirmations and testified various synchronicities (events of unbelievable "coincidences"). Those signs are mostly doings of faithful followers, helpers and protectors: angels. At least in my case. I am not sure if work with angels would qualify as a spiritual technique, but it seems only logical to write this here. Given the religious character of my upbringing, I have been listening about and praying to angels since I can remember (Guardian Angel Prayer…), but until recently, I could not say I totally believed in them. I am not sure how I have started to research about angels at some point, but I've started to implement them more into my life, to follow the signs along the road and to test the whole story, so to speak.

I had just moved to another apartment because of my divorce, and one morning I found the first feather at the table of the small loggia. The feather was little, grayish-white, fluffy and at the middle of the table. My first thought was: that was angels contacting me. However, the next moment I started to rationalize – I said to myself that the window was open and there was a great chance that pigeon's feather just flew in. Next day the same thing happened. The third day a big pigeon's feather was lying in the middle of carpet in my bedroom (almost five feet from the window), and it must have somehow flown in through the window that was ajar on the top. I felt as if I was going mad (fortunately, I photographed everything for evidence, for my own sake). Then I said: O.K., if all those feathers were angel's, they would have been white (as angels usually are), and not grayish or speckled. You can probably guess, the next morning I found completely white feather at the middle of the table in loggia. I can't explain the feeling, I just know I stopped doubting then. To make things more interesting, I have never found feathers in my apartment after that.

Then one day I noticed the book called *Stairways to Heaven* on my shelf. The book was a present for my PhD from a dear colleague from my Faculty, and it is the second book by Lorna Byrne (■ 45). It tells a story about angels, just like Byrne's first book *Angels in My Hair*, which was translated to 20 languages. Angels were the ones to encourage Byrne to write books, and she claims she has been seeing them and talking to them every day since she was a child. In her books, you can get to know different kinds of angels, you can read her life story and find out how angels work in the world. It wasn't long before I discovered more people who communicate with angels, organize workshops, testify. I have to mention books about angels by Sylvia Browne (■ 46), who have been researching angels for more than 40 years. Her work I recommend to those who doubt the existence of angels or have certain prejudices (today, it is easier to believe in Santa Clause than in angels). You might think you are too mature to believe in something so "unreal" as angels. Meanwhile, that is so easy for the children. You tell them they exist, and that's it – for them it is the truth, they won't ask hundred questions and start doing combinatorics. My son believes in angels; whenever we have to park, he says: "Angels, help, parking lot." And we find it every single time. Moreover, we believe angels protect us 24/7 and sometimes whisper to us what to do. We notice feathers outside, we see number sequences... There are many ways to notice angels are with us all the time.

That is how spiritual quest led me to angels, and they are a part of my life ever since. The reason could be my favorite prayer, which I have been praying for as long as I can remember. Who knows? If angels got you interested, you can begin your own search. Better yet, test everything and see for yourself. You can ask them to find "lost" things for you or to contact you. In fact, you can ask them anything, there is always an angel that can help. However, angels won't help us until we ask them to. It's crucial to remember that. You have to ask them from your heart, and only then they can act. Well, try, what can you lose? As I said, numerous books were written about angels (it wouldn't be fair not to mention Francesca Brown (◼ 47) and the book *My Whispering Angels*). Your search, therefore, shouldn't be hard. Those who search will find. Besides, angels will lead the way; you just relax and let yourself go. And believe.

QR 47

Mini challenge

Do you see feathers or number sequences? Decide to pay attention to the signs on your path of happiness. Call for help from your angels; what can you lose?

Today, there are many spiritual techniques; it would take several pages just to write them down, and I don't think there is value in that. I have told you about the things I have personally had experience with and the things I practice (alongside relaxation, which is our next challenge); everything else I cannot present in so many details. I can tell you what my friends/acquaintances say they like and find helpful, and you should research further if you are interested. There is a method called wing-wave, which quickly and effectively eliminates stress, raises the level of creativity, mental skills and self-confidence – by working with emotions. Then there is the emotional freedom technique, which is based on belief that the source of all problems in our body is the disturbance of the energy flow (energy blockade). It is also referred to as tapping, because the meridian hot spots are stimulated by finger tapping. This technique is simple and free. The next technique is subconscious communication, i.e. neuro-linguistic programming (NLP). The root of this technique lies in the fact we are fully responsible for solving challenges in our lives. NLP focuses on communication techniques and skills, the ones that enable us to get rid of negative habits, the ones that control our emotions.

I have started my spiritual quest by this thinking: if subconscious controls unbelievable 90% of our actions and if it accounts for 90% of that iceberg – then it must hold the key for happiness. That has led my spiritual journey because all techniques are based on reprogramming the subconscious. In the end, there is no right or wrong technique, they are all right and they are all wrong – it depends on us and on our beliefs. I practice them because they were helpful to me, they made me healthier and more satisfied than ever before. They helped me live in a different reality of higher vibrations, where, by the law of attraction, I enjoy more of the same. The best would be if you could find suitable method for raising vibrations yourself, because this is the only way to get to the place you want to be. Everything else is following someone else's path, which leads to some other, someone else's place. Of course, our paths may cross (after all, we are all one), but every one of us has his/her own path and experiences that he/she is here to collect. Therefore, get going and be courageous. If you feel this is not for you right now, that is fine too. I cannot change you; all I can do is to work on myself and to change others by the example I make – when they are ready for it. Maybe the data from the next challenge will make you think, and consequentially act.

* * * * *

We are at the end of the first group of challenges: healthy and cheerful spirit – life in the present moment. We have talked about four challenges – the need to be healthily selfish, to find more time for ourselves by reducing screen and media time, to differentiate spirituality from religiousness and to become spiritual seekers – that have led us to some of the spiritual techniques of my choice. Next part is dedicated to healthy and serene mind, where we will first talk about probably the most important life challenge – everyday relaxation of mind – and then about relationships.

❧ Recommendations to inspire you on your journey of happiness ☺

- [QR 41] Ho'oponopono Dr Hew Len and Joe Vitale part 1: https://www.youtube.com/watch?v=k_s0jBNeXTA&list=+PLKettaSfWNEY_aP-VMrDXH-ED-vxXLPCJs
- [QR 43] Introduction to Kinesiology: https://www.youtube.com/watch?v=NN1dctmPYqw

- Web sources and articles:
- [QR 42] Kristijan Husarek, Wake-up Method, e-mail: wakeupmetoda@gmail.com
- [QR 44] Color Psychology: https://www.colorpsychology.org/
- [QR 45] Lorna Byrne: http://lornabyrne.com/
- [QR 46] Sylvia Browne: https://www.sylviabrowne.com/
- [QR 47] Francesca Brown: http://www.irishministryofangels.com/

- Zero Limits: The Secret Hawaiian System for Wealth, Health, Peace, and More, Joe Vitale i Ihaleakala Hew Len, 2007.
- The Easiest Way: Solve Your Problems and Take the Road to Love, Happiness, Wealth and the Life of your Dreams, Mabel Katz, 2014.
- Stairways to Heaven, Lorna Byrne, 2012.
- Angels in My Hair, Lorna Byrne, 2010.
- My Whispering Angels, Francesca Brown, 2013.

A HEALTHY AND SERENE MIND - LOVE FOR ONESELF AND OTHERS

CHALLENGE 5:
DAILY RELAXATION
OF THE MIND

Take control over your mind, or he will take over you.

Although daily relaxation of the mind, i.e. practice of state without thoughts, can be considered as practice of spiritual techniques, I have singled it out as a separate challenge because I believe it is highly important. In addition, it is not just the relaxation of the mind, but of the body as well. I have already said that the challenges are intertwined and it is impossible to separate them strictly by the trio "spirit, mind, body". Regardless of what you believe or don't believe, whether you raise your vibration by certain techniques or not, whether you are religious, spiritual or neither – you need to relax (everything else leads to various illnesses). Therefore, you should better learn how. Sadly, big part of world population doesn't know how to relax (there are people 60+ that have never relaxed completely and consciously), and they wonder why nothing is going as it should, why they are constantly angry and frustrated, vulnerable and depressive, etc.

Life today has an accelerated pace, every millisecond something new happens, and media serve it to us through all windows and channels. We are constantly busy, we generally, as I have already explained, "lack time", especially for relaxation and practicing calmness and stillness. You know those situations when you can't remember the last 10 minutes or so – you must have experienced that sometimes. For example, you were driving your car, and you can't recall the past 10 minutes, like you have wandered somewhere and everything was on autopilot. It means you were not in the present moment, you've got lost in your thoughts. The goal of all spiritual techniques, actually, is to prevent the brain from unnecessary thinking, because it pushes us either in the past or in the future, while life unfolds in the present. Additional challenge is the fact that most negative thoughts are related to past or future. Mark Twain said, "I've had a lot of worries in my life, most of which never happened." Therefore, if we don't train the brain to work for us, he will automatically work against us. Mind constantly drags us back to what happened or makes us worry about things that are yet to come. Our mind is like a restless monkey jumping from branch to branch, from tree to tree. It clings to thoughts firmly as monkey to a branch/ tree, and it does not give up the need to be right all the time. It is called monkey mind. That monkey is quite active, preventing people to think consciously – and that is how our mind starts to control us.

Thoughts emerge with great speed. According to some research (National-al Science Foundation, U.S.), we daily have up to 60,000 thoughts, and some think the number is even higher – 100,000. Be as it may, let's say we have a new thought every second or two (as if they fly with the speed of light; actually, thought is a light form of energy that changes quickly and easily). Imagine the sheer numbers, and 80-90% of it is negative in most people. That is why it is said that primary cause of misfortune isn't the situation itself but our thinking about it. Every such thought consumes our precious energy (even thinking about that amount of thoughts makes me tired) and provokes a physical reaction (affects the functioning of our body). Big part of those thoughts is unconscious and to me the strongest aha-moment was when I found out that as much as 90% of those thoughts we have every day, repeatedly, and they reflect our thinking and beliefs that have led to this kind of thoughts in the first place. Once our subconscious accepts certain idea or concept, it stays there until we replace it with another. Besides, our thoughts are energy, vibration, and they affect our lives greatly, especially the ones we think repeatedly, the ones with strong emotional background – those thoughts leave a strong mark in our subconscious. Thoughts are powerful, they can make us ill, but they can heal us as well. That is why it is important to develop positive thinking, and that process should not be taken lightly. Remember the stream: our thoughts become our words, our words become our actions, our actions become our habits, our habits become our character, and our character becomes our destiny. Our mind, therefore, always has something to think about, and the things we think about, i.e. thoughts become our destiny. That is why it makes sense to control it, isn't it? However, if you try to tame the mind a bit – for example calm it with one of the relaxation techniques – It will immediately start making excuses. Mind is never calm, it always complains about something and it will not stop even when we do everything we need to do; in fact, it will never stop because the inner critic never sleeps. Therefore, either we control the mind, or it controls us. There is no third option.

Mini challenge

What do you think about the most? How many of your thoughts deals with past, and how many with future? How much of your day do you spend in the present moment?

The person who has influenced change of my opinions the most and encouraged me to meditate daily is Joe Dispenza, popular doctor I have mentioned before. He has written several books and he gives exceptional seminars around the world. However, I was particularly impressed by his life and work probably because my mind, which is accustomed to think scientifically and analyze everything, needs exactly this kind of approach. I especially recommend you to read (if you haven't already) his book *You Are the Placebo: Making Your Mind Matter* (■ 48). Dr. Dispenza believes the placebo effect is actually us – our thoughts, opinions, beliefs and perceptions that shape our reality and health as well. Dispenza's book is the result of his own experience, i.e. paralysis diagnose and serious operation of six crushed vertebra. After three months he started to walk again and returned to normal life (without any intervention), proving to himself that body intelligence was real. He began to study spirituality and decided to spend the rest of his life exploring the connection between mind and body, and the idea of the superiority of the mind over matter. If you study his work, you will understand how human brain works and you won't have many further questions. You can choose to practice his meditations daily – which he sees as the key for change – and reprogram the mind through this process, or you can choose not to do that. In other words, you can make a step forward or stay in the comfort zone despite the incredible information and scientific facts you have heard from him. His meditations and courses have enabled incredible life changes (up to spontaneous remissions) for numerous people, and all this speaks in favor of trying it out. One of my favorite interviews with Dr. Dispenza, conducted by Tom Bilyeu, you can find at the link (◼ 49).

QR 49

Mini challenge

Watch the interview with Dr. Joe Dispenza at QR 49.

Thus, we talk about relaxation, or thoughtless state, or meditation, or mental training with the sole purpose – peace (serene mind = happy mind). Some see the meditation as science, something you need academic knowledge for, something impossible to accomplish. However, it is not like that, I have to encourage you. If it were the case, very few people would meditate today (and that is very far from the truth; reportedly, only in U.S. more than 10 million people meditate daily, and the number tripled from 2012). Meditation isn't some novelty; Buddhists meditate for thousands of years and they are very well aware of positive aspects of daily mind relaxation. In 1978, World Health Organization recognized officially and admitted the role of meditation and other traditional medicine techniques in population's health. With that, it supported a holistic, i.e. systematic approach to medical practice. It is estimated that between 200 and 500 million people meditate worldwide.

Starting and ending point of any meditation is breathing, and numerous scientists (especially neuroscientists) at various institutes and centers have been studying meditation. The number of scientific studies that focus on meditation is constantly increasing, and new modern machines that enable scanning and analysis of brain function confirm the benefits of this method. The benefits of meditation have become the subject of numerous studies, and those studies confirm that meditation reduces stress, improves immunity, brings more joy and laughter and less nervous agitation, improves sleep, allows us to get to know ourselves better, to depend less on other people and love ourselves more. It also fosters inner peace and relaxation, allows for greater concentration, enhances creativity and intuition, etc. According to Dr. Dispenza, one of the important characteristics of the brain is neuroplasticity. Groups of neurons that have fired and wired together forming a community of neurosynaptic connections are called neural networks. Neuroplasticity, therefore, is the ability of the brain to alter these neural connections and networks by learning new information and recording experiences. This results in physical changes and the ability to maintain the altered state. Neuroplasticity allows us to further develop our actions and modify our behaviors in order to achieve better results in life. Scientific research on neuroplasticity shows that the brain changes at the physical level with every new thought, every new choice, every new experience, every new behavior and every new emotion. Chemical and physical changes occur, changing the brain itself.

Video *Train Your Monkey Mind* explains meditation in a simple way (■ 50). As it is very important, I will recount it now. We can relax the mind, i.e. informally meditate, anytime, anywhere. As we walk, while drinking coffee or tea, even while we are at meetings. Many people misunderstand meditation; they believe that meditation QR 50 requires blank mind and focus, so they just try too hard. It is hard or even impossible to block thoughts and emotions, which we actually need within us in a way. Whether we will listen to our monkey mind, which constantly babbles something, is another story. The mind gives us an opinion, and we can decide for ourselves whether to listen to it or not. By relaxing, we actually want to make friends with the monkey mind, but not by just giving him a banana. Therefore, the right method is to keep our monkey mind busy by using a simple relaxation training: we need to be aware of the breath and tell the mind to observe it, and then we have to begin inhaling and exhaling consciously. While doing this, different thoughts will emerge in the back of our minds, but this is not a problem – we just should not care for them. As long as we do not forget to focus on the breath, everything is fine, and we do not need too much concentration for that. Just be aware of your breath, inhale and exhale. Even two or just one conscious breath is fine, and that is why we can relax whenever and wherever.

Mini challenge

Inhale through the nose and exhale through the mouth, and count ten times (inhale-exhale 1, inhale-exhale 2…).

Many public persons have admitted eventually that they had spiritual teacher on their journey, and all of them said they practice relaxation daily. Even planetary famous Dr. Mehmet Oz talked about the subject and he said that his five-minute meditation work wonders for mind and body (■ 51). The thing is, only five minutes of relaxation can relieve you of accumulated stress and restlessness. There are more and more schools in the world that have introduced meditation instead of punishing the unwanted behavior of disobedient pupils and this has led to astounding results: from a smaller number of reprimands to calmer and more placid pupils. Relaxation is more often on the agenda of kindergartens, which have a corner or a place to relax. Some schools still send children into a corner for punishment, and some (e.g. in Baltimore) have equipped a special colorful room (Mindful Moment Room); children go there when they need to blow off steam (and we all need it, regardless of our age) and relax in a quiet environment on pillows. Meditation, therefore, leads to better results in school – and in life in general as well.

In order to prevent our own mind from distracting us and to stop living in the past, we need to get out of the comfort zone and exercise relaxation – and we have to be persistent. Relaxation has changed my life, and that is the reason why I have written that this was probably the most important challenge. I started relaxing around 2013. The best part for me is that I always have a technique that gives me a way out in crises, and it is worth more than anything. There seems to be something in the saying: stand still, breathe deeply, and count to 10.

Therefore, taking a few minutes a day to relax is crucial; it's like a mental training that has to become a habit, just like teeth brushing (in fact, teeth brushing can be meditation as well). It is important to become aware that we are alive and to look at the world around us with new eyes (for example, as you walk around the city, look around you, feel what you are sitting on or lying down, try to pay attention to everything that is happening in the present moment). Try not to live automatically, but in full awareness. As soon as you start living in the moment, you are already there; it is not a destination. People often have unrealistic expectations of relaxation and want to achieve certain results, and when they don't, they give up. Being in peace only five minutes and monitoring your breathing is the perfect start – which has to be followed by persistence.

Casual breathing can be classified as informal meditation. If you are more fond of animated video, take a look at *Meditation – How to Meditate* (■ 52). As I began to relax, one thing led to another, so I have

QR 52

started to search for different options and relaxation techniques. Internet, especially YouTube, is full of videos that can help you relax. Just type relaxation or meditation. I find guided meditations excellent as well. You can search guided meditations on other languages too, depending on your knowledge and inclinations.

Mini challenge

Listen to my guided meditation Love, Peace and Joy (■ 53).

QR 53

Since I have mentioned affirmations, let me share few words about them because I use them every day. Affirmations are in fact positive thoughts, autosuggestions, sentences we say to ourselves. Everything we think about, eventually is being projected to the screen of our lives. Affirmations can be expressed either in your head or out loud, and it is good to combine them with some other activity because that way they will be transformed into habits more easily (e.g. during the exercise, brushing teeth, washing dishes, while climbing up the stairs, walking a dog, driving – anytime indeed). You can repeat affirmations for as long as you want, the more the better, because with every new repetition of positive statements your mind will resist less and less. You can also write affirmations down, and then read them every day. They actually enable us to change our subconscious patterns (those 95% of thoughts that are the same every day because of the patterns), and they are especially powerful if we say them while looking at our reflection in the mirror.

It has been scientifically proven that affirmations can heal spirit and body (remember L. Hay). When creating your affirmations, keep in mind they should be positive (don't say, for example, I won't be sick), they should be in the present (don't say I will be healthy) and they should be personal – i.e. I am healthy (which is positive, in the present and personal). You can try repeating this famous affirmation daily, whenever it pops in your mind: "Money comes to me every day from expected and unexpected sources", and then just observe what will happen and what you will attract. Affirmations are truly simple, useful and fun way to make your mind busy; therefore, I don't see any reason not to try creating better and more meaningful life with their help. Except laziness, of course. In my planner there is a special page I call wish list, and on it I write all the wishes (even the craziest ones) that pop in my mind and that resonate with me. And you know what? It really works: write a sincere wish and let it go (because your happiness doesn't depend on it to come true), and it will come true in time. As you reflect on affirmations, remember that you become what you read or listen or whom you socialize with.

Mini challenge

Display motivating messages and/or inspirational sentences all over your living/working place.

Many people meditate with mantras – sort of vibration, combination or set of sound waves (the thing is, it has been long known that sound has an effect on matter, ■ 54). Mantras can consist of a single letter or of an entire song. You can recite or sing them, aloud or in your head (no one has to hear it), you can listen to somebody else reciting them or look at the written mantras. In numerous religions of the world, you will find the practice of repeating certain prayers, invocations, songs, chants etc. certain number of times. It obviously works. That is why they say mantra is a broader term than the prayer, even though today it is mostly related to Indian tradition. I have read somewhere a nice metaphor for mantra, which likens it to a stick for elephant training. A 132-pound man leads an elephant weighing several thousand pounds, and he controls it by poking it with a stick when it doesn't listen. Metaphorically, mantra is the stick, and our thoughts are the elephant; i.e. with only few letters or words we can control our thoughts, which hold a great power. Personally, I do not have mantra, but I know one of the most famous is Om (symbol of primordial vibration). From the ones set to music, the most famous is Gayatri Mantra, which I like the most when sung by Deva Premal (■ 55).

When it comes to relaxation and music, it seems convenient to mention gong therapy, i.e. gong baths / massages. It is a sound therapy, a form of meditation performed on a popular ancient (supposedly most powerful) instrument called gong. It originates from the Far East, along with other percussion instruments and various bowls. Our body is mostly made of water, and the sound, i.e. vibration, makes the water in cells vibrate. Gong vibrations cover all body frequencies and energy centers. Since gong has a proven beneficial effect on health, therapies are also used in some hospitals around the world for cleansing the body and soul. I take gong baths whenever I can, and I find it extremely positive, comfortable and relaxing experience after which I feel calm, rested, fresh, relieved from stress and negative emotions. You can listen to the sounds of gong (■ 56), but it can't be compared to the experience of gong vibrations in person. Gong is an excellent method for relaxation, cleaning and raising vibration.

QR 56

The effects music has on our body, health and mood have been proven long time ago (you know how some songs cheer us up, some calm us, some reactivate memories of certain moments or people, some relax us…). You should not neglect the meaning, intensity of influence and the power of music in your life; therefore, be careful and choose what you listen because it affects your vibration greatly. Since that is the case, let the music work for you; for example, as I type this book, I am listening something from the playlists called inspiration music, writing music or something at 432 Hz (instead of unnatural 440 Hz, which is mostly the frequency of music today). The right music transfers beneficial healing energy because it is a pure tone that is mathematically based on nature and vibrates in accordance with the golden ratio. You just have to type 432 Hz music in YouTube search bar and you will step into completely new empire (most of the famous songs you can find in 432 Hz version). That music, i.e. frequencies will help you in everyday relaxation. Given that we are exposed to a variety of sounds for the bigger part of the day, try to put at least some of them under your control – to help you relax and raise the vibration.

While you are relaxing, it can be nice to apply some of the creative visualization techniques. Those techniques will work if you believe in them, and they say they are much more powerful than knowledge. Let me repeat, we do all this in order to reprogram our subconscious, which influences our lives and actions greatly, as I have already said. Visualization is the common tool for athletes' psychological preparation, because it enables creating an experience in their conscious. The method itself, in the end, is not that much different from writing down certain wishes and goals, but visualization means going deeper and it is helpful to engage all senses while doing it. It is actually something we've naturally possessed when we were kids – and if you have children or you are in contact with them, you can witness it daily. Children are true connoisseurs when it comes to fantasizing and visualization because their brain is in theta state by the age of around six. It's not hard for them to imagine anything, in one thing they see 10 others, they transform everything into a story, they create anything they want in a second, they can easily drift off in their world for an hour playing make-believe with their real or imaginary friend. Guided meditations often use visualization techniques as well, so that can also be one of the possibilities for combining techniques.

How to (creatively) visualize? Easy, because it is similar to fantasizing. This tool is free and everybody can use it, which we actually very often do – we are just not aware of it because the process happens spontaneously. That's why it is good for us to become aware of our thought processes (everything starts from thoughts) and to engage them in making our desires or goals true. We can visualize while sitting or lying in a comfortable position. First, we start to breathe deeply and relax thoroughly. Then we begin to visualize what we want, try to get into the desired situation. We should imagine as many details as possible, involve our senses – everything we see, hear, smell – we should smile… The idea is to imagine everything as if it is really happening, as if we are dreaming a dream we would like to come true. In doing so, it is important to have only positive thoughts and to deal with ourselves. We can visualize as much as we want; there are no limitations. We just have to let our imagination run free. Given that we visualize all the time (e.g. about the car we want to buy), the process itself isn't necessarily space-related, we can visualize anywhere (especially when we get a little practice). During those visualizations, the key is to stay in the present moment, to control our minds and lead them towards the realization of a certain desire or goal. We can finish the visualization with affirmations that are related to a wish we want to come true. You have to understand that not all your desires will come true, just those that are for your own good. The ultimate goal of the spiritual path is a state without desires, because every desire creates a new one, and that new one creates another one, making us spin in a circle. When we are without desires, living in the present, we let higher consciousness guide us through life. This does not mean that we should not have plans, or goals, or desires; it means we should not be attached to them, dependent on them.

Mini challenge

Try to take a few minutes each day for creative visualization.

We are what we believe we are. By changing our convictions, we change ourselves. I myself, for example, always had somewhat wider hips and about nine pounds more than I should (not by some beauty standards, but by my own perception). I have faced the hips issue several times, as I was satisfied with everything else about my looks (e.g. small waist). I've tried exercising, different treatments, dietary changes, everything. Then, I solved the challenge about two years ago. How? Excess fat disappeared by itself after I had changed my convictions. I realized that by telling myself I had wider hips and by being reconciled with what I considered my standard looks – I attracted that in my life. You know how some people say they can eat and eat and yet they never get fat; then there are those (myself included) that say they get fat from just one dinner, as everything makes them gain weight. You know what? Both groups are right. And that is the living proof of the power of belief. I realized that one day, while looking in the mirror. It was a real aha-moment. First, I had to accept and come to love my wider hips and myself, and then I had to start changing my beliefs. I complemented everything with exercise and a different diet, but the key was to repeat affirmations and visualizations (because I had been on diets and exercised before, but with no result). I started to believe that I ate well, that everything I did benefited my body, that I was healthy (more on the subjects in the last two challenges). I repeated affirmations every day and I visualized myself without the excess fat on my hips. And there you have it, it happened, that was it. I can't recall the exact moment, but I know I am now satisfied with my looks. All that, obviously, had to happen in order to make me a living example of success.

I believe it is important to mention something else I use: hypnosis. This word may seem dangerous and intimidating (I too thought of it that way before), and this false image is often the result of the Hollywood movies we have watched. However, hypnosis is essentially psychotherapeutic technique that deals with our subconscious, i.e. it is the bridge to our subconscious. I hope you have a clearer picture now: again, we deal with circumventing the conscious mind in a way, through the natural method. Some believe hypnosis is like a trance – the state in which we stop noticing external events because we are absorbed by those within ourselves. Hypnosis often goes hand in hand with regression, which provides insight into past lives and the resolution of problems from the past (though it is not necessarily related to hypnosis). I am not competent enough to write about hypnosis, but it is enough to remember what I've said, and if this method resonates with you, you can find some of the numerous hypnotherapists, complete hypnosis course, or read books about it. What I do is relaxation hypnosis: I often find a hypnosis on YouTube in order to relax or to help solve an ongoing mini challenge.

Some of my acquaintances say they had so-called lucid dreams during meditation, or they had experienced astral voyages etc. I will not talk about those topics because they are too wide and their focus goes beyond this book, but let me say this: there are all sorts of things out there, and the fact we are not aware of something does not mean that it doesn't exist. For technology lovers among you, the good news is you can choose between numerous free apps for meditations, affirmations, hypnosis, and breathing. Do a little research, see what is on offer, try it out. On the path of happiness towards the magic zone, we slowly discover different things and we are never bored.

At the end of challenge 5, I can say that relaxation is of utmost importance if you want to know yourself and be happy. Start with the breathing and complement it with whatever suits you; I have merely presented you what was beneficial to me and what serves me daily. All those methods for relaxation and for living in the present moment enable mind control – because, what mind expects, often happens. The fact is, as you grow and mature spiritually, you need less and less techniques, because you discover that all knowledge and all the power lies within you. That is, we have come to this world fairly well equipped. Techniques help us reprogram subconscious and awake the creative power within us. They remind us that we create our lives ourselves, that we are 100% responsible for it and that we aren't observers (unless we decide to be, and let those 60,000 thoughts per day control us and steer our lives). Life is a game, so play it.

At the end of this important challenge, let me tell you the story called *Gods from Olympus* from a book I have read. After creating the world, all things and living beings, humans and animals to serve them, Olympian gods had an excess of creating power. They sat with Zeus and started to debate what to do with it. They had to prevent humans from possessing it, because that would make them their equal – human beings would be as powerful as the gods from Mount Olympus. While they were contemplating, Zeus said: "We have to make sure this creating power never ends up in the hands of humans because that would make them better than anyone on Earth, and they would be just like us. We are the rulers of all things and living beings on Earth, therefore we have to hide this creating power and let humans live by their own means, without having the power of creation." One of the gods suggested hiding the power in the skies. However, Zeus decisively declined and said: "It is merely the question of time before humans, which are curious and ready for challenges, decide to reach for the stars, sun, clouds – and then they would find the thing we wanted to hide from them." After little more contemplation, Poseidon had another proposition: "Let's hide the power of creation into the depths of the ocean, in the darkest corners of my kingdom; they will never find it there." Zeus declined this idea as well: "Humans are too adventurous and they want to understand the world around them. It is only a matter of time before they dive into the depths of the seas and at their bottom find the creating power we try to hide from them. There must be some more secluded place where they wouldn't dare to look." Then Athena, the goddess of wisdom, suggested to Zeus and other gods to hide the power of creation into the human itself, into the depths of his soul where he wouldn't dare to look while trying to achieve something. He would always wonder whether he is able to do something or not, not knowing that he carries the greatest creating power within. And while wondering about success and failure, he would be weakened. Gods accepted Athena's suggestion, and Zeus put the creating power in the soul of every human being – to carry it and pass it from generation to generation, without ever daring to look for it in himself and thus becoming equal to the gods of Olympus. Hence, from the ancient times and the creation of world, humans walk the Earth with the greatest creating power – without ever daring to really search for it and use it in order to achieve their goals.

৶ Recommendations to inspire you on your journey of happiness ☺

- [QR 49] How to Unlock the Full Potential of Your Mind | Dr. Joe Dispenza on Impact Theory:
  https://www.youtube.com/watch?v=La9oLLoI5Rc
- [QR 50] How to Train Your Monkey Mind:
  https://www.youtube.com/watch?v=4PkrhH-bkpk
- [QR 51] 5-Minute Meditation to Reduce Stress and Anxiety:
  https://www.youtube.com/watch?v=4r9eRgLX770
- [QR 52] How to Meditate - Er. Rohit Sharma:
  https://www.youtube.com/watch?v=e0rSmxsVHPE
- [QR 53] Best Meditation Ever: Love, Peace and Joy – My Happiness Doctor Anita Freimann:
  https://www.youtube.com/watch?v=ziNed_jcEDY
- [QR 54] Cymatic Experiment:
  https://www.youtube.com/watch?v=GtiSCBXbHAg&feature=player_embedded
- [QR 55] Gayatri Mantra, Deva Premal:
  https://www.youtube.com/watch?v=UlnHON3tAXo

- [QR 56] * Incredible Sound * Deep Journey * Close Your Eyes & Listen Earth Gong 62" by Tone of Life: https://www.youtube.com/watch?v=5L8hct4XFdE

- [QR 48] You Are the Placebo: Making Your Mind Matter, Joe Dispenza, 2015.

CHALLENGE 6:
HEALTHY RELATIONSHIPS
WITH YOUR FAMILY OF ORIGIN

If it can be solved, there's no need to worry,
and if it can't be solved, worry is of no use.
Dalai Lama

Following challenges deal with relationships, the ones that, one way or the other, consume big part of our life, time and energy. Those relationships include our parents, children, partners, friends, acquaintances, working colleagues. Before we tackle the topic of challenge 6, and that is family we were raised in, I would like to share with you several thoughts about relationships in general. One of the most comprehensive studies on happiness in U.S. showed that money, fame or job weren't the most important for happiness. The clearest message researchers got from 75 years of study is this: good relationships make us happier and healthier. People who have closer bonds with friends, family and community, generally are happier, physically healthier and they live longer. On the other hand, loneliness (greater than what a person desires) is toxic (see the result details and interpretation from research leader by scanning ◼ 57). No surprise there, as we are social creatures and, just like some animals, we like living in a "pack".

QR 57

Mini challenge

Name relationships that have the biggest influence on your life. Just say the first ones to cross your mind.

Relationships are extremely important because they shape our lives constantly, there is no question about it. Famous world billionaire Jim Rohn said we are the average of the five people we socialize the most with, i.e. we spend the most time with. Although it might seem trivial, it is truly the case, at least in my life and my reality. Allegedly, our earnings are close to or about the average of the earnings of those five persons. The same is with our intelligence. Therefore, we have to be careful whom we socialize with, because this is what we will become. Among those five people, it would be wise to have 1-2 persons that know or have less than us, in order to inspire them or help them lead better lives. Next, we should have 1-2 persons similar to us; they would be our reference group. And last but not least, we should have 1-2 persons that have more than us or that are much better than us in the field we are interested in (and want to become excellent in). People often lack the later, and that can be the comfort zone as well, limiting our growth and progress.

Mini challenge

Name your top 5 people, with whom you socialize the most. Do they live the way you would like to? Can you draw a parallel between your life and theirs?

The top five persons with whom we spend the most of our time usually are people that are very similar to us. There is nothing wrong with it. However, if we want to prosper and become excellent in certain area (virtually any area of life: profession, intimate relationships, health, diet, parenting…), it is wise to be among people who know more about it than we do. This will give us boost, we will benefit from other people's experience and leadership. I know many of you will say you don't have such persons in your lives, or you do but they aren't in the top five (perhaps they practically couldn't be). I understand that, but this digital age enables you to have around any person you want, all the time. Even if you don't know him/her personally, if they aren't physically close to you, you can still include them in your top five. You can follow their work, watch their seminars or available videos, you can read all their books and implement what you have learned. Very successful people often share their entire journey, all their small and big secrets of success, presenting them openly and honestly in their books. Therefore, it is up to you to get moving, to leave your comfort zone, to think about your top five and to push somebody out literally, in order to make room for the person that inspires you in the field you find important and in which you wish to prosper. Does this make sense to you? I have done it many times myself, and changed (some) people in my top five, depending on current situation. If you don't do that, you will in fact stay deeply inert and you will literally limit your opportunities for change.

We believe that we choose some relationships by ourselves (for example, partners or friends), and that we can end them any time we want; but other relationships we accept as given (e.g. parents or children), and we can hardly break them (because, as people say, they are our flesh and blood). I mean, we can end it in a way that we stop communicating and seeing someone, but we will stay connected energetically nevertheless. Hence, it is important to think whom you let in your top five, and to make sure you have at least one person who constantly encourages you to act, i.e. to be in the action zone. Now we will get back to the main topic of challenge 6.

Of all relationships, our parents have the greatest influence in shaping the course of our lives. Therefore, they are often the source of our biggest life lessons. Although family includes parents, siblings and other relatives, parents still have the most powerful role for most people (like the queen in chess). They create the first fabric of our lives, and they teach us everything. As tiny, newborn babies, we are completely dependent on others, and during those first days and months adults instill in us certain habits, patterns, norms, beliefs, and more (in the first five minutes we are given name, nationality and religion, without being asked about either of it ☺). It is true that the first three years of life are the most important and that the things we absorb then, define us the most as adults. It's fascinating how parenting impose certain standards on children (which is actually fine; it can hardly be otherwise). During growing up, and later in life, we stick to those standards firmly because adults/parents are our moral and every other compass – and because in time those standards become our own. If we don't break free from that way of life and from those standards during growing up, it will become solid part of us. Even when we stop living with our parents, when we become independent, all those teachings will continue to live in us. We will earn our living, no one will tell us what to do anymore – but we will still stick to the things we were taught, because our parents' paradigm has been installed in us and become a habit (reflected partly through conscious, but much more through unconscious mind). As if we have become our internal judge, judging all our actions constantly and tirelessly – by the old rules that were imposed on us long time ago.

Today things have started to change partially, because the generation sociologists call millennials or generation Y (born between 1980 and 2000) is more and more prone to put themselves first, not to fit in usual schemes and the way of life. For example, millennials would more often buy experiences than build/buy houses or flats (their parents might have wanted that too, but they weren't courageous enough; they followed other people's rules and tried to fit in). There are numerous studies on the topic today, because the habits of this generation affect the economy greatly. Read the article at ■ 58, and maybe you will begin to understand yourself, your children or grandchildren better. Going to extremes isn't good – and millennials often do just that – but it is good that they are more free in expressing them-

QR 58

selves and their views, in fighting for it (of course, it often makes their parents' hair curl because they cannot understand their children and they keep asking themselves about the direction this world is going ☺).

In comparison to prior generations, to the members of generation Y career is more important than money, and they focus on their own happiness more. Because of that, they are often considered selfish. However, let me repeat something from the first challenge of healthy selfishness: to take care of ourselves isn't selfish, but responsible. Some of you may not understand the parenting context of this, but if you have started an independent life yet stayed connected to your family in the sense of energy and behavioral patterns – you will understand perfectly. From my experience, people are often unaware of this challenge. I can tell a mile off that several friends of mine have their parents complicate things for them and make their lives harder (even though those friends have their own families and children now), but they are completely unaware of that. Even if I mention that to them, they fail to understand.

Mini challenge

Think and try to apprehend how much influence your parents have or have had on your lives.

I had an aha-moment related to this challenge after I had read the book *Geometry of the Divine Spark* by Serena Alba. That book came to me "accidentally" just after I had started to practice relaxation regularly. The thing is, we constantly search for energy. That is why we rest, sleep, drink or eat – we need the energy to function. Therefore, we often steal this energy (especially when we are not well, i.e. when we are low on the vibration scale) from people around us, mainly from those closest to us. And there are no better and stronger relationship than the one between parents and children. Why is this so hard to detect and comprehend? Because, we call that love, because every parent loves his child more than anything and it is hard to understand that this love can be suffocating. Because, even if they think that parents torment or burden them, children will not think of it as something bad – they will look at it through the prism of love, and they will think that it is fine because they "owe" a lot to their parents anyway.

Geometry of the Divine Spark says that everything we do, we do out of fear or out of love (I have talked about it earlier, but after this new information I invite you to watch this extraordinary video about fear and love, made by top experts ▣ 59). Where there is fear, there is no love; and vice versa. You cannot love and be afraid at the same time. Alba describes her own life and family journey full of illnesses, the entire course of events that led her to start researching energy. The book is actually based on the concept of psychic and energy vampirism (presented by Joe H. Slate, psychologist and professor, in many of his books). The idea is that some people live of the energy of others, by drawing it (the same as vampires draw blood). Usually, one person is the vampire (with low level of energy), and the other is the victim. Psychic vampires do not have special powers and they act from the position of weakness; they cannot generate energy they need by themselves, hence they desperately look for it in others. Anybody can be vampire – neighbor, working colleague or a friend, but vampiric relationship is common between parent and child, because parents love us "the most". Even if you are the victim in one relationship, you can be a vampire in another (because you are drained, you start drawing energy from others; vampire career always starts while we are the victim).

QR 59

This is completely unconscious and instinctive process. Instead of loving us, parents fear for us and, in addition, often want us to succeed where they had failed. While trying to be good enough, a child actually tries to become perfect in order to earn love, in a way. At some point, children become adults, but few parents are willing to accept and respect that fully. They may say they do, but they aren't in reality. Moreover, if and when you muster enough courage and means to leave parental home, your parents start to suffer from "empty nest" syndrome. Regardless of how far you go (in terms of miles), vampirism can continue. Well, if you aren't at hand, it is a bit easier for you, but if you continue with daily contacts and if your parents remain very well informed about your life (almost as if you are still living with them) – it's pretty much the same thing.

For me it was like this: I had a happy childhood and parents who almost without exception supported my actions. In time, I have developed a deep belief that I needed support and approval of my actions from my parents, and that became my pattern of functioning. It affected all my big, life decisions, as well as those daily, smaller ones. Given that I have always been very close to my mother, I used to tell her everything and ask for her approval all the time. Sometimes I would act differently than she had expected, but that required enormous efforts and lots of thinking and doubts. Interestingly, when I talked to her about it, she would say that I always did things my way, i.e. I was a true Aquarius. Paradoxical, isn't it? By trying to please others, you subordinate yourself, and those others are often dissatisfied with the result (remember the healthy selfishness).

If you have moved out from your parents' house and started to shape your independent life, ask yourself how many things you do in accordance to the habits and patterns from your parental home. Are you fine with that? Can things be different? This could be about trivial stuff, literally – from the kind of pasta and linen you buy to the cars you drive or wish to buy. Ask yourself how many things in your home today is the same or similar to the home of your parents: wall colors, do you have flowers or not, which kind of food and how you eat, how you spend your time… Even the patterns of functioning with your partner – surprise, surprise – oftentimes just kind of coincides with what you have watched from your parents from the earliest days. One of my friends once shopped with her mother and picked up a bag of pasta from the shelf, provoking her mother to ask somewhat angrily, why she had chosen that pasta when they always buy other kind. My friend then asked: "Who are we, mom, I haven't been living with you for the past 15 years, who are we? I, in fact, always buy this pasta." You see, this example shows how much our parents want us to be dependent on them and on the patterns they had instilled in us. It is a harmless example, but it reflects the overall behavior patterns perfectly.

Mini challenge

What else do you do the way you have learned from your parents, even though you know for a long time you want to do it your own way?

I know a man at the age of 45 who is divorced, has a child and another wife – and he has only recently figured out that his mother has a huge influence in his life, that she more or less subtly continues to shape his life and that she is a burden to him. She keeps telling him that he doesn't visit her enough, that he is not giving her enough money, that she is miserable and he does not care about it, that this new girlfriend of his is lame, that he should not have ended his first marriage, that his child is suffering – in short, that he isn't worth anything. And the man is 45! You see, these are emotional blackmails, and the person who stands firmly on her own two feet, who isn't in desperate search for energy, won't do that to you. It made him crazy because he loves his mother, he doesn't want to hurt her and he feels responsible for taking care of her – but, on the other hand, he cannot listen to her anymore. However, at least he comprehended that, and now he only has to work on it. Better late than never; some people spend their whole lives and never realize they have been living in this comfort zone.

Parents actually have certain expectations from their children, and if children do not live up to it (which is often the case, because they have different idea of life) – problems occur. Meanwhile, expectations, whether real or not, never end. Parents will never be completely satisfied, because your life is probably different from theirs (not to mention all the changes caused by technological and other progresses). Mother of my colleague from IT sector (application developer) fears all the time that he will end up in prison because he earns money (considerable amounts) in very strange ways: with his computer and this internet thing ☺. My parents never expected me to achieve the things they had missed to accomplish. Nevertheless, they unconsciously tied me to them and to their behavioral patterns, which eventually became a burden to me. I am not sure I was clear; they didn't make me do this or that, and they would more or less support everything, but since I knew their opinion on certain subjects and I knew they would do things differently if they were me – that was enough to torment me. I don't blame them at all (after all, they did their best at the moment), it was all my doing.

Once, my father told me that I was being silly and that he couldn't believe I worried that much about everything. He said that I was constantly in some kind of fear and that I had to live my life. That was a little aha-moment for me as well. In fact, dad let me go usually, but mom was the one whose approval I sought even when I really shouldn't. Quite simply, if I made different choice than my parents, I would feel bad – if I told them that, I knew they would not approve, and if I kept quiet, I would feel bad for not saying anything. Moreover, when I started living with my boyfriend, I actually stayed very connected with my mother. It was a life in a sweet comfort zone, in "golden cage" of sorts, which I had created in my own head. That love was actually conditional in some strange way, and based on fear. Mom cooked meals and did everything she could to relieve me from additional workload (which, at the time, I thought was great). She tried to help me as much as she could while I was working and studying for my PhD. Instead, it contributed to delaying the moment I finally took responsibility for my life. When I realized I have been living in a cage, I decided to find a way out and search for keys. As much as it is good to know there is a way out, you start to panic when you discover the keys are in your hands.

I left the cage completely when I decided to divorce my husband; that eventually led to sort of "divorce" from my parents as well. However, my decision was firm and clear, and nothing could have changed it. I've chosen a new life and I was ready to let go of all those who weren't fine with that. Once I made the decision (with lots of other energy work, meditations, breaking ties and attachments with wake-up method), things started to fall into place and everybody accepted my decision. Ever since I have taken responsibility for my life, I have truly started to live. Then I experienced magic – I realized I have been earning my own bread for 10 years and nobody should tell me what to do or make decisions for me because nobody lives my life but me. As one of my colleagues put it: "Those that don't feed or dress me aren't allowed to tell me how to live my life." True.

I have already explained how our lives and the decisions we make shouldn't depend on what others think. Our wish to be liked by everybody is doomed from the start and it leads to failure (there is no person that can please the whole world). However, we often give that special place to our parents, i.e. we put them on pedestal. Don't get me wrong, our parents are, of course, entitled to give us advices because they love us. But, you are entitled to choose whether you will take those advices or not, and you have to figure out how to react if they start to criticize you because you haven't done everything the way they had advised. In the end, it is irrelevant who was right, and it doesn't matter even if you are wrong all the time. Those are your mistakes, your lessons, your experiences – it is your path. I know many parents say something like this: "While you are under my roof, you will do as I say." Although it may seem a little bit harsh, it is understandable in a way – they shape and define their lives in accordance with long-established habits and circle of cognition. You just have to endure until you move out. But after you do, don't let them control your lives. Don't let them tell you where you should work, how, how much and for whom. Don't let them make you buy this or that apartment or tell you that you shouldn't rent. Don't let them criticize your actions and the way you spend holidays (especially if it is different from theirs). Don't let them comment on your choice of partner, torment you with questions about grandchildren, tell you what and how much you should eat… I could go on forever. Eventually, it is important for you, your parents and the rest of your family to understand that it is fine to have an opinion (and we often have one), that it is fine (and sometimes advisable) to express it – but it is not fine to assume that others will act accordingly, so we shouldn't and mustn't do that.

Therefore, parents are allowed to give you advice, but you have to think about it and make the final decision. They shouldn't and mustn't impose their opinions on you all the time, and expect you to dance to their tune. When you grow up, you should treat your parents' advice the same way you treat advices from other people – you should ask yourselves whether they are competent to give you that advice. The question isn't whether they have the right (they take it anyway), but whether they are competent. Can they advise you about starting up and running a business if they have never done it? Can they tell you how to follow a vegetarian diet if they eat meat? Can they tell you not to spend your summer in this or that way if they don't go on holidays during summer? Can they advise you how to do your job or manage finances… You get the point. When we are little, they advise us on everything because from them we learn about life; they know everything, and we don't know anything. However, as the time goes by, the ratio slowly changes. Everybody understands that process in theory, but some do not accept it in practice.

This topic reminded me about extraordinary short book *Four Agreements: A Practical Guide to Personal Freedom* by Don Miguel Ruiz. Those four agreements are: be impeccable with your word, don't take anything personally, don't make assumptions, always do your best. While I was reading the book, I was especially intrigued by the second agreement: don't take anything personally. The author reminds us that nothing other people do is because of us. What others say and do is merely the projection of their own reality, their own dream. The key is to take the stand and lead such a life that the opinions and actions of others cannot reach us, because then we will no longer be victims of needless suffering. This applies to parents too; so do not take everything they tell you personally. As the saying goes: The road to hell is paved with good intentions.

It is generally hard for parents to understand that their children have suddenly become adults and that they don't have ultimate influence on them as they used to. It is hard to accept that children have grown up, that they have their own experiences, their own path. I have seen numerous students that truly didn't want to study (at all), but their parents wouldn't hear of it. Those students suffered, really suffered, they lacked motivation for studying and their heart was somewhere else. A child should be guided until a certain age, but after reaching adulthood (which even the state admits), he or she has to learn to be responsible for his or her life, and parents need to develop that before that crucial point. Parents who hold their grown up "children" in bonds (often by helping them financially) and constantly direct them – actually harm them. At the time of admissions at my Faculty, we often see students with parents that knock on doors instead of their children, ask around, fill out papers, taking "kids" at the age of 18 by the hand!? How crazy is that? Parents, let your children get lost in a new city – that way they can learn how to orient themselves. Let them knock on the wrong door – that way they will learn how to stick up for themselves. Let them feel hunger, and they will look for the canteen. They have to grow up! If parents fail to understand that, they turn their children into invalids. Those children are in chains, building wider and wider walls around their comfort zone. They too often don't understand where all this leads, because they don't see anything wrong in having their parents pay for everything and in living with them safely by the age of 30. Oftentimes, this brings about that bad side of children's life choices, which leaves parents bewildered, of course – they have given everything for their child, and, somehow, he or her ended up in a bad company. Because they aren't allowed to make their own choices, some children accumulate so much anger that, when they become independent, they do everything exactly opposite from what they have learnt and done before. It's as if they act out of spite and with the sole purpose to have things differently than their parents.

Whenever I think and talk about this topic, I remember legendary Croatian journalist called Goran Milić and his opinion on "kids". As he said, he has traveled the world, and compared Croatia to economically successful countries such as Denmark, Norway and Switzerland. He claims those countries, even though they are four times richer than Croatia, don't have certain economic or social parameter to give them fourfold advantage (neither four times higher salaries, four times more real estate ownership, 4 cars per 1 Croatian, nor their students know four times more than Croatian, nor is their health service four times better). The key to understanding the differences Milić sees in the way children and youth become independent – in engaging in the working process, acquiring working habits and leaving parental home. Thus, it's about taking responsibility for one's life – as many as 40 times more adult Croats (under 30) live with their parents than in Denmark. Of course, when a child becomes independent, at first they will have a significantly lower standard than they had with their parents, but that is the whole point. Soon they will be able to reach the desired standard (and exceed the prior one) because they value earned money more, because they have become responsible members of society.

Parents think they can protect their children from everything – starting with crossing the street (teach them how to cross the street, be by their side for a while, control them a little and then let them go; if it's meant to be, it's meant to be, you can't wrap them in cotton wool forever). The worst thing our parents can do is to protect us from life challenges. It's fine to help children, but it's not fine to have them expect this help. I believe that parenting is about teaching children to live independently and supporting them later on (without emotional blackmails and self-esteem attacks such as: you are still green, you don't know anything about life, you cannot change anything, we told you so, that's what you get for not listening…). When given improperly, support can ruin you – in fact, it can be the best way to be ruined by those who love you. Numerous things between parent and child are wrapped up in a wrapping paper called good intentions. As children, we are constantly being served all sorts of baits, but we have to choose whether to take it or not.

Today I do what I want and what I think is right. I can say that untangling the situation with my parents was a challenge for me, but today we have normal, nontoxic relationship – true love in which everyone lives their own lives. I still talk to my mother on the phone more or less every day and my parents babysit for me from time to time – but it is all based on mutual agreement and on a lot of respect. My experience taught me that we cannot do much about the actions of our parents and relatives – they do what they do. The only choice is to accept it if it is within the limits we consider normal, i.e. if it is acceptable to us, and to arrange our life the way we want. There is no universally good relationship, with healthy boundaries for your and your parents' behavior; this is something you have to set for yourselves. Just you for yourselves – not the way you were taught, but the way you think is best. Put things in the right place and, more importantly, call them by their name.

If the things your parents do and/or say aren't acceptable for you and if they lower your vibration, you have to be brave. You shouldn't stay in the comfort zone, but face the fear and challenges. You should arm yourself with courage in the action zone and start talking and redefining your relationship. If that doesn't work, you need to do as you see fit so that it does not compromise your life and decisions. Some could say any living parent is better than none. I agree up to a point, however, there are parents that are so alive that they live both their own and the lives of their children – with often not so great consequences (I invite you once more to read the book *Geometry of the Divine Spark*, and as an introduction short article at ▣ 60). I sincerely wish you to recognize the importance of that challenge, that is, to become aware of the existence of that comfort zone and to set clear boundaries for the relationship. In order to have healthy relationship with your family of origin, thank your parents for everything they have done for you, tell them you love them, occasionally call them when they aren't expecting it, surprise them with something, hug them when you see them. Praise them, praises are very powerful and we don't use them enough. Make all those nice gestures of love and gratitude and do it every time you feel like it. Forgive everything you resent because it is necessary for your happiness as well (in order to release pain, anger and other negative emotions). I know you have all sorts of experiences with your parents, but this mini challenge you will do for yourselves, not for them. You have to free yourselves from the burdens of your past.

Mini challenge

Call your parents as soon as possible (if they are still alive) and tell them you love them, that you are grateful for everything they've done for you and that you forgive them for every bad moment or misunderstanding.

In any case, do not regret anything; everything happens for a reason. However, continue trying not to do the things you shouldn't, and not to fail doing the things you should. That way you won't regret anything tomorrow. If, regardless of the reason, you don't talk to your parents, it will eat you up inside. You have to forgive and unload the burden of the past in order to start living normally. It doesn't mean you have to have perfect relationship with them, but between not talking and energy vampirism there is a wide range of possibilities where you can find your place. If your parents passed away and you still resent them something, you have to forgive them. The tools from challenge 5 can help you with that. Send peace, love and light to their souls, and whenever you think about them, focus on the positive things that happened. Be grateful you had them. From where I am now, I wouldn't change anything from my past, not a single thing, because it made me a person I am today. I am grateful to my parents for everything they have done for me and for what they still do, and I am grateful for every circumstance that made me realize I have to take responsibility for my actions as an adult. Today we function out of love and we have a healthy relationship.

Although the family of origin can be a big life challenge, I believe it is more beneficial to focus on how you will do as a parent or partner (or how you are already doing). Would you rather have great parents or be one? Let's concentrate on the later.

Recommendations to inspire you on your journey of happiness ☺

- [QR 57] What Makes a Good Life? Lessons from the Longest Study on Happiness, Robert Waldinger:
https://www.ted.com/talks/robert_waldinger_what_makes_a_good_life_lessons_from_the_longest_study_on_happiness
- [QR 59] Fear vs Love - Joe Dispenza, Bruce Lipton, Tom Campbell: https://www.youtube.com/watch?v=jPuwwzfcyHc

- [QR 58] Millennials Would Rather Spend Money on Experiences than on Things:
  https://www.businessinsider.com/money-advice-spending-tips-experiences-boost-happiness-jean-chatzky-2019-3
- [QR 60] How to Spot (and Deal with) an Energy Vampire:
  https://www.nbcnews.com/better/health/how-spot-deal-energy-vampire-ncna896251

- Geometry of the Divine Spark, Serena Alba, 2008.
- The Four Agreements, Don Miguel Ruiz, 2001.

CHALLENGE 7: INSPIRATIONAL PARENTING

Your children are your mirror.

embers of generation Y (people born from 1980's until 2000) often become parents because "the time for having children has come". On one hand, it is lame, because it means we have succumbed to influences and expectations of our society; but on the other hand, it is good, as without this influence birthrate would be even lower. All joking aside, the fact is we are hardly ever fully ready for a child, and one of my colleagues says it's for the best – because if we knew how it's going to be, we would definitely never be ready. I've already said I became mom at the age of 30. Some will say 30 is late, but for me it was the exact right moment.

I think pregnancy and child's first few months are wrapped in some kind of myth, open secret or general lie, so to speak. The thing is, publicly everybody claims it is wonderful to be pregnant, it is the most amazing period of life. Media and social network profiles are full of lovely expectant mothers and toddlers (often professionally photographed), and everything around them looks marvelous, beautiful and idyllic. The truth is somewhat different from that idyllic picture, I believe, and once you realize that, you feel even worse – because you are the exception, apparently. It's awesome for everyone but you, you feel horrible. What do I mean by that? Well, I haven't found much "romance" in being pregnant, even though I was active as much as I could and should, I was eating healthily, I had the attention and the help from my husband etc. The fact was, my body changed significantly because I gained 26 pounds (which actually isn't that much), and I experienced pain and swelling daily. In addition, I had 1000 questions (and fears, often) but very few answers; I wanted everything to be perfect but there weren't guarantees. Moreover, I had to buy ton of stuff for that new creature etc. Finally, I mostly lacked someone to talk with about that, because every expecting mother around me was delighted with everything that was going on (or at least that was what she said).

I remember how one of my acquaintances said she adored her unborn child, how she loved him more than anything, how he would become this and that… I can openly say I didn't have much feelings for my child before I gave birth to him. Of course, intuitively, motherly, I loved the child that was part of me, and I did my best to provide him with everything he needed, but it would be wrong if I say I had enormous love for someone I hadn't seen or met yet (that love, greater every single day, came after the birth). It's exciting to feel your unborn baby playing soccer in your belly, because it allows you to feel interaction and connectedness. And, even though women are afraid of giving birth, ultimately a moment comes when they would rather have the baby out of their belly, as they can't bear that kind of cohabitation anymore. Postpartum period is full of challenges, given the poor conditions in most hospitals around the world, breastfeeding and all sorts of newly created challenges.

Therefore, I appeal to all new parents among you: stop telling things that aren't true. Why have false smile after sleepless night (and most new parents have many such nights) only to hide your weaknesses and parenting challenges from others? I don't know whether you are aware of this or not, but pregnancy and first few months with child are followed by the myth that everything is great and you shouldn't feel bad (although postpartum depression is the reality for 10% of parents). One remark for everyone: if your life isn't like the one pictured on the covers of magazines, and your friends tell you theirs is – don't lose your sleep over it as it is far from reality. True love for a child, at least from my experience, comes somewhat later, because it needs to develop just like any other (even love "at first sight"). Therefore, pregnant women and new moms, don't worry. Like my friend would say: "Take it easy, everything will fall into place."

And while you try to manage in those first days, know that parenting is a challenge. I have called it inspirational parenting because I believe parents should be exactly that: inspiration and mentors for their children. If there is something you resent your parents, so to speak, don't nurture anger; instead, remember that and ask yourselves how to act and do differently as a parent. Even if you haven't remembered most of the things from the previous challenge, you must have realized that as parents we have absolute power in shaping those little and fragile beings. If we call the blue – green, they will accept that (at least to a point they start receiving different information through social interaction). Oh, if only colors were the biggest challenge! Given that the role of parents is essential for life, upbringing and orientation of children – the fact that there are no schools for parenting (as one of the most important roles) is one of the biggest paradoxes of our time. We are on our own in the game called being a parent. Fortunately, numerous books were written on the subject, but the downside is that it all comes down to parents, i.e. there are no systematical mentoring and help. That is why we often raise our children the same way our parents raised us, i.e. we repeat the patterns we have learnt from our parents.

And if our parents interfere in upbringing of our children, things sometimes complicate additionally – often inducing big decisions. New grandparents are often true manipulators, because everybody has certain wishes and desires. However, you are not jukeboxes with the sole purpose to fulfill those wishes. One couple I know got a divorce because grandmother (wife's mother) had insisted to see her grandchild every day – as she had made or bought him this or that. The husband endured it for a while, but then he simply told his wife: "Look, honey, it's either us or them." They got a divorce, so you can guess what she had chosen. She didn't see anything wrong with taking her child to her mother every day, and she even accused her husband of not loving her family of ori-gin. Unfortunately, this isn't an isolated case.

It can be especially complicated if grandparents babysit for you, because it becomes an open arena of conflicts. From the point of energy, it's ap-parently the best if grandparents don't babysit regularly. There is truth in that. I'm not saying that this can't be good, that grandparents can't take care of grandchildren well, that they won't give their best, that they won't spend quality and educational time with grandchildren. I also know that some of you want things to be different, but you just don't have other option. However, once you realize you had enough and de-cide to take responsibility for your child, you will find the means. Until then, stop complaining in vain; either change something or stay silent. How will you know that everything is fine with grandparents babysit-ting? They have to listen to you because you are responsible for your children. You are mother/father and you have to decide what your chil-dren will wear; when they will wake up or go to sleep; what, when and how they will eat; whether they will use walkers or not; what kind of diapers they will have and why; when they must see a doctor; what they can or can't do; when and how much time they will spend outside, etc. Your parents don't have the right to tell you how something should be or what is better for your child. Don't let them tell you anything of the following: I believe it should be like this; your doings are wrong; you are to strict; it wasn't like that when I was young; why do you do it like that; you will raise them wrong; I brought you up and you turned out well, so I must know something. Alas, many young parents fall for the last statement, giving in eventually and accepting the situation. Today, with fast pace of life and tons of stuff we have to do, challenges lurk around every corner, making us believe that children's safety is the only thing that matters. We are satisfied if things are more or less fine and we just don't have the energy to face the "unimportant" stuff. However, it's not unimportant at all. I know lot of grandmothers that are in charge and that have usurped the role of child's mother subtly. The key is to set very clear rules for the things you consider important. And not to back down there. On the other hand, you can give in with the things you don't regard as that important. If your parents don't respect your methods of upbringing, even though you have explained everything and did everything, then you have to come up with another solution – as much as it may seem hard or even impossible at the moment.

Child will turn your world upside down, however it's one thing to be mother and father, and being husband and wife is something completely different. Even though there are exceptions, having children isn't something that can improve relationship between partners (it can only bond them emotionally and legally). Instead, life with children can even instigate genuine understanding about the nature and character of partner. Around me, I see more husbands who sleep in other room to avoid being awakened by their babies than those who get up at night. I see more husbands unwilling to change diapers (because it's "phew") or help their wives do house work, at least in the first months with child. More husbands who almost never participate in the care for children… I could go on forever. It's not uncommon for women to move in with their parents during the first few months, as their marriage becomes untenable. I will not get into reasons now, but I can say this: my experience was different. My husband took good care for our son and there were virtually no activities (besides breastfeeding) we didn't do together, i.e. not a thing he couldn't do by himself. Given the fact that babies bond with mothers in the beginning, I insisted he took part in everything. And it has been like that ever since, even after divorce. But the birth of our child didn't improve our marriage. As I became more and more dissatisfied, my child felt it. Then, as I have already said, after a

QR 61

two-month battle with colic (by the way, a great method for calming relentless crying you can find in the book called *The Happiest Baby on the Block* by Dr. Harvey Karp, ■ 61) I have started to face other topics and challenges.

Now that we have realized that as parents we are solely responsible for our children (until they reach certain age), we have to see how to be parents in practice and how to inspire children and guide them through life. I can't give you specific recipes that will definitely work for your child, but I can tell you what and how I do today. For start, it's important to accept you have made mistakes (i.e. wrong moves) as parents, and you will make them in the future as well. I'm not sure how you as (future) parents feel, but to me the statement that first three years of life are the most important sometimes sounds obligatory. There are no perfect parents, but that doesn't mean we should give up and stop trying to be better, best in the world even. We have to work on our growth, because parents are the first and most important teachers to children. Therefore, if you like something I said, great, start changing things. It's never too late, no matter how old is your child. Do not even think of blaming yourself for this or that (as that way you will be going back to the past). Instead, focus on the things you can do better and differently as of today, as of this moment. Children are constantly in the present moment, especially when they are very little (before the system shapes them and before their brain waves go from theta to beta state). If we want to be close to them, therefore, we have to do the same.

Mini challenge

Think whether you resent something to yourself as parent and release those resentments and negative emotions with some of the techniques I mentioned earlier – in order to prevent them from growing in your mind, spirit and body.

That period after I had finally taken responsibility for my life and moved with my son to another apartment wasn't easy for me. Around that time, I experienced the first challenging phases in parenting (around the age of two). That, and Matej's inexhaustible curiosity, made me act. Search led me to the book called *1-2-3 Magic: Effective Discipline for Children 2-12* by Thomas W. Phelan (■ 62). If I were to recommend you only one book about parenting, it would be this one. You won't regret the time you spend reading it. For little children we are "gods" they mimic and they learn much more from what QR 62 we do than from what we say. They watch us, they don't listen to us. Along the lines of that, Phelan, as clinical psychologist and an expert for disciplining children, gave parents three clear steps (copied here from the book description): *Step 1 is controlling unwanted behavior – learn incredibly simple counting technique which will make children stop doing things you don't want them to do (wining, arguing, tantrums, sibling rivalry etc.). Step 2 is encouraging wanted behavior – learn several effective methods for encouraging children to start doing things you think they should (cleaning their rooms, cleaning after themselves, going to bed, doing homework etc.). And step 3 is strengthening parent-child relationship – learn four powerful techniques that will strengthen the bond between you and your child.* In the book *1-2-3 Magic* you will also learn how to manage six kinds of testing and manipulation, how to act if your child disobeys you in public and how to avoid talk-convince-argue-yell-spank syndrome, which I believe we see all too often today. And you will learn that silence can speak louder than words.

I took the advice I gave to you and read the book with pen in my hand, writing down several pages of notes as a reminder. I read it from time to time, and I have even sent it to several friends as a little help. The method really works, but I have to mention that every parent knows their child best and everything has to be adjusted to the needs of the child to a certain point. The book is basically about consistency, the fact that children need clear guidance and parental authority, and the fact that parenting approach differs depending on whether you want certain behavior to start or to stop. The program is effective and easy, and it will teach you how to deal with unwanted behavior routinely, gently, but firmly. The goal is to enable children to grow happy and to be capable of existence and coexistence with others. I especially liked how the author emphasized many times that for every chastising (i.e. counting for misbehavior) we have to have five praises – in other words, the least possible ratio is 1:5. Every punishment or discipline measure should be followed by five praises, because they are water and fertilizer for children's self-esteem (which is one of the basic parenting tasks). The book underlines the importance of active listening as well, i.e. it encourages conversation with empathy and sympathy. In the end, discipline should take up 20% of time, and the rest 80% should be filled with sympathy, fun, praise and listening. Today we have the epidemic of permissive parenting, and parents have lost their leading role in many homes. Fifty years ago, parenting was much more authoritative – parents merely had to look at their children, and they would react. Today, on the other hand, parents are permissive, and they aren't keen on sanctioning unwanted behavior.

Mini challenge

No matter how old your child is – praise him. If you criticize or scold him, don't forget to praise him five times more. Try to use this ratio (1:5) for some time and observe does that make sense or does your relationship change and how.

Personally, I don't lie to my son and I show him my feelings openly. In other words, through my example I show him how to live – we all do that, actually, but the question is do we want our children to live the life we are currently leading. Every morning he exercises a bit, and then we make fresh juice or smoothie from fruits and vegetables. In doing so, we learn about fruits, vegetables, seeds, nuts and other ingredients. While we eat, we always express gratitude (because there are those who don't have anything to eat). We hug and kiss a lot, and we keep saying to each other things like "I love you" or "You look beautiful". We don't skip cuddling in bed in the morning, and we say beautiful affirmations constantly – mostly with one lullaby melody, to which we just add new words. I teach my son how important is to relax and breathe deeply; he often listens to my guided meditations for children, and every day before sleep we take 10 deep breaths; we also have little fellow that travels along the body before sleep and turns off part by part at every major joint. Moreover, bedtime is the time for stories (I sometimes read to him, but more often I just invent stories in order to comment something important that happened that day or to prepare him for something that is about to happen). Besides, we often do role-plays because it enables my son to get into the story and tell me things from different perspective.

I let my son make some decisions on his own, with all the consequences. For instance, when he was little, he used to bite his pillow, and no matter how many times I warned him about that or used "enough" (following the 1-2-3 method), he kept doing that because he found it amusing and because it was his way of joking with me. Then, in one story, I told him about bad and good bacteria, where they lived and why – in order to make sure he understood the concept. Next time he bit the pillow, I told him he had just eaten tons of bacteria but I respected that. I brought him more pillows asking him to chew on all of them, so that they would be free of bacteria and dust – and I wouldn't have to wash them. Of course, he looked at me in wonder saying he wouldn't do that, but I kept encouraging him. When he started to decline categorically, I returned everything to its place. I don't know how old children have to be in order to do this, i.e. to realize the harmfulness of certain actions, but try as soon as possible. First, find a way to explain them certain notion or concept (whatever is on the agenda) through a story, and then use their new knowledge when you need it. Of course, it's wrong to explain why it is not a good idea to cross the road at red light and then leave it to trial and error (you have to follow common sense and feel your child).

Before I became a mother, I often observed parenting methods of my friends/acquaintances, i.e. their behavior towards children. I never understood statements like this: "My son adores chocolate and sweets in general, he just can't manage without it, he is simply like that." Or: "She doesn't go to bed before 11 p.m., she just can't fall sleep, it's genetics." "He doesn't eat anything; I have a celebration if he eats cheese and pretzels." "Kids are crazy about my smartphone; I have to hide it when I'm at home." "She is four now, and she still sleeps in our bed; no we haven't been apart for more than an hour." "They are completely indifferent to educational games; all they do is playing with toy cars whole day long." "She watches cartoons for two hours every day; if I turn them off, she goes nuts, she is simply like that." My views on that were quite radical, so I kept my mouth shut. Besides, people would tell me, wait and you will see once you become a parent. Therefore, I absorbed everything I saw and I kept away from parenting topic.

Great, and after I gave birth and became a parent, everything I pictured – absolutely everything – came true. By some miracle, my son has been sleeping in his own bed from day one (in big bed since he was 10 months old), and in his own, separate room. He stayed overnight at my parents' for the first time when he was only three weeks old – my husband and I needed one night of good sleep, and he lacked nothing, he had all necessary care and plenty of stored breastmilk. Grandparents took him to the seaside when he was 10 months old, for three weeks. He never used a pacifier. He started eating everything when he was nine months old, and he never ate store-bought baby food. He loves all seeds, nuts and fruit – fresh, dried or in home-cooked compote. He eats everything, absolutely everything (cooked, baked or raw) and he expresses gratitude for it. He is in bed by 8 p.m. during winter and by 9 p.m. in the summer. He never touches my smartphone, so I can leave it wherever I want. We haven't reorganized our homes because of him (e.g. my parents have a house full of plants and cactuses, and everything is fine). He started to watch cartoons (mostly in English and educational) at the age of two and a half. He doesn't care much about toy cars, but he loves to play with Lego, paint with water colors, cut with scissors, put together puzzles, search for differences in pictures, solve mazes, create his own games, role-play, help in everyday chores. He dresses himself from the age of two, he writes letters, likes to listen calming music (■ 63), to sing and dance. All this things and activities characterized his first seven years. In addition, I have to mention he never drank sodas, he doesn't eat sweets (cookies, bonbons, chocolate) or chips and puffs – that is how he is raised. Besides, he has gluten, lactose and white sugar sensitivity. People sometimes ask me what does he eat? Well, all sorts of things, but healthy. I make him raw chocolate, cakes, ice cream, bonbons… Moreover, it ideally fit into my 3H Food diet, which I also radically changed. More on that in the challenge 12.

QR 63

Mini challenge

Think about how you feed your children, what sort of example you set to them, and dedicate your effort, time and energy to make your diet as healthy and as natural as possible.

I didn't share this in order to praise myself or my son; who am I to say what is right (time will tell), let alone universally true. I have many challenging moments with my child and I don't consider myself supermom, but I have set certain frame and parenting methods – so today I know how to react 95% of time (I am rarely "unprepared") and we face less and less challenging situations (although every life stage brings its own challenges). However, I can share the things we do and I can say that I've confirmed what I always knew: this has nothing to do with genes. Even though some parents (obviously!) don't believe it, i.e. accept it – children don't come to this world with congenital need for chocolate or sweets or puffs, for staying up late, for watching cartoons and movies, for using smartphones, for sleeping in parents' bed, for consuming screens. You have learned them that! All of that. Your children are your mirrors. To say that your child is like that and that you can't do anything about it, is nothing but staying in one big comfort zone that will cost you a lot – these excuses have great consequences, mostly for this young life.

I admire Phelan's book because it shows and proves that consistency (both in parenting and in the context of personal behavior) is the most important thing for children around the world. Every day I see parents saying to their children: "This is the last time you did this or that" – and then repeat the same sentence 15 times in the next two minutes. Well, how do you expect your children to be respectful if you do that? It's impossible. 1-2-3 method is, therefore, great because on 3 you have to, without exception, make a break. I know it is sometimes hard because it means you have to leave the store in the middle of shopping, cancel planned activity, put your child in bed earlier, stop the car in the middle of drive, finish a phone call, move the child away from the table, etc. However, this happens mostly when you start practicing consistent parenting. Once your child realizes you are serious and after the age of three, he will experience consequences no matter where you are and what you are doing at that moment – he will start behaving differently. Therefore, when you decide to become consistent, be tenacious, and the results will start to motivate you soon. You aren't doing anything bad, because 80% of your time with child consists of playing, having fun, praising and bonding. And it is known that children learn the best by playing. This applies to adults as well, because we have our inner child with us all the time, even if we (too) often forget about it.

I got the confirmation that I was on the right track during one workshop for children and parents. I was shocked when I realized how many parents never told their children that they loved them. Many of them didn't have a habit of commenting on their children's day, asking them how they felt or whether they were good parents and how they could be better. (Uh, there were so much genuine emotions and shed tears, both from parents and children.) Fortunately, the participants felt the need for improvement and they must have applied later some of the things they saw and learned. One of the best ideas I got from that workshop was the box of gratitude. It is so simple (as all the best thing in life are), yet so effective and fruitful given that gratitude is the key for a happy life. We wrapped old shoe box in lovely wrapping paper, made a hole on it, prepared pieces of paper – and every (or almost every) night we write down all the things we are grateful for. The idea is to write down at least three things, but children get the point very quickly – so now I have to write in small letters in order to squeeze in all those thank-yous. At first, Matej thanked for everything he saw around him (Legos, paintings on the wall, window), but eventually his gratitude became deeper (he started to thank for breathing, for having each other, for not being cold, for having the gratitude box to thank with – this last one is one of my favorites). When you encourage children, you are astounded at how humble they are in their appreciation and how big their hearts are. Eventually, I started to say thank-yous with Matej. Today he, my partner and I do it together – everyone mentions the things from that day he is grateful for. Children mimic us all the time, and by doing this they learn a lot about life, emotions, perception, understanding of situations they have experienced, etc. In order to practice the box of gratitude with your kids, first you have to cultivate gratitude yourself.

Some parents told me they don't know what to be grateful for. You can't convince me you don't have anything to be thankful for – you are breathing, you probably eat something every day, you are alive, you have access to clean water, electricity… We can be grateful for the important things we have been given – sun, rain, air, water, weather… Think about all the things you take for granted. You know there are many people that don't enjoy all the benefits you enjoy, therefore you should be thankful for that. Here is a great tool I use on my seminars: I tell participants to imagine someone will take everything – everything! – they miss to thank for today. They often comment how from that perspective it is possible to be grateful for virtually everything. See how the perception of gratitude can be changed? Gratitude doesn't come from happiness; happiness comes from gratitude. I dare to say gratitude is the key for a happy life. Gratitude brings us back to present moment and puts focus on what we have, rather than nurturing a consumerist approach that constantly focuses on what we don't have. That's why it is important to practice gratitude every day and to instill this concept in

QR 64

children from early on. I warmly recommend watching this beautiful video on gratitude that will encourage you to cultivate it in your life and give you some ideas (▣ 64). You can watch it every day and observe incredible changes that will happen soon.

> **Mini challenge**
> *Make a box of gratitude for your family and start filling it every night with the things you are thankful that day (and/or in life in general). You will receive many times as much.* ☺

Matej knows that we attract what we radiate, and that by the law of action and reaction we receive many times as much for everything, I mean everything. If you say it and live by it, life will give you situations to confirm it. And Matej connect the dots by himself. For example, in one phase he refused to greet our neighbors, so I explained in detail and with examples he would be repaid multiple times (e.g. even if someone doesn't greet us, we should greet him because that way we will make his day better with a smile). Two days after he started saying hello, he "coincidentally" received a bonbon from our neighbor in the elevator; she just spontaneously took it from her coat. "Mom, look, I was good and said hi to everyone – and I got many times more!" He was thrilled although he gave the bonbon to his friend. He didn't need further proofs, even though we experienced enough similar situations for writing a book. However, you don't have to write a book, a letter of gratitude will do. If you lack motivation, imagine how nice it would be if you had a letter of gratitude from your parents. Don't miss a chance to do that for your child (and parents; why wouldn't you write a letter to them too). Here is what I wrote to my son.

Dear son!

This is my letter of gratitude to you, Matej, for coming to this world and for choosing me, as you like to say, of all the moms in the world. With your arrival, much has changed in my life; in fact, little has remained the same. Although it may seem that we adults teach children how to live, every day I am more aware that we actually have to learn from you kids, because you are always in the present moment and you are much closer to the source. Indeed, it isn't easy to rise to the level of a child.

Thank you, son, for choosing me. Thank you for teaching me to fight for myself. Thank you for making me realize I have to take responsibility for my actions. Thank you for being so special and for teaching me to be in the present moment. Thank you for being my mirror and for always showing me what I am like, whether I like it or not. Thank you for accepting my choices, even though you sometimes disagree. Thank you for always catching my kisses and sending them back. Thank you for sleeping in your room from day one and for always being big no matter how little you are. Thank you for remembering everything you've been told, and I am proud you can't be fooled easily. Thank you for teaching me how to play (life). Thank you for teaching me that it's not important what other people say. Thank you for believing in angels and for encouraging me to go on a spiritual journey. You have also taught me what creative mess is and that I could miss much of your joy and laughter if I strived for perfect neatness and perfectionism. Thank you for dancing and singing with me. Thank you for coming to my bed every morning and giving me the gentlest "ouch" kiss. Thank you for looking forward to the box of gratitude every day and for knowing that everything in life is being repaid multiple times. Thank you for always being here for me. Thank you for being stubborn sometimes; it's not easy to handle you then, but at the same time I am proud for knowing you have yourself.

I hope I already am a good mother to you, but as long as I live, I will do my best to be even better. Your mom loves you more than anything in the world, to the sky and back countless times. And no, it can't be shown or measured. Kiss.

Mini challenge

Write a letter of gratitude to you child (one for each).

Parents often exaggerate and overfill children's weekly schedule with all sorts of activities. Things get even worse when children don't enjoy them, when they, for example, go to tennis lessons from the age of three because their fathers think it's right and they will someday be top tennis players. I agree that children today sit too much (in front of the screens, unfortunately), but they say that at such a young age a child should not be directed to a particular sport. If your child isn't involved in an organized physical activity, you can still spend time outside with him as much as possible, play, run or at least walk and talk about everything around you. It's very important to be careful about what you say and how, because a random sentence such as: "Come on, you a ballerina, don't make me laugh", can, and often does, play a key role in later life and life choices. For example, if you tell your child at early age he is tone-deaf and he sings poorly, he will probably stop singing. O.K., he may truly be tone-deaf and music certainly won't be his future profession, but that doesn't mean he shouldn't sing whenever it is appropriate. I often remember Cesar Millan (dog whisperer), who said in an interview how his career started because his father didn't laugh at him when he told him he understood dogs; instead, father told him he believed him and gave him his support. Sometimes one sentence can make a huge difference and lead us at the crossroad that will determine our life.

Children love to talk openly; they love to share what they experienced, how they see the world. It's important not to look down on them while communicating, not to belittle their ongoing challenges because they are not real or big enough. It destroys their self-esteem. Negative sentences or comments from authority figures (especially parents) can change children's world forever, so make sure you are not addressing children in a toxic way (◼ 65). To be completely present, to raise children by examples you give and out of love (not fear), to be life coach and available when they need your support – those are the main tasks of parenting. It's important to work on child's emotional development from early on, because studies have shown that big part of future success (more than 70%) depends on emotional abilities. Emotional intelligence is the most important thing when it comes to raising a happy child (watch a video showing one dad preparing his daughter for school by saying positive affirmations in the mirror, ◼ 66). Of course, it is easier to leave everything to chance, and today this mostly means to give kids the access to screens. I have to say a few words about that, even though we have already covered screen diet. Before, we have talked about you, but now we will discuss it from the perspective of those little ones that you are responsible for.

QR 65

QR 66

With the development of technology and the ubiquity of television in people's lives, companies realized that children are an excellent channel for encouraging additional consumption of adults and that they themselves are a large, untapped market. Modern marketing, therefore, sees children as future consumers, because consumer opinions and habits they adopt during their consumer socialization remain for life. Rule of modern marketing is: a brand should be imprinted in children by the age of 10, because that way they will automatically buy such brands when they grow up as well. In some countries, marketing addressed to children directly is completely forbidden. In the mid-1960s, the strategy of multinational companies shifted from manufacturing according to the needs of consumers, to the production of the needs themselves and their necessity. When desire replaced the need as the dominant aspect of consumer preoccupation, the activities of consumer society underwent a transformation, because the desires are psychological and inherently limitless. Television, of course, marked a turning point in marketing communication, which changed further in the early 2000s.

It was a time of the development of neuromarketing, which focuses on the subconscious part of consumer decisions. It's up to you to decide is that ethical or not, but I want to focus on children here. They are increasingly influencing family purchases, and the reasons for this noticeable increase are: increase of average amount of money per child (there are more and more mothers on the labor market), number of children in families is decreasing, parents are usually older and more situated (postponing marriage), divorced parents (new partners and more people that buy for a child), single parents (going shopping for the first time earlier), guilt factor (parents are absent a lot), etc.

With the media, children grow, communicate, raise themselves, mature, and adopt habits. Children and adolescents spend about seven hours a day with different types of media – much more than in any other activity. A Harvard University study found a signs of atrophy in deep-brain regions of teenagers, which means a lifelong decrease of cognitive abilities. You could say that humanity is collapsing cognitively because we rely on cell phones and technology. For the brain, screens are similar to drugs, especially in children, because as they move their fingers across the screen, dopamine and endorphins are secreted. The brain is naturally drawn to things that happen and change quickly; and that is exactly what modern media counts on. Whose responsibility is it? It has been proven that the most important factor in long-term consumption of media content in children is long-term consumption of media content by parents. Children, especially those under the age of nine, noticeably mirror the behavior of one or both parents.

Mini challenge

Ask yourself what you mirror to your child in the context of screen and media consumption.

I know parents who are proud because their three-year-old children use smartphones almost on their own – and that, apparently, makes them smart. I don't believe that could be the definition of wit or ability, especially if parents didn't direct it nor limited, as is the case often. Those skills children will acquire later in life, like it or not, because screens and technology are all around us. Some parents put TV sets in their four-year-old children's rooms, and they see no need for certain control (studies show today's children will have spent 7-10 years of life watching television by the age of 70). Meanwhile, studies clearly show that children shouldn't watch screens at all until the age of three, because it affects proper brain development and forming of synapses. And what about playing outside – Chinese jump rope, tag, hide and seek and all the other games my generation used to play? Why was that forgotten? Why is 14-year-old son of my colleague meeting his friends at 7 p.m., and virtually? And then they play videogames who knows how long (with the least possible control or without it). Why parents today know little about social networks for adults, and meanwhile children under the age of 13 use them regularly? They know equally little about social networks intended for small children, and the children use them, of course, without being instructed how to behave properly. The challenge is this: children often know much more about technology, i.e. they are more computer literate than their parents are, and that enables them to manipulate easily. You need understand the virtual world children are growing up in. Many things depend on parents; if you have children, inform yourselves and take control, it is your parental duty. The most important thing is to develop children's self-respect because self-confident and secure children will resist to advertisements more easily.

However benign this topic may seem at first, it actually isn't. Our children are so addicted to screens already that they are rarely able to resist temptations themselves (remember those ruthless numbers on addictions from challenge 2). Even the most impoverished parents, who struggle to make ends meet, will buy their children a cellphone just to keep up with the trends and allow the children to spend a few hours a day in front of the screen (which causes inadequate development of certain brain regions). Inform yourselves, talk to your children about these challenges before it's too late, set clear limits of technology usage and control the process, act on time. We live in the world of perverted values, but remember that we ourselves create them every day and constantly. I am not against technology, especially for educational purposes, but I consider the question of limits to be crucial. And children cannot set boundaries on their own.

Mini challenge

Set clear boundaries for your children regarding screen and media time. In doing so, first make yourself well aware of the opportunities and dangers of technology used by your child. Learn about parental settings for your TV, cellphone, specific apps, etc.

An NGO in Croatia launched the "10 Days without a Screen" project back in 2008, in order to encourage elementary school children to use screens selectively. The project was modeled on a similar project in France, where children use screens excessively. The project had certain media coverage, so the NGO started to realize the idea of raising and implementing the project at the national level. I will list some of the comments participants made upon completion of the project as I consider them extremely important. Comments of pupils:

- After a long time I was telling jokes with my sister.
- I am proud at myself. This project opened my eyes!
- I didn't have the desire to watch some fun shows on TV; I realized I could do without them.
- I realized days go in vain when I am on screens all the time.
- I liked that I really played more.
- I could ask something at any moment because TV was off, and my parents weren't busy with screens.

And here are some of the comments from parents:

- There is no need to watch stupid things on TV any more.
- If there were more projects like this, I, as a parent, would be the first one to suggest others to try it because it is perfect.
- It was so good the whole week that we will try to continue.

- I thought it would be impossible to do that in our family, but I was wrong.
- 10 Days without Screen project brought more smile to my child.
- Project was good because it brought our family closer, and we talked more.
- Children go for screens only when they are bored and when they don't have company.

You can encourage changes in your surroundings too. Talk to kindergarten teachers, schoolteachers, homeroom teachers, other parents – be the change you want to see. Dedicate yourself to your children, give them yourself, this is what is most important and what they need the most. Studies show that brain establishes 75% of all neural synapses by the age of seven, of which 50% occur by the age of five. That is why children have to be as active as possible. Furthermore, since technology is ubiquitous, let us, as parents, be wise and use it to work for us.

Paradoxically, we go to school many years and learn all sorts of things, but there is no formal and compulsory education for being a child or a parent – we just manage along the way. That's terrible! There are courses to prepare you for marriage, but a course for parenting – um, who needs that. Consequently, our society is how it is; we deserve it. For now, everything relies mainly on parents, and on educators and teachers as well. But I like to think that this too will change sometimes. Since I have been following people and channels I talked about, read the books on the topic and use technology in educational purposes – things gradually change in my world. Meanwhile, dear parents, there are no excuses, your (small) children are your responsibility; in this aspect of life you will reap as you saw more than elsewhere. If you have grown-up children, be supportive, praise them (remember the 1:5 ratio). Whatever you have instilled, they have it now, and there is no return ticket. However, it doesn't diminish the possibility of growing together in all areas of life. Just don't force them (or, even worse, emotionally blackmail them) to do this or that, this or that way. It will only induce resistance and move you away from the goal you have set. Encourage them to live authentically, make sure they know that you love them (tell them), that you care, that they have a refuge in you, that you are their parent no matter what.

I know parents have hundreds of questions daily (is this right, am I doing things correctly, should I have reacted the way I did). I also know that being inspirational parent isn't easy sometimes – but it is far from impossible. I hope my example inspired you for action, i.e. resonated with you and woke you up. You are your children's biggest inspiration, all the time, because most of the time they are not listening, they are watching you (of course, it doesn't mean you are allowed to be shouting or swearing mom or dad). Since that's the case, try to be the inspiration you want to be and spend a lot of time having fun.

For motivation, watch the video (◼ 67). With tears in your eyes, you will get the proof for everything and conclude that Thomas Alva Edison really had a killer mom and that parents have extremely important role in our lives.

QR 67

In the end, I am aware that some of you don't want to be parents at all, and that is fine. Don't produce children just because others expect you to or in order to save your marriage or to get married. I know people that can't imagine themselves with children in any combination (from all sorts of reasons). Although some may say it is selfish (it might as well be), I believe it is much better than to have a child without accepting him fully, a child you won't care for properly, a child you will raise sporadically and leave that task to the street and technology. It's better to admit the truth than fulfil other people's expectations. Speaking about that, it's not easy to live in truth, but it's very liberating. Especially in intimate relationship. Therefore, let's step out of the comfort zone once again, in the challenge 8.

⚡ Recommendations to inspire you on your journey of happiness ☺

- [QR 63] Mozart for Babies brain development:
https://www.youtube.com/watch?v=XjbJZ-8vH8Q
- [QR 64] Say "Thank You" - A Motivational Video On The Importance Of Gratitude:
https://www.youtube.com/watch?v=7uzynHWxn5Q
- [QR 65] 8 Toxic Things Parents Say to Their Children:
https://www.youtube.com/watch?v=GS_mATLF7BE
- [QR 66] Dad Motivates Daughter for School:
https://www.youtube.com/watch?v=42aF-bL_lRE
- [QR 67] The Power of Words!
https://www.youtube.com/watch?v=Z9UQldMGgdA

- [QR 61] The Happiest Baby on the Block, Harvey Karp, 2007.
- [QR 62] 1-2-3 Magic: Effective Discipline for Children 2-12, Thomas W. Phelan, 2005.

CHALLENGE 8:
TRUE PARTNERSHIP

Yes, everything is simple. It's people who complicate things.
Albert Camus

Every relationship is made of two persons – us and some other person, i.e. mother, father, child, partner, friend, acquaintance, colleague, relative. No matter how much time we spend with someone, we can never truly know what's going on in their head. We don't know what they believe to be the truth, what they are thinking, what is their reality, what they believe in, what conclusions they make. Besides, we change constantly. This challenge affects most people, hence you will probably recognize yourself here. Love, they say, is the strongest power, capable to change everything (especially if it is unconditional). We will focus on intimate relationships (without going into gender differences or making judgments on same-sex relationships). Regardless of the type of intimate relationship, there are many challenges that always pop up along the way.

The concept of love is woven into the very core of our being and it is probably one of the biggest inspirations to everyone. No wonder we fall in love from an early age, in many ways. We often ask children whether they have a boyfriend or a girlfriend, letting them know it is something natural that will come someday. All of you probably experienced puppy love, as well as more serious love afterwards, although there are no rules here. Some people have lots of long relationships, some several short ones, some (few) have been together since elementary school and married for 40 years (I know one such couple), some marry after a short dating, some never marry, some marry several times. Some people say we fall in love in only three persons during lifetime. The first love occurs while we are very young – say in high school – and we idealize it. The second love we try hard to hold on to, which is challenging because it's a difficult love we have to learn some lessons from. And the third love is the one we don't expect, the one that comes easy and sweeps us of our feet. This love destroys the ideals we have, the notions of what love should be and what is the true love. But the variety of possibilities in a sense of quantity and quality of a relationship shows there is no universally accepted course by which our love relationship should and must develop.

In most countries, it is common to crown the love we think is true with marriage – sacred bond between two people. Almost every religion has some kind of ritual related to marriage, but they somewhat differ in rights and obligations. That way, religions, as institutions, have created new institution of marriage with its own rules. It serves all religions perfectly well to be present at that crucial step for each individual, to set specific standards there as well. It suits the states too, so the definition of marriage is even included in the constitutions of some countries. If you look at it more closely, marriage is quite bound by laws, regulations, customs, beliefs and attitudes – which regulate rights and obligations of those that sign the papers. They want to live happily ever after and produce offspring, while marriage becomes a social mechanism for regulating partner and parental duties and obligations. I won't go deeper into this, because this subject requires separate book. It is enough to say that marriage didn't exist forever as an institution; the name and the meaning developed with time, mostly in order to create and bring up the offspring (although today some married couples decide not to have children). Beside church and civil marriage, there are many more interesting and creative types: arranged marriages, child marriages, forced marriages, temporary, informal, wild, posthumous marriages etc. Marriage became institution sometime during Middle Age, under the influence of religions.

However, regardless of beginnings and the types of marriages, some-things seemed to go wrong in the definition or equation of marriage – because there are more divorces today than ever before. The statistics is unrelenting; fewer and fewer people around the world are getting mar-ried and more and more are getting divorced. The most often reasons for it are: inability to live together, irreconcilable differences, unwilling-ness to compromise, unwillingness to respect other's needs, an accentu-ated division of labor, then abuse, alcoholism and infidelity. No wonder young people find marriage less and less attractive, and often decide not to finalize their love in an institution that have been losing its value in recent decades. Today is common to live in a cohabitation, modern re-placement for marriage – partners live together without being registered at city hall or church.

I won't tell you whether you should get married and when, i.e. in what kind of union you should live and for how long, or whether you should live like that at all – because that would be irresponsible and somewhat crazy. Obviously, there are numerous possibilities, and you will find your own eventually. What I do want to say is this: you should know why you have chosen certain option, i.e. you should muster courage to do what you want rather than what is socially acceptable or what your family or whoever think is right. For that, you will need a serious amount of courage. In other words, intimate relationships are one of the most common comfort zones, and people become aware of it as soon as they start to question themselves. Dealing with intimate rela-tionship is quite a feat, but my story and experiences might help you direct your thoughts about that.

Mini challenge
Think about your relationship – do you live in the comfort zone? Can you describe it in short and reveal the most pressing areas?

I had several relationships in my life, and they usually weren't short. I can't say whether I fall in love easily or was I constantly searching in others for the things I myself was missing. By that, you could conclude that I had gained certain experience and knew what I was doing when I married my ex-husband. Our relationship started during our master studies (this is where we met). We were often together because we attended intensive lectures every other weekend. We also had many tasks we had to finish, we traveled together and socialize often during events I had organized as a course coordinator. You may say mutual interests connected us and we started to feel affection for one another. Damir was kind, kind-hearted, always ready to help, constantly ready for a joke or two. During those first months of our relationship, we traveled a lot, passed exams and finished our masters. Gradually we were spending more and more time together, so I moved in with him. Afterwards we got engaged, and I thought it would ease the feeling of living "in sin" I had. At work, it was a time of marriage for my generation (young assistants at the time), so we sometimes had as much as three weddings per month – the same people sat around the table, only the newly-weds changed. I felt somewhat pressured by that – I kept thinking why I live "in sin" when other people were getting married. My ex-husband and I got married in 2011. Nobody forced me to that, and I didn't have the reasons to oppose it because everything was well-arranged and it was only logical to get married.

My thinking how that just wasn't right, often reflected in the form of dissatisfaction (later I realized that words and thoughts are powerful, and that we attract what we radiate). Damir had second thoughts as well, but he didn't pay them much attention; I was the one to think about everything because I was writing my PhD thesis on happiness at the time, and happiness became my obsession. Consequently, I started to analyze everything (I am generally inclined to that) and to study what psychology says about that. No wonder I experienced system failure every now and then. Still, I continued to reside in the comfort zone because I kept comparing myself with people around me and every way I looked at it, I was doing better (at least when it came to visible, comparable things). Then I would think I was being ungrateful and selfish. Actually, I was a challenge to myself. I tried to talk about that to the people close to me, but the comments were always the same: I was being selfish; I was looking for the better bread than is made of wheat; I should be content with my marriage because my husband wasn't beating me, drinking too much, gambling or cheating on me; he wasn't wasting money or go out all the time; he respected me. I was also told I should pay more attention on how others lived, I was still green, I didn't know how life was and what the real problems was, I was aiming for perfection that didn't exist, everybody had it the same as I did or worse, etc. Those were the reasons that kept me in my marriage, and I didn't dare going upstream. Nonetheless, something stuck in my head; my heart was telling one thing, and my mind and everybody around me the other.

The next move was to have a child, so we did. It was meant to make our marriage better. However, as I have already said – our son and his colic steered me to the spiritual journey instead. As soon as I got back to work (Matej was six months old at the time), everything accelerated. I had been meditating and practicing certain spiritual techniques, so, obviously, I attracted people with the same vibration to my life. With my team at Faculty, I started to work on a project very intensely, and meanwhile we absorbed new spiritual knowledge like sponges. We looked forward to each of the insights you have the opportunity to read about in this book, we studied the law of attraction, that is, we were like a pendulum (when more than one person emitted the same frequencies). When we were together, unbelievable things happened, i.e. we were manifesting more than ever and, most importantly, we kept receiving confirmations for everything we did. During that time, I sometimes came home feeling cheerful and on high vibration, but Damir didn't share my enthusiasm. Those circumstances limited my personal growth more and more.

Then I started to think about the difference between compromise in a sense of coming to an agreement and compromise in a sense of making a disreputable concession. I reflected on what it means to love in a healthy way (others, but more importantly myself). In short, this made me act. The only thing that bothered me was a question of child, that is, how he would accept it and should I have stayed married because of him. Definitely not! Children, we have figured that out already, learn by examples, and we have to ask ourselves what we are teaching them with our marriage. After some thinking, my ex-husband and I decided to divorce because I didn't want to live a life that didn't satisfy me, no matter what anyone else said or thought about it. Only the two of us knew about the divorce because I didn't want anyone else to tell me what to do, given that in both outcomes I was the one that had to live with the decision and its consequences.

Damir and I have somehow always been (and remained) mostly friends. We committed to do everything in order to make things as peaceful as possible, if not spontaneous. And so it was. The marriage ended without noise and yelling, in a very civilized way, without lawyers and drama. We are one of the few couples who ended the story with a divorce by mutual consent (which happens in approximately 3% of cases) and everything was settled in a few months. Throughout the divorce (up until now), we didn't experience tension. People often wonder how both of us managed to went on with our lives so quickly and how we didn't end up going to psychotherapy or taking antidepressants (because, beside the death of loved ones, divorce is considered to be the most stressful situation in the life of an individual). They marvel how we never talk about each other badly and how we don't talk about the divorce and the reasons for it in general. They comment how it is all strange because we did not have solid reason for a divorce (by whose criteria, please?) and how we can still function normally. The judge told us we were an unusually rare example of a peaceful divorce, and at the Social Welfare Center the counselors could not believe how normally we function and communicate. After answering all their questions, I gave them a little lecture on happiness, and they said they had never had such a couple before (there is a first time for everything) and that our child was happy to have such parents. Hence, not every divorce is a sad and difficult story, and it is by no means the end of the world. It all depends on the way you approach it. It depends on our perception.

You may be wondering how I did it? By practicing spiritual techniques. That is why I talked with such enthusiasm about spiritual techniques and the importance of spiritual practice. That is why I am so confident today that all this is true and it really works. I confirmed it with my own life. To clarify, making the final decision was not easy for us, but once you make a decision and reconcile with it (that is, you no longer doubt it or think "what if"), then the entire Universe is engaged to help you and facilitate your journey. We explained everything to our son, we did not lie to him, and he accepted it as normal – again, because we acted normal and because it really was normal, no false behaviors. Damir and I are constantly in touch because we will continue to be parents forever and we try to function in these roles as best we can. To end this story with a joke: I always talk the best about my exes - be as it may, they knew how to choose a partner. ☺

Whenever I talk privately with my friends or acquaintances or during my counseling sessions, somehow everyone initially hesitates to talk about marriage or relationship, because I got divorced and stepped out of the norm. Because they know my opinions, because they immediately realize that they live in a comfort zone, because they know that I know too much about their relationships. Indeed, when you understand a little about psychology and combine it with spiritual knowledge, the situation is clear from afar. Something has gone terribly wrong with today's marriages – because for people around me it is normal to cheat, lie, hide, not care. Or, maybe they don't consider it normal, but they accept it nevertheless – because they live in the comfort zone despite all these insights. I'm not saying that you need to get a divorce or that marriage shouldn't exist; I just urge you to ask yourself again, for the hundredth time, whether you are truly happy with your partner and whether you live the life you want. If you are not happy, and you do not change anything, you are responsible because you reap what you saw. And if you are not happy and you want a change, know that there is a solution and it is not impossible to have a healthy and good relationship.

So, what are my current insights on partnership? I will share some thoughts that I follow. The motto of any partnership should, in my opinion, be "to grow together". Indeed, as I am on a strict diet of screens, I have time to grow. The key is to encourage each other as partners to read and study new content. And if the new content is of common interest, that's great. That is how you can truly grow together and develop your relationship every day. Actually, who we are, depends on who our partners are and what they are like, because they more or less directly influence our development. Love is not a magic wand to make our wishes come true, although we all too often find ourselves in this situation. Everything, including love, begins with us (remember, if you do not love yourself, you cannot love others).

The foundation of love is actually freedom, and jealousy is not a part of it. As this challenge is called true partnership, it is obvious that it has to include adultery or cheating as well. The question is what is cheating? One look, several looks, the thought of wanting someone, correspondence, a video call, a kiss, sex (once "accidentally" or repeatedly, real or virtual), double life? Here I have listed only a few possibilities, and our time is continually opening up new channels that are constantly lurking. This make sayings "the devil never sleeps" and "the opportunity makes a thief" even more true. Everyone has their own definition of cheating or adultery, and I believe we cheat every time we avoid telling something to our partner, every time we hide something. It can be a simple message, which we would rather keep to ourselves because the partner will "misunderstand" and there is nothing there anyhow. Living with someone in truth implies that you can openly say anything that is happening without fear. In fact, jealousy is at its core a completely pointless and toxic phenomenon and if you tell your partner everything, there will be no place for it. But for such a relationship you have to be with a person who is on the same wavelength as you and live in your agreed microcosm.

The truth is, if love is real, there will never be room for a third person in it. In other words, if something is going on (even if it is just a message), this is a good reason to question both yourself and your partner, because you have both attracted it. When you think like that and look through the prism of spirituality, a third person can never harm you and your partner. If your love is real, you will only be stronger after an honest conversation; and if it is not real, that is good as well because you will leave a relationship that was not what it needed to be. If love is real, there is no room for a third party, and if the third person appears nonetheless, it's time to put the cards on the table. Because, whoever is hungry at home, eats at a restaurant. Therefore, take a look at what, how, when and how much you cook daily. Some couples don't mind the third party, and there are those who live in open relationships, or cultivate polyamory – there are so much possibilities you could write a whole book about it. Without going into all these combinations, I want to say that it is important to live in truth and not lie to partner. If you are both in truth and in peace, it is nobody's business what you are doing behind closed doors and whom with. That's why love is always freedom. Sometimes, it is necessary to know what love isn't in order to know what love is.

Let's be clear, if you want to cheat, you will cheat, regardless of the place and age you live in. However, think for a moment how much effort it took to cheat 50 years ago compared to today. Life has accelerated and changed with technology unprecedentedly, so today you have literally the whole world in your pocket, which makes everything much faster and easier. The author of an article I read goes as far as to mark technology and 24/7 availability as the main reasons for many failed marriages. Everything is faster, so people walk into our lives faster, leave them faster, and all our interactions are faster. Before, you would be on a date and arrange to meet again in 2-3 days; today you communicate with that person hundred times in between, revealing many things about yourself and sometimes even canceling the next appointment. That's how things are. However, one should always keep in mind that the glass is half-full, and I testify with my own example that it is possible to control things and make technology beneficial. I can say that in my current relationship there is no control: we do not check each other's cellphones, but we do not hide them either – there simply are no secrets. I didn't have that kind of bond in all my previous relationships, but at a certain stage of spiritual development I realized that if you lie to others, you actually lie to yourself. In other words, lies are like a boomerang – they all end up where they have started.

Mini challenge

Ask yourself is there anything you keep from your partner, anything that nibbles you inside, even just a tiny bit.

I have a colleague who has a second (secret) cellphone for communicating with her other love (and this has been going on for years). Ten years ago, I was with a friend of mine at her friend's wedding, and this friend of my friend cried because she was with her lover that night and they love each other, but he has a wife and she is marrying someone else. Another colleague of mine is married, and constantly engaged in extramarital activities; her friends cover for her. One man has another wife, which the first one does not know about, so he constantly goes about his "hobbies" (e.g. fishing, even though he never once actually fished – he just keeps all the equipment for credibility). One woman constantly lies to her husband how much money she is making because she gives some of the money to her family, and the husband would not understand it. Another one has to justify every receipt to her husband, literally for stockings she bought. One of my colleagues hasn't been sleeping with her husband for many years; instead, she sleeps with her son in another room (although they are on good terms and, as she says, have a great marriage, and the child is fine too, and healthy). One woman caught her husband in lie and adultery, but he eventually convinced her otherwise; she believed him and even apologized for following him (in this case, he did wrong, but the truth was that everyone involved in the story is responsible for what happened). One woman is addicted to typing with other men, this is her passion and she can't help it even at the cost of her marriage. One woman told me that she would never divorce, no matter how much her husband cheated on her, beat her or neglected her children; she just couldn't stand the shame and looks from people around her. I could keep listing such examples forever.

I do not condemn any of the above because people do the best they can. After all, let him who is without sin cast the first stone. However, it is unfortunate that all these people suffer so much, that they live false lives, some even double (or triple) lives, that they are constantly tense because they don't live in truth. If they would just expand their circle of knowledge a little bit and start working on their personal growth – they would still be doing the best they could, but that would be more than before. I know several couples who are facing a divorce and people around them have no clue about it. Actually, I believe more marriages would fall apart today if people had conditions for divorce. Some women, for example, live with their families in in-laws' houses; women don't work, they have children, husbands cheat on them. Since those women have no income, they have nowhere to go and they are trapped. I know there are sad life stories, but the fact is that when there is a will, there are ways. Always. The question is why someone attracts such experiences to his/her life, and what they have to resolve with it. No one says resolving the situation will be easy, but it is far from impossible. A colleague of mine, who recently divorced, moved with her son to a rented apartment and was left without a penny literally, but she showed that it could be done. It was very difficult, but she realized that she had to take her life into her own hands and stop relying on her rich ex-husband. She opened every door, she contacted every person, but everything is fine today, she is working and she is happier than ever. The key, therefore, is to take responsibility for everything, absolutely everything that happens; think of Ho'oponopono and try to do that (if you haven't already). Then just observe how your lives start to change and how everything wrong goes out.

Today, everyone seems to have something to hide and most people hide something from their partners and family. Recently, I watched a great Italian movie *Perfect Strangers* (■ 68), which tackles the question of how much we know about the people close to us. It also shows what cellphones do to us in intimate and everyday relationships. In this comedy/drama, seven friends over dinner decide to play a game and put their cell phones on the table in order to make all communication public (because no one is hiding anything, of course). The situation starts to develop in a very unusual way and when you think this is it, something new happens again. Although this is a movie, it is inspired by real life and if we decided to put our cellphones on the table for one night at least, all sorts of things would emerge. Do watch the

QR 68

movie (with a partner if you have one and if you are brave enough), because it really captures today's society and confirms that we know very little about each other because we have two faces: the real and the virtual one. It will really make you think.

Mini challenge

Do you have completely honest relationship with your partner? If you have, arrange a few open days in which you will have full access to every communication (cellphones, computers). If not, what prevents you from following the truth?

When it comes to movies and the truth, it always remind me of a movie that most of you have watched, because it is a classic based on the novel *Count Monte Cristo*, which has had numerous remakes over the years (supposedly as many as 40; here is link to one of them ▣ 69). The movie sends a message that everything comes back to us sooner or later and that we will be judged by our actions (although I'm not sure how wise and healthy is to plan revenge; there are many other ways to act in a dharmic way – I recommend Jack Hawley's book *Reawakening the Spirit in Work: The Power of Dharmic Management* - ▣ 70). However, what has been etched in my mind is the inscription engraved in the prison cell in the final shot of the movie: The truth will set you free. If you start following the spiritual path, you will see that nothing but the truth is the right way to live. Not to mention that every lie often creates a new lie, and before you know it, you find yourself in a spiral of lies from where it is harder and harder to find a way out. The worst part is that by lying (or concealing the truth; it is basically the same), we primarily harm ourselves – we lower our vibration and could get sick.

QR 69

QR 70

It is therefore very useful to start a relationship with a pure heart and in truth, because if it starts in the wrong way, the way out is even further. However, it seems that it is not easy to insure a good start, as in the process of selecting a partner we are guided by programs created in early childhood. Some psychologists claim that our behavior with a partner is determined in earliest childhood, and the key is, you have probably guessed, in our subconscious. Besides behavior, it affects every choice we make. What kind of person we will attract to our lives can be determined by searching for long-suppressed events, when we were 2-3 years old (with the help of a simple experiment). At this early age, we shape our beliefs, adopt behavioral patterns, and realize what the world is like. This is how we develop (at unconscious level) into four types (which will manifest in our intimate relationships later): a rejecting type, a needy type, a timid type, a confident type. We actually bond by subconscious image, and I found it very unusual to comprehend.

I somehow sought (and obtained) full equality from my partners in all areas of life. I do not believe in the male-female division of labor. Women are emancipated today, at least more than ever before, and co-existence with someone should be just that: coexistence. Household chores aren't something a woman does and her husband helps, because together (if everything is right) they should take care of everything and maintain the space they call home. They need to be partners in that area as well. Even today there are extremes to whom marriage is the embodiment of a patriarchal relationship (in my surroundings I know several such examples), but I am glad that there are more and more others – where partners are equal, or at least strive to be. And women are often both mothers and queens, and are actually guilty of not including partners in everyday life (especially when they tell them *you're didn't do that right, I'll do it faster and better*; this destroys in men that little atom of will to help).

Mini challenge

Dear women, try to get your partners involved in household chores for at least a week and praise them for everything they do. Dear men, get involved in household chores for a week (if you can't see for yourself, ask your partners how you can specifically help them and persist in getting answer) and don't act as a guest in your own home.

In my opinion, partnerships is best covered in the book *ScreamFree Marriage* (◼ 71). If you want to have a better marriage, develop your relationship, or you know someone who would like advice in the area, give them this book. It was written by famous marriage and family therapist Hal Edward Runkel and his wife Jenny Runkel. The book will literally turn upside down everything that you thought you knew about relationships. I'm not going to reveal what the book says (you will have to study it for yourself), but I will single out four fires of marriage: the fire of time accountability, the fire of the extended family, the fire of household management, the fire of sexuality. These are the issues most often disagreed with by partners, that is, inevitable areas of conflict after two lives come together. However, the authors emphasize that these fires must be addressed if we are to establish the meaningful, lasting and deep relationship that we all desire. You see, again this is about getting out of the comfort zone because we all generally yell too much at each other. Each partnership entails confrontation of everything that two individuals carry within themselves (character, habits, beliefs, rules, perspective, and the way of using time – just about everything). Reading this book, you will understand that we all yell at partners very often (sometimes even when we are silent), you will learn the simple formula for creating and maintaining the relationship that you have always wanted (which really works). We have indirectly already gone through most of these areas throughout this book, but with a slightly different approach. What this book has in common with *ScreamFree Marriage* is the fact that both call people to grow up, take responsibility, learn to calm themselves first (master their emotional reactions no matter how the other behaves) and then only act through the concept of honesty.

For most people, honesty and openness may be hardest to accomplish in the part of a partnership called sexuality. Although we live in a society where sexual revolution happened long ago, where sex is sold and offered (and even imposed) at every turn (even in content for children), where there are less and less taboos because our society is pornified – It is bizarre to see how sexuality between partners is often taboo, something that only happens sometimes (less frequent as the time goes by),

QR 71

in the dark and according to same, established patterns. Where is the truth in that, what happened to opening to partner, where is the spontaneity, where is the fervor? We said earlier that everything is energy and one of the biggest causes for losing energy is sex! Fortunately, it doesn't have to be that way, in fact, a sexual act can actually even be the basis for spiritual and personal growth.

Long before us Westerners, Eastern cultures knew this and shaped it into what they call tantra. It's a huge area that I won't even try to summarize in a few meaningful lines. It's best to visit the website (▣ 72), and take a peek into this sexual expanse yourself. Basically, everything you thought you knew about sex would be turned upside down. ☺ The male population can learn how to strengthen and maintain prostate health, increase sexual power, and enjoy a sexual act without losing energy (having a real orgasm). The female readers can learn how to get rid of the menstrual cycle and menopause problems completely naturally, how to manage, extend and prolong their orgasms, how to use natural contraceptive methods, etc. After you master it, the sexual act becomes a source of energy that at the same time strengthens your immune system, deepens emotional relationships, and makes you more resilient. I warmly recommend you to reflect on this topic, to transform your sexual experiences and practices into art and to release your kundalini.

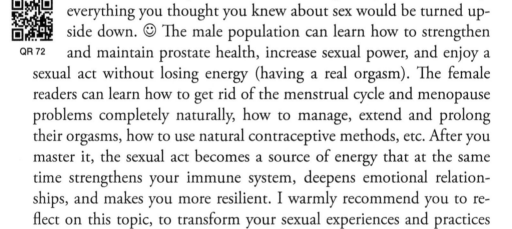

QR 72

Mini challenge

Look yourself in the mirror and define, that is, openly describe your sexual life for yourself. How much different is it (in sense of quality and quantity) from the things you really want? Why is it like that? Are you willing to change it?

They say that one of the greatest enemies of marriage/partnership is actually boredom – when everything starts to happen according to the usual schedules and patterns (you know by now that I must emphasize how this is also a comfort zone, and of course it is). Do you know why we feel great at the beginning of relationship? One of the key reasons is that we have fun then, we go out to the movies, theater, walks, dinners, we socialize a lot, maybe travel… Well, that's the key. No matter how much time, money, or whatever you have or don't have, these aren't and should not be excuses that prevent you to have a good time with your partner. Work together on mini challenges, make a list of desired activities, and encourage yourself to leave the comfort zone.

Ultimately, when we take everything into consideration, if you have decided to have a partner in your life, you need to be able to look your partner straight in the eyes (and hold that look), and precondition for that is a 100-percent truth. We have come to the end of the partnership section. However, you are probably only at the beginning and you are wiggling in the comfort zone, small or bigger one, where only you know the complete truth. It's more comfortable that way, but it's not better in the long run. Set a true partnership for a goal, everything else is lying to the others and, worse, to yourself. Besides, everything in life is being repaid multiple times, remember.

Recommendations to inspire you on your journey of happiness ☺

- [QR 68] Perfect Strangers - Trailer:
     https://www.youtube.com/watch?v=kqX0-xn8j1g
- [QR 69] The Count of Monte Cristo - Trailer:
     https://www.youtube.com/watch?v=gzRSVl8UewM

- [QR 72] Somananda Yoga School: https://somananda.org/

- [QR 70] Reawakening the Spirit in Work: The Power of Dharmic Management, Jack Hawley, 2002.
- [QR 71] ScreamFree Marriage: Calming Down, Growing Up, and Getting Closer, Hal Edward Runkel & Jenny Runkel, 2011.

CHALLENGE 9:
STIMULATING FRIENDSHIPS
AND ACQUAINTANCES

Considering how much I want others to respect my freedom,
I have to respect theirs.
Françoise Sagan

If you think for a moment about a statement, or the fact, that we are the average of the five people whom we mostly socialize with (as we mentioned in the challenge 6), you will immediately realize how important is to have the right people around you. Much easier said than done, especially today. Family of origin is given to us, same as our children, but friends and acquaintances are a very variable category, and it's quite liberating to know that. We are social creatures, and with given relationships and people around us, many of us are surrounded with people from early on, starting with nursery, kindergarten, elementary school, high school, university, working environment, neighbors, people with the same hobbies or activities (running, fishing, training, certain seminars…). People constantly come into our lives – that's perfectly normal. I have a friend who asks me from time to time: "Who is your best friend now?" I usually laugh and say that best friends don't exist because that term reminds me of elementary school and the time we filled each other's scrapbooks – at that age, we always emphasized who is our best friend. To me, this is a non-existing category because what we would call BFF (i.e. best friend forever) is BFF at certain point in our life.

In this context, we may ask ourselves what is the definition of friendship in the first place? Who are our friends, who should they be and what is their role in our lives? Above all, friendship should be a relationship between two people that is inherently positive and based on correct, shared values and mutual respect. More than ever before, I believe – again caused by technology and social networks in particular – the definition of friendship is completely distorted. Not so long ago there was no virtual friend category. If we were to look at numbers only, I have many "friends" on social networks, but are they really my friends? It's been almost 20 years since Mark Zuckerberg very cleverly, marketing-wisely and thoughtfully put "Add Friend" button on then most popular social network, instead of "Add Acquaintance" or "Add Contact" buttons. It seems that this has created new definition or paradigm of friendship and devalued it in a way. Recently, I watched a great video *Real Life Facebook* (◼ 73), which shows in a clear and funny way what real life would look like if we treated our "friends" the way we behave on this social network. The video is funny, but it's also kind of sad, because we've distorted values. Of course, technology is a great tool for maintaining friendships when someone moves away, for example, as it can help you overcome the physical barrier, i.e. distance, in seconds. However, among all those virtual "friends" there are few who stay your friends even after the screens are off.

QR 73

I think we should rethink our notion of friendship and differentiate our friends from acquaintances. Every friend was once, at the beginning, an acquaintance; in order to become friends with someone, one has to eat a measure of salt with him. In other words, friendship develops; it is not an overnight occurrence. The Latin proverb says that the friendship established over a glass of wine is usually fragile (literally: glass). An acquaintance of mine says that distinguishing friends from acquaintances is easy: his friends are the ones he invites to his birthday parties and important celebrations – along with his family, they are the most important people to him. Everyone has their own criteria. Whatever your criterion is, it is important not to call all people friends because they are not. In doing so, we give them the importance they don't have, and we degrade true friends. Actually, the term we use is not important, nor it is necessary to put people in certain categories, but it makes sense to consider to whom we give our time and energy, and why.

Mini challenge

Think about what friendship means to you, and who might not belong on your list of friends if you apply your true criteria.

Regardless of terminological differences, both friends and acquaintances can play important roles in our lives, and they often do. They even say that a value of a human being is equal to the number of his true friends. True friends will listen to everything we have to say, everything we have on our minds. According to certain studies, most people (approximately 80%) are more inclined to talk to good listeners (not to big talkers), so it's clear what kind of trait we value from a friend: listening. Besides being good listeners, friends should always be there for us, because they are elected category, not imposed one. I believe you can't have a bunch of true friends, because friendship takes time and everyone's friend is actually nobody's friend. In our teens and young age, it is easier to share everything with our peers (especially if you are a girl) than with adults or parents. Why? Because they rarely if ever judge us, they do not discipline us, they do not reprimand our behaviors, they understand us, and they often go through similar situations themselves. Even when we are older, we sometimes find it easier to confide in friends than, for example, in a spouse. Is that good or not, it is for you to decide, by taking into consideration all the insights from the previous challenge. Although the definition of friendship does not seem to be universal, the need for friendship is something everyone feels. The proof for that is the popularity of one of the most famous series ever: "Friends".

Since I was an only child, I always had a house full of friends, children from my street, and later from school. They were often at my place and we would study together. I liked to help them in subjects I was good at (e.g. mathematics), and I always did. This continued when I was older, when I used to manicure and polish my friends' nails for free, give makeup tips and free makeup, pluck eyebrows, give advices on hairstyles etc. Moreover, I always had a car at my disposal, so I took them wherever they needed to go. It has never been difficult for me to do something for others, from smaller to larger favors, and my parents used to say that our house sometimes looked like a promenade.

It is said that a friend in need is a friend indeed. That is, it is easy to be good with someone when everything is fine. This is an honest truth, and that's why all those famous people and celebrities (from musicians to politicians) have challenges with relationships. They have trouble discovering who their true friends are and who are just newcomers claiming to be "relatives" in the 5th generation. If it's 3 a.m. and you have an emergency, which of several hundred cell phone contacts (except family members) will you call for help? Hard question, right? And which one of them will answer you at 3 a.m., or better still, really come to your aid? A true friend is someone with whom you can remain silent or talk for hours, who knows what you love, who supports you, who makes you a better person, who accepts you as you are but has a constant positive influence on you as well, to whom you can confide in, who is like a sibling to you, with whom you are totally relaxed. I like to joke that if you want to make a quick and easy clean-up of your circle of friends and all those who call themselves that, it's best to get a divorce. Within a week, everything will be solved. ☺ I'm kidding, of course, you won't divorce just to test your friends, but the fact is that some of the big life changes will surely cause certain reactions in your circle of friends as well, and you'll quickly realize who's thinking what.

Maybe all this about friendship is pretty clear to you and you wonder what the challenge here is. Well, the challenge is encouraging friendships and acquaintances. Admit it to yourself: do you sometimes go for coffees, get-togethers or birthday parties because you promised, you feel obliged to or you think it could be useful to you – even though you don't really want to go? Do you go to weddings that you consider lame, but you have to go for one reason or another? In fact, in all these situations, you are lying to yourself and by doing that you are likely to lower your vibration. As we get older, especially after we become parents, we have an increasing list of commitments and less time for wasting, i.e. spending on irrelevant things. However, there are many who still do that – I see it in everyday life, and I have done it myself before. If you put yourself first, you will never again go anywhere out of sense of duty, not if you truly don't want to go. Indeed, as you start appreciating yourself more on the path of happiness, you will be less inclined and willing to dedicate your time to the people who are not worth it; that is, you will focus more on doing what you truly want.

It is a pity that this area of life often has a comfort zone too, hence some people constantly linger in our lives, we just don't have the courage to push them out. Friends can be energy vampires as well, and they can affect our lives considerably. Maid of honor of one of my friends arrived at the wedding at the last moment; she was late for one reason or another (she is always late). She is, generally, so disorganized that my friend had another person as a "reserve" from the beginning, that is, she had a replacement in case the first one wouldn't appear. I couldn't hide my bewilderment and I asked why she chose her in the first place, given that she wasn't satisfied with her and given that her maid of honor obviously did not respect her at all. She said that she was returning favor because she was her maid of honor as well. Apparently, they had agreed upon it a long time ago (in elementary school). In the meantime, everything that had to be done during the months of preparation for the wedding, she did with the "replacement". To me, that was and remained incomprehensible. To whom are we adapting, whose expectations are we meeting, where does it say that you have to return the honor? I also know people who literally chose their made of honors and best men out of anger or caprice, and I won't even mention those who choose them by how fit and/or financially savvy they are. All these perceptions and motives are distorted, but even here everything always comes back to us as a boomerang. In the end, we know deep down that this is not right and that is disrupting enough for our inner peace.

Different friendships bring different lessons. Not all our friends – not to mention acquaintances – have good intentions and they often act out of jealousy and envy. There are those who take advantage on us, and that can become toxic too if we fail to realize that on time. Sometimes your friend is exactly the person your partner has an affair with; sometimes the persons you would least expected to, have been passing on information you asked them to keep for themselves; sometimes they spread bad and untrue information about you; sometimes they are twofaced.

Gossip is another story, psychology phenomenon even. Maybe some of you did experiments on the subject in school, as I do sometimes with my students. All of us know how fast the rumors spread and how most of them consists of inaccurate information, which in the end turns the story into something else. For example, I select five volunteer students, and send four of them out of the classroom. Then I read a fictional story that I made up to the fifth student and the rest of the class. The fifth student has to tell the story as accurately as possible to one of the four students who comes in the classroom; he then has to pass it to the next one, and so on until the end. Each time, without exception, the story is reduced to at least 1/5 of the original, the characters are mixed up, the whole story is twisted and, in the end, it no longer resembles the one from the beginning. Even though the students try their best to tell the story as accurately as they can (for extra points) and no one has the slightest motive to change or subtract anything. Imagine how this goes when it is a real-life story, when people you know are involved, when those involved have all sorts of motives, and when emotions are a part of it. It really can be ugly and sometimes tragic.

The movie *Gossip* from 2000 (watch the trailer at ▣ 74) clearly shows how one gossip can be fatal. After seeing it, you will think carefully about whether it makes sense to gossip, especially about your friends and/or acquaintances. In addition, if we gossip about others, we poison ourselves with negative emotions. It is said that if a person cannot say anything good about himself and wants to say something, he will start speaking badly about others. In any case, it may be better to leave the rumors to those with lower vibrations and to deal with your own life. I know it's hard sometimes, but people will always talk. You simply don't have to pay attention to it, because it inhibits you in every sense, you pay unnecessary attention to it and you lose energy. You don't have to prove anything to anyone. Every attack is actually a cry for help – this is a sentence worth remembering. Besides, whatever someone does, he does it to himself. That goes for everyone, including ourselves.

Mini challenge

On your next get-together with your friends, try not to gossip at all and observe the reactions from your friends, as well as how that makes you feel. Repeat this as often as you can, and remember that everything we say, actually speaks about us.

It's important to know that friends are our mirrors too, therefore you attract whatever you radiate. If you don't like something in your friends, take a peek at yourself – they point to something. If you have friends, or "friends" who accuse you for not calling them enough, who keep record who contacted whom and how many times during last month, with whom you always have to arrange a meeting weeks ahead (and you live near to each other), who never talk about themselves but want to know every detail of your life, whom you suspect to leak the information about you, whom you aren't keen to answer the phone, whom you aren't comfortable with... – I am sure you know those people aren't really your friends, and you throw pearls around. The question is why you do it and what for. Those people are in your life with a reason, and if they are truly like that, and you socialize with them nevertheless – doesn't it say something about you as well?

One sign of distorted friendship may be if you always, without exception, pay for a drink, and your friend never takes his wallet out of his pocket (unless you have agreed on that for some reason, say until he finds a job etc.). Or if you always hang out at your place, if you always do your best to host your friends and prepare something for them, and they never make an effort for you, they never or extremely rarely invite you to their home (however small it is). Or if they constantly need something from you, but they get evasive and dodging when you need their help or service. Or if they socialize with others, but only call you when they need a shoulder to cry on or when they need some help or benefit. Or if they don't respect your life partner, if they reject you because you have changed your beliefs, religion, partner, etc. Or if they are always late, thus letting you know that they don't appreciate you and your time.

Mini challenge

Think – do you have a toxic friendship, some person that suffocates you and you feel that your relationship isn't honest? The answer is the first thing that pops on your mind. What can you do about it?

A true friend doesn't have to be someone you talk to on the phone every day; I have a friend whom I don't hear for a month sometimes, but when we meet, it's like we met yesterday (and I know I can always call her). There are people who have been in my life forever, but I certainly couldn't call them friends. On the other hand, there are those whom I met by chance one evening and with whom I immediately clicked and exchanged some symbolic gifts, whom I care about in a strange way, as if we already knew each other "from before".

The dog is, they say, human's best and most loyal friend. Ever wondered why? Dogs really love their owners unconditionally, they always follow them, they look forward to them even though they have only been away for five minutes (this is because they live in the moment). Besides, they never reveal secrets, they understand their owners, they say they can even take certain diseases from them (I loved the documentary *Secret Life of Dogs*, ■ 75). I agree with Corey Ford that if he is properly trained, a man can become a dog's best friend. ☺ And, can we be like puppies in friendship? Cicero said that life without

QR 75

friends is nothing. However, the focus should be on how to be a good friend, not how to have good friends. They say that friendship can also be spiritual, and I confirm it with my life. Therefore, it is not a bad idea to ask ourselves are we a true friend, can our friends talk to us about anything? Do we criticize constructively rather than destructively? Do we make our friends feel understood and listened to? Do our friends think we can be fully trusted? Do they think we respect their boundaries, we are forgiving and we don't hold the grudge? Do they think we see the best in others and we will be there in good and bad times? Being a true friend is not easy; if that was the case, anyone could do it.

While I was growing up, I felt angry when at some points certain friends walked out of my life and we weren't on good terms anymore. Life tells unbelievable stories, so it took time before I realized that people constantly come and go, and more importantly – it is perfectly normal. Perhaps it is the concept of "best friends" from early childhood why we think that friendship has to and should be forever. It shouldn't, however, and it was totally liberating realization for me. Sections along our path follow in some way the stages of our growth and development, that is, life stages. Each of these stages are marked by certain people. We have friends from elementary school with whom we are still in excellent relationships; we have those whom we invited to "our birthday party" only once; we have those who are related to us through a business environment; and we have those whom we met for just a few days (or even hours) but they have left a mark forever and touched our lives. There's no need to bother with that; they did their leg. Maybe we occasionally turned left or right precisely because of them, which led us to where we are today and we should be grateful for that. Moreover, sometimes our lives become intertwined with certain people again, which is also nice – a new story based on old foundations.

Ergo, some people stay in our lives for just one day, some for a few years, and very few will be here for a lifetime. We change constantly, so why should we expect from others to stay the same and satisfied with our company in the long run? Friendship should be based on reciprocity, that is, both parties should be equally willing to receive and give. It takes courage to face this challenge and end relationships that are not right for you, no matter who it is. You should speak to a person whose role in your life has changed, you should put the cards on the table and clarify the situation openly. If the person is honest, he/she will understand, respect your sincere intention, and probably be relieved himself/herself. If the person misunderstands, becomes angry and blames you for this or that, or starts playing the victim – then he/she has not understood and is not really worth your nerves or your time. You should concentrate on those with whom you feel comfortable and relaxed, and with whom you have a relationship based on trust. It is the trust that is the key linker, the glue and connective tissue in all relationships.

The challenge is to admit to ourselves openly what relationships actually stifle us and are not friendly at all. That way we can create space for new people in our life. When you close the door, a window opens, the saying goes, and that's the way it is (hence, you shouldn't look at the closed door because you could miss the open window). Through the spiritual path, change happens by itself, which is a happy circumstance. All my friends will tell you that I have changed a lot lately; yes, I have, I am quite different than I was 5-6 years ago and this process of change has miraculously removed certain people from my life. I just don't feel like listening to people complain, lament just to lament and create drama constantly. I don't have the energy for those who need to be lifted constantly, and when they are offered a solution, they just "overhear it" and continue to cry. Once or twice is fine, but with s third time I draw the line. I've made quite a lot of radical decisions lately, therefore I find it hard to force myself to chat with people, telling them things they want to hear if that doesn't resonate with my "new" life. And as much as I try to tactically verbalize certain things, some of them considered it too much nonetheless, so they stepped away immediately. Some stayed and we are in even better terms than before (and boldly go ahead to discover new paths). Others are still somewhere in between; I'm not weird enough for them to go away, but at the same time not attractive enough to stay.

Other people who work on their growth, who think, who don't live by default in the comfort zone, but stick out for themselves will tell you the same. As soon as you start digging deep into yourself, you begin to clear your relationships and things inevitably change. You see the world from different angle, and unlike before, you are now ready to let certain people go their own way without hesitation. There is nothing wrong with that; when you enter a new section of your road, some people go with you because they change themselves, some stay on the old road, and some you will yet get to know. Thus, the beauty of life has brought some new, wonderful people (friends or acquaintances) into my life, people who are at my frequency exactly and who stimulate my further growth and development. Moreover, we grow together. Surround yourself with positive people, have fun, socialize and don't forget: friends are always your mirror, whether you admit it or not.

൙ Recommendations to inspire you on your journey of happiness ☺

- [QR 73] Kinne – Real Life Facebook:
       https://www.youtube.com/watch?v=Xzxt1sJ3RzI

- [QR 74] Gossip:
       https://www.youtube.com/watch?v=BVeBO-ahVGU
- [QR 75] Secret Life of Dogs:
       https://www.youtube.com/watch?v=ze7ILC8-b2w

CHALLENGE 10:
DO WHAT YOU LOVE

Doubt kills more dreams than failure ever will.
Suzy Kassem

We live in a modern, consumerist society whose main manifestation is the hyperinflation of desires and cravings and it is therefore sometimes really challenging to put them under control. In order to fulfill our desires (past, present and future), we generally think that we have to work hard because money doesn't "fall from sky". Consequently, if we are among those lucky ones who have a job and have to get up on a Monday morning (by the way, this is also the period when the most heart attacks happen), we have no right to complain about anything, according to general opinion, because at least we work and make money. I want to clarify a few things in this challenge in order to explain why I am convinced that all of us have a purpose here, a calling that is not good or even healthy to ignore.

Let's start with the money that makes the world go round, which is why most people work in the first place. First, money is a paper that we have given a certain agreed value, and it often has no intrinsic value. Money, like everything else, is vibration and there is a lot of money in the world, it is only distributed unevenly. If you want to understand how money is made, check out the animated documentary *Money as Debt* (◨ 76); I always advise this to my economics students. Money is therefore a means of exchange, and although the idea itself is

QR 76

not bad, because it facilitates daily life, today things have gone too far. The world is ruled by money and banks. Everything we do and create, we usually do to be happy (sometime in the future, when we achieve everything we want and buy everything we need). We don't do it to run in a circle – in so called rat race (I warmly recommend a nine-minute video on the subject; you can watch it by scanning the ◼ 77, and it will open your eyes in many ways). You will fully

QR 77

understand the rat race after reading the book *Rich Dad Poor Dad* by Robert Kiyosaki; I think everyone should read this book; especially persons focused on economics (◼ 78). The general, widespread paradigm is that more money means more happiness.

QR 78

Mini challenge:

Think what money means to you. How much money would you like to have and why? What would you buy with it?

People have the misconception that winning a lottery would make their lives perfect, comfortable and problem-free. However, believe it or not, this is often not the case. Winning a lottery is one of the worse things that could happen to you (besides, you are statistically more likely to be hit by a meteor). I know this is hard to believe, but based on many studies, science says that's the case. Research shows that the majority of lottery winners shortly after winning do not have a better life than they had before (big money – big problems). On the contrary, life is actually worse for many of them. If you still don't believe me, check out episode or two of the show *The Lottery Changed My Life*. There are many talks of lottery winners' curse because millions gained overnight can ruin everything. Watch excellent movies *Mr. Deeds* from 2012 (◼ 79) and the 2010 comedy *Lottery Ticket* (◼ 80). Take some time and check what the internet will tell you about the lottery winners. Among them you will find the few whose stories are positive and who, for the most part, went on living their usual daily lives, going to work and everything else.

QR 79

QR 80

I am not trying to talk you out of buying the lottery ticket; anyone can do whatever they want with their money. But let me clarify what lies behind it. Ask yourself why do you want money. Do you want money? What are you going to do with it? Shower with it, eat it for lunch, take it for a walk, go to sleep with it, make love to it, talk to it? Um, well, that can't be done with money, you may say. Certainly not. Therefore, you do not need money per se; rather, you want the things that can be bought with money. It is very important to understand that. For example, you want a special shower cabin that massages while playing music, you want food, heating, textbooks, a comfortable bed, medication you need, fun, socializing, traveling, a boat or just a decent standard of living. Now, you can have a great deal of things without money or with much less money than you think. Under the illusion of love for money, all of us, in fact, want experiences. If you want to buy a boat for example, you should ask yourself why. To keep it in a port? Probably not. To drive it? You actually want the feeling you get when riding on board. Or you deal with a confidence challenge, and you want to enjoy the moment when others envy you on the boat, you want to see their facial expressions in order to be proud of yourself. When we start banalizing everything we do, and asking ourselves at deeper and deeper levels why we do it – we reach the very core and understand what keeps us trapped. We come to the final answer that we must somehow survive, and that we essentially want to be happy. The question is how big is the gap between what we want in our life and the level at which we are surviving. In any case, money is and should be a resource, not a goal.

There are two psychological phenomena of happiness that I want to share with you. The first is the phenomenon of social comparison, and the second is the phenomenon of adaptation (i.e. increasing aspirations). Namely, people have congenital need to compare themselves with people around them who represent their reference group (that is, who are similar to them). Most people sleep peacefully and do not care too much – if at all – for the billions of dollars of the richest people in the world, but they worry whether they are better than their neighbors (whose grass is always greener), their work colleagues or their peers. Such a comparison is inherent to people who earn less or more than the reference group. We can witness, therefore, a kind of ubiquitous rivalry and comparison; it is actually in the foundations of modern society in general. Hence, more money does not necessarily mean more happiness, because we have a habit of comparing ourselves with others constantly. Yet, comparison with others does not necessarily have to be bad; sometimes it is good to compare ourselves with others so that we can assess our situation more realistically and as a form of motivation for further progress and improvement. It is useful, therefore, to follow a good example (but not to be obsessively inclined to make comparisons, as someone will always have more than us). Meanwhile, we have to be aware of ourselves, our position and capabilities (that is, we have to stand on our feet firmly).

Mini challenge:

Recognize the people you compare yourself with, ask yourself why you do it and what for. Are they really more successful than you, in what domain and from whose perspective?

We mostly evaluate our present situation in comparison to the recent one, that is, with the last level of satisfaction reached. In addition, we always need and want something, no matter how rich we are. Simply, our needs are unlimited, and we constantly need more because we quickly get used to what we have (remember how modern marketing sells us desires, not needs). The fact that we adapt increasingly fast to new, better situation and living conditions is exactly why happiness doesn't grow proportionally to the increase in economic well-being (we shouldn't overlook the fact that increased workload, which supposed to bring us higher income, carries opportunity costs as well, such as less free time). A new car, house or cellphone (especially tangible assets) causes short-term happiness (the first scratch on a car or the first cellphone drop is the most painful; afterwards those are just "old" goods and we already want new things). In other words, at every new level of life standard, the period of satisfaction with material things we own is shorter. This phenomenon of adaptation means that we get accustomed to higher incomes because their effect on happiness "evaporates" over time. The lottery winners are therefore happy only shortly after winning, and their happiness quickly returns to the initial stage. Oscar Wilde said nothing gets old as fast as happiness.

The relationship between relative and absolute income, i.e. the effects of irrational beliefs about money, must be taken into account as well when considering the relationship between happiness and money. Would you rather earn $50,000 a year while other people make $25,000 at the same job, or would you rather earn $100,000 a year while other people get $250,000 at the same job? Assume for the moment that prices of goods and services will stay the same. Research in behavioral economics shows that respondents often opt for the first option because they do not look primarily at their situation ($50,000 or $100,000), but rather base their decision on comparison with others (looking at relative incomes they compare to other people's). They would rather earn twice as much as others, even if it means earning half of what they could. It is not very rational to decide on the first option because with second, they earn twice as much and they can buy more given that the prices of goods and services are fixed. This example shows irrational decision-making and beliefs about money, which in turn can affect evaluations of the importance of money for happiness.

Even though the money makes the world go round, it cannot buy everything. I read somewhere that money can buy a house, but not a home; a bed, but not a dream; a watch, but not time; a book, but not knowledge; position, but not respect; medicine, but not health; sex, but not love; blood, but not life. Therefore, money is not everything. On the internet, you can find numerous tips on how to live with a lot less money. Even the famous travels – which people often consider as something unattainable, something they would be happy to do if they had large amounts of money – do not have to cost a lot. Some people even travel the world for free. Hence, get informed if you are interested, because when there is a will, there are ways.

Having said that, let me share this information: numerous communities in the world today have already abandoned conventional money systems and developed their own, alternative currencies. There are time banks in which you don't invest money, but time – one hour of one's work, regardless of his profession and level of education, is equal to other person's working hour. That way people exchange goods and services within the community (all followed by different computer systems). For example, you translate some text and someone gives you a haircut in return, or you help someone to do something on the computer for an hour and he massages you for an hour, etc. Local currencies or a time bank may seem like unfeasible concepts to you, but they already exist in communities in different countries nevertheless.

Mini challenge:

Write down what you would do if money weren't the issue, if you had everything you need and if your existence was secured. What is your calling, where does your heart wish to be?

Now that we have completed the story about money and understood some of the psychological phenomena we are affected by, we can further develop the story about this challenge. Watch Alan Watts' speech *What If Money Was No Object?* (◼ 81). Indeed, stop for a moment and wonder what you want to be in life? What do you want to do? Some people never wonder about that because they have no courage, some think about that when they reach old age and some

QR 81

never. How about you? Do you know what you want to be when you grow up? No matter how old you are, it's never too late to ask yourself that question. When did we begin to believe that we had stopped growing, that is, growing up? We're growing all the time, aren't we? When we perceive life like that, we realize that every day is a new opportunity to take a different path, to go where our heart wants us to be. Regardless

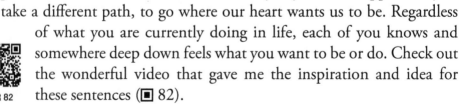

of what you are currently doing in life, each of you knows and somewhere deep down feels what you want to be or do. Check out the wonderful video that gave me the inspiration and idea for these sentences (◼ 82).

QR 82

A woman I know works as an accountant in one school, even though she always felt that her role and mission is to make cakes, special cakes (proven to be wonderful and delicious). Life just led her to a different, safe path. I have already mentioned a few students who study even though their heart is pulling in a completely different direction. One of my acquaintances is a professor, but she wants to have her own orchard and grow organic apples very much. There are countless examples such as those, and only few who dared to transform their calling into business. Why? Not because it's not possible, but mostly because they haven't tried it. Because they act out of fear of change and the unknown (what if I fail, what if I couldn't do it and people mock me, what if I lose my livelihood), and sometimes even because of the fear of success. The system we live in has taught us that success is measured by financial results, i.e. money. However, if we act out of love and do the things we are passionate about (regardless of our previous education and age), then we would be supported, that is, the chances for success are very high.

If you see money as a product of successful work and not a goal, you can open yourself up and try to figure out what your calling is. Job is what we do every day and what pays our bills (more or less). Some like their jobs, some don't (or they don't care or think about it), but when I look at the people around me, it seems to me that there are more of those who don't. Furthermore, there are those who are, you could say, careerists. They "pursue" a career that usually involves more responsible tasks, i.e. constant improvement and progress. Both those with a job and those with a career can be happy or unhappy; it all depends on their perception of life. However, there is also the (life) calling, something your soul strives for, something you want to do regardless of financial reward. It is what occupies you completely, where you feel the best, what you are born to do, what you are talented and gifted for – it is your meaning of life and mission. That's why the goal is to do the job that you feel is your calling. That way you do not consider your job to be a burden, you enjoy doing it and you are doing it excellently. The key is to apprehend and recognize what our vocation is and then begin to accomplish it.

I have many examples for that as well. One of my colleagues left a stable job in a ministry and moved back home to an island to develop a local community there. Another one left Zagreb with her husband, moved to the seaside (although they both had excellent jobs and positions) and now they are producing olives and jams. The third has a great CV, but now she is teaching yoga and slowly retiring from the company she works in. One of my friends (from student days), who has a master's degree in economics and has worked at several companies on various positions, realized that cynology was her only logical life course because dogs have always been her passion. I remember all the challenges she went through and, believe me, it was not easy for her to become a dog trainer, i.e. a dog whisperer, especially in a small town like Osijek. However, she left her comfort zone with bold steps and embarked on the uncertain and unknown. She put in a lot of effort and work, she was incredibly persistent, and eventually she opened her own business, which is very successful today. Doing what she loves has no price; she has turned her life's calling into a business and you can see it in her approach to business, both owners and dogs can feel that. There are many such examples, and if you pay attention, you will certainly find them in your communities (one cute and extreme you can find at the ■ 83).

QR 83

Ergo, beware what you wish for, as it might come true. All these people left their comfort zones; they were brave in the fear zone, persistent in the action zone and then found themselves in the magic of life. No one says it was easy. They probably stumbled upon a bunch of obstacles and additional challenges along the way, perhaps they lacked support from the people around them, and they had to make sacrifices and work hard. Often, especially in the beginning, you will earn less than in a standard job, but you will be happier and more satisfied, much less stressed, and therefore probably healthier. When you do what you love, then events just go to your advantage and you have a support for making your dream come true. The similar was with me; I have been working at the Faculty of Economics for 15 years and I really love my job (especially students and lectures) because I think (and I have a feedback to confirm that) I have a positive and inspiring influence on most of them. It is one of my channels for influencing the lives of young people. Some people wonder why I decided to write a book about happiness and expose myself like that, why I started something new when I already had everything settled. Well, I felt it was the logical next step out of the comfort zone, and numerous people whom my advices have helped pointed me to it. I lack nothing, I really have the life I've always wanted, but I have come to a stage where I want to help others, be a catalyst for their change, an example of a happy and content life. We usually come to this stage gradually: we realize what makes us happy each day (with me it's the notion I made someone else happy), and then we want to do more of that.

I thought about writing the book earlier (encouraged by the people I helped), but the trigger was the making of my *jyotish* chart. An acquaintance who made it for me is also one of those who changed careers – he was a building engineer before his spiritual pursuit led him to *jyotish* and *vastu*, and now he successfully combines all his knowledge and expertise. One summer he made me a *jyotish* (which means "light") chart, confirming me that I am on the right path, that I have support and I just needed to continue boldly. This is not some fashionable, popular and sometimes trivial horoscope from the daily newspaper, but Vedic astrology. The thing is, when we were born, the planets were in a certain position (a natal chart is made according to that position) and that determines our entire life. Through that position (and 12 houses), one can easily read the whole life in detail, with astonishing precision. More importantly, it can help us choose the right moment to start any activity, especially the bigger ones that mark our whole life (choosing business partners, spouses, buying real estate, etc.). *Jyotish* will not tell you that this or that will definitely happen to you, and that therefore you need to do this or that; but it can give you a broader picture of your life, that is, enable you to understand your personal purpose and meaning in life.

It was priceless to me and it happened at the right moment. *Jyotish* will illuminate your path and help you take responsibility. Then it is up to you to make choices every day in accordance with the free will that was given to you. Anyway, if you are interested, check it out. Don't believe a word I say. In any case, just a few days after I got my jyotish chart, the idea of writing a book became clear, and everything else is history. I am a woman of action, i.e. I act immediately if I can, and thus you have this book now. Speaking of help, let me mention one other thing: a lunar calendar based on the moon cycles. I find it amusing how some people do not believe that planets have an impact on us, although they know (and accept because they learned it as children) that the moon and the sun cause tides. But no, they do not affect us (even though about 70% of our bodies is water). ☺

Mini challenge:

Find out who can make you a good jyotish chart and order it if you can.

It is not necessary to feel a calling or have a career (some people don't even have a job because they explicitly don't want one). It is important that we do whatever makes us feel good, that we are not stressed, and that we are at peace with ourselves. The thing is, no matter how much money we have, it will not automatically make us happier. Money will not make you happier, but happiness will bring you more money. I remember one study about happiness at, I think, a hospital in America, where they asked staff how happy they were. Researchers were astounded when they realized that the person who showed the highest level of happiness and job satisfaction was not one of the doctors or the director, but a cleaning lady. When asked how that was possible, she said that her role at the hospital was paramount because patients would be even more ill if she did not clean as good as she did. You see? That's it, she has found her purpose: she does what she loves, and in that she has found a higher meaning. That's magical, because no work is less valuable as long as it is done honestly, ethically and responsibly. Being a mother (especially inspirational one, as we've talked about before) is certainly responsible, honorable and, you can say, the most important job. It is unfortunate that women today are often torn between work and family. Only one (husband's) paycheck is often not enough for a normal life, so women are forced to go to work as well. Every rational and realistic person among you knows how much work a woman and a mother really have at home. If we want the house to be tidy and clean, meals fresh and healthy, and children well brought-up – we have to dedicate time to it, which means we don't have much time for another job. Or if there is another job, this first part of the story suffers. Finding a balance is not easy, as I have already commented throughout the book. We cannot do everything, nor are we talented for everything; therefore, it is wise not to follow modern trends, but to arrange life in a way that satisfies both our personal desires (growth, development, vocation) and the commitments we have assumed (family). Find your own way.

In the context of work, the challenge is that some jobs are paid unbelievably much, and others lot less, even if they are much harder. This is the result of a system we live in and its distorted values. We live in a time when new jobs are evolving exponentially, jobs that did not exist until a few years ago, especially in information and communication technology (e.g. bloggers, digital marketing experts, application developers). In the meantime, there are also those that do not exist anymore because they are outdated. It seems to me that today there is a lot of hierarchical differentiation and categorization of people – those in higher positions we value "more", others we see as "just" workers; those with more titles are worth "more", those without titles "less". It's all upside down, and ultimately this is not a measure of satisfaction at all. These are situations in which the bad side of the human ego comes to the fore, and some people think they are superior and better than others, they are entitled to manage others – like modern slavery (as if it is not enough that we are already slaves to the system through the loans). As a university professor, I often see students outperforming the teacher, so to speak. Personally, I want my coworkers to do better than me. I really incorporate myself into their story; I give them everything and ask for everything, so I see their success as my own. I believe we haven't accomplished much if with my mentorship they did the same as me. If they did more, then we have succeeded. Leonardo da Vinci said: "Poor is the pupil who does not surpass his master." However, some teachers don't have the courage to admit they are surpassed because they have every possible egoistic program in full operating mode (usually – the higher the position, the less will for acknowledging the success of others). I believe we constantly learn from each other about life. But society today collectively suffers from the hierarchy imposed by systems. The movie on this topic I always recommend is the 2015 *The Experiment* (■ 84). It shows one of the most important social experiments of all time, led by psychologist Stanley Milgram: how much we are unwilling to defy the authority of an authoritative or superior person and act on our own conscience and moral principles. The movie doesn't have particularly tense plot, but in a brutal way and through real-life experiments it shows how people sometimes act as sheep and how unquestionably and automatically we trust authority. It's so easy to manipulate people, it seems.

QR 84

However, others seem big just because you are kneeling. Stand up! And when you get up, try to paint every day in your colors and play your own movie as much as you can. In your business environment, try to be as cheerful, smiling and kind as possible because kindness is contagious, it opens all doors, even the steel ones, and stimulates the brain to release the hormone of happiness. Moreover, it will bring joy into your life. Why not be the person everyone remembers as always cheerful? At least sometimes, wear cheerful colors, break the monotony of the gray day, be different, dare to live differently. On average, we spend as much as one third, i.e. eight hours a day at work, and the retirement age is increasing, so most of us spend a lot of time in the working environment. We meet acquaintances, friends and lovers at work; yet we often hear people say how their colleagues are like this or that and that it is unsustainable. This is not surprising, because knowing how to handle people is one of the biggest difficulties a (working) person faces. For that, one has to be wise, because having good relationships is a skill that can be learned in psychology. Research shows that about 80% of job success is determined by emotional intelligence, and it is wise to work on its development from an early age. Check out a great video by internationally renowned psychologist Daniel Goleman on the topic of emotional intelligence (■ 85), whose book is dubbed the world's bestseller.

QR 85

Reading challenge 10, some of you have probably perceived money differently for the first time. Others have become aware of the difference between job, career and calling. Some have felt the inner voice that whispers to them: "Come on, move ahead, you are well aware of your path and your calling." Some may decide to stay in the comfort zone because they are fine with that and do not care that much (as long as they have any work). Some have realized that they are quite satisfied with what they have. Some have learned how one can find out what is his role in this life. Some have realized they listened to authority too much. Either way, I hope this challenge has sparked at least some thought and raised some issues that will inspire you to change.

* * * * * *

This concludes the second set of challenges called *A Healthy and Serene Mind*, where we have mostly dealt with relationships. At the end, here is another comprehensive recommendation. In my opinion, the best book about relationships is *How to Win Friends and Influence People* written in 1936 by Dale Carnegie (the most renowned applied psychology author in the world). The book has been sold in over 15 million copies over the course of 80 years and had several editions since, the most recent being *How to Win Friends and Influence People in the Digital Age* (◾ 86) – adapted to modern times. The book is a true gem because it shows numerous examples of real-life situations that have occurred throughout history, with famous and less-known people, and the recent edition is full of well-known and recent examples. The book is a treasure trove of numerous experiences, covering topics such as tips for winning people's affections, getting people to think like you, complaining without offending and expressing hatred, writing a business letter, having a happier family life. It really makes readers realize how little they know about relationships. I recommend you to read the book, but it can be a perfect gift as well, for the people dear to you, as it has a proven potential to save and/or maintain a certain relationship.

❧ Recommendations to inspire you on your journey of happiness ☺

- [QR 77] The Rat Race Explained – Life's Financial Trap:
    https://www.youtube.com/watch?v=jcFN-lQPIb4
- [QR 81] What If Money Was No Object? – Alan Watts:
    https://www.youtube.com/watch?v=khOaAHK7efc
- [QR 82] Idris Elba + Purdey's Present: #ThriveOn:
    https://www.youtube.com/watch?v=aJ4sIo3UZfw
- [QR 83] The Russian Hipster Who Lives Like a Hobbit:
    https://www.youtube.com/watch?v=ahBIeVSqnTc
- [QR 85] Daniel Goleman Introduces Emotional Intelligence:
    https://www.youtube.com/watch?v=Y7m9eNoB3NU

- [QR 76] Money as Debt:
    https://www.youtube.com/watch?v=2nBPN-MKefA
- [QR 79] Mr. Deeds:
    https://www.youtube.com/watch?v=5aB1aJrxfvw
- [QR 80] Lottery Ticket:
    https://www.youtube.com/watch?v=TBtplgiBm2k
- [QR 84] The Experiment:
    https://www.youtube.com/watch?v=O1VOZhwRvWo

- [QR 78] Rich Dad Poor Dad, Robert Kiyosakij, 1997.
- [QR 86] How to Win Friends and Influence People in the Digital
    Age, Dale Carnegie, 2015.

A HEALTHY AND POWERFUL BODY - LOVE FOR ONESELF

CHALLENGE 11:
CARING FOR
THE PHYSICAL BODY

Those who think they have not time for bodily exercise
will sooner or later have to find time for illness.
Edward Stanley

The 12 challenges that this book deals with are actually inter-twined, as are all the topics we have tackled, because it is something all of us face in this journey we call life. Moreover, all of us are on our own particular life journey, some walk on the path of happiness and some not. In addition, we are on a different level of awareness. In this challenge of caring for the physical body, I will suggest a few more techniques and methods that can help improve your health (primarily physical, but emotional and mental too), as well as the quality of your life. This requires changing your habits and starting something new, which causes a lot of resistance in all of us, especially in the beginning. It is said that only a wet baby loves change. ☺ Why is that so?

I experienced one of the aha-moments during a lecture on habits by John Assaraf. He is the founder and CEO of NeuroGym, a company dedicated to using the most advanced technologies and evidence-based brain training methods for helping individuals unlock their full po-tential and maximize their results. John said every question has been answered today and we can find every answer very quickly by using the internet. For example, we can find out how to eat healthy, how to lose weight, how to increase sales, how to record a video, how to fish, how to give a lecture... You see, every "how" has already been answered, someone has done it before us. And if one person could do it, most others should be able to redo it. It is clear to all of us that almost every one of us can achieve most of what we aspire to; the only question is whether we are truly determined to act, to do everything we need and everything we can, and to be persistent enough to achieve the desired goal and result.

John wanted to know why in a world where almost every "how" is already answered and the process is known, people still do not achieve the desired results. In the context of this challenge, for example, we can talk about achieving optimal weight, i.e. losing weight, which is a big challenge and comfort zone for many people in the world. If you want to lose weight, it is obvious what bad habits you need to eliminate and what needs to be changed. However, the fact is that most of those who have been on a diet and have lost weight, regain it soon, sometimes even more than they lost. A sort of yo-yo effect happens. This is a point in John's lecture where my aha-moment came from, where I realized how powerful brain is. Beliefs (which begin to create immediately after birth) create behaviors, and behaviors create habits. Research shows that as soon as we start to change (any) habits, the brain says a big NO to everything because it's his way of protecting us. Safety is number one for the brain; everything new the brain literally perceives as a mistake because it loves habits and life in the comfort zone. Everything we are accustomed to, our brain considers as safe. It thus encourages us not to make changes, but to step back and protect ourselves from perceived danger. Our brain acts like that because every new and unusual activity consumes a lot of energy, and its mission is to conserve energy. Therefore, by using hormones and other ways, the brain literally persuades us not to change. (This is the voice in your head that says: "You don't have to exercise today, start tomorrow or Monday", or "Eat another piece of cake, after all it's just one piece.") If our beliefs are messed up as well, that is, if we are not 100% certain we want change – it is as if we push the throttle with one leg and the brake with the other. The brain is confused. If there is no clarity in the brain, it always returns to the comfort zone and safety. These two brain functions (safety and energy conservation) are good for our survival, but they also drag us back into the comfort zone.

Once you understood these, in my opinion, extremely important concepts and the way the brain works, firstly you can relax because you are not the only person who has a hard time managing change, and secondly you can try to outsmart the brain. The clearer your vision is and the less you confuse your brain with doubts – the better. You have to believe that you can do it, you have to constantly empower yourself with the various techniques that have already been shown in the book. Do you remember what was in the top drop of the action zone image, that opening through which we go into the magic zone? It was persistence, and not by accident. Research shows that it takes about 66–365 days for the brain to fully adopt new ideas, habits, behaviors, and ways of thinking, that is, to replace old habits with new ones. Eureka! This means that besides a clear vision, you need persistence. Try to commit yourself to doing a new thing for 21 or 100 days (because it's a shorter and more realistic period than a year) and then persevere. At some point in the process, your brain will give in, it will stop talking you out of a new habit, and it will realize that it consumes more energy to talk you out of the change than to yield and accept it. Then the magic will happen because new neurons will form and you will literally become a new person (this was confirmed by the scientific work of the aforementioned Joe Dispenza). I wanted to emphasize this once again because it is crucial, especially in the context of changes outlined in this challenge. Keep in mind that your brain will discourage you, embrace that fact from the beginning. You should have a clear vision and idea of change, and just be persistent in new actions outside the comfort zone. The brain will soon adopt this new way of life as a new habit.

We have already talked about the mind and emotions – two things that are connected through our vehicle, i.e. the physical body that has been entrusted to our care. I do not know if you have noticed that the last thoughts we have before bed, the ones we go to bed with, are most often the ones we wake up with the next morning. Our first thought in the morning is not random – it is related to both our dreams and the subconscious, and it is said that the morning shows the day, that is, the first thought creates our day. Therefore, it is important not to look at the screens for at least an hour before going to bed and to sleep as relaxed as possible. Long before, people woke up with the sunrise, and ended their activities at sunset. Our biological clocks are no longer in tune with nature; the situation has changed radically, and today we go to sleep later, many people work at night or mid-day shifts at work, etc. Nevertheless, it would be very good for your body to establish your own routine (if you have not already) and to stick to it. This also means setting a nearly fixed time for going to bed and waking up in the morning. And since finding 15 minutes for yourself during the day is the key, the source of any change, I suggest you just get up earlier if you still think you can't find this time (but want to work on yourself). It has been proven that if you get up 15 minutes earlier, it will not put you off track or cause lack of sleep. Meanwhile, you can use that time for yourself, for some of the mini challenges, for planning the day, for reading, for watching encouraging videos and similar activities. Getting up 15 minutes earlier is unlikely to be (too) difficult, and when you see what you can gain by it, you'll want even more time for yourself (and you'll find it, believe me, it's universal law).

Mini challenge

Set your alarm clock 15 minutes earlier for tomorrow, and do it right away. Dedicate that time to studying something new, for example some of the topics from this book.

A few years ago, I was introduced to the concept of early rising, *The 5 a.m. Club*. It is actually an informal club, popularized by one of the most respected management consultants, Robin Sharma, who is also a motivational speaker and one of the most widely read authors in the world (known for bestselling books *The Leader Who Had No Title* and *The Monk Who Sold His Ferrari*). The members of that club (and you can become one from tomorrow) get up every morning at 5 a.m. and begin their day with rituals. You devote the first hour to yourself and, at Robin's recommendation, divide it into 3 x 20 minutes, namely: 20 minutes of exercise, 20 minutes of planning, and 20 minutes of learning. You can exercise any way you like (it will warm you out and wake you up nicely); planning refers to the activities of that particular day and setting goals; learning refers to acquiring any new knowledge – reading books, portals, watching videos, whatever. It takes a while to make a habit out of getting up early and to adjust your metabolism and biorhythm. Getting up early will certainly increase your efficiency because the brain and body are in great shape during that time of day, you are more focused early in the morning, more concentrated and you have the highest energy levels. Therefore, hours from 5 to 8 a.m. Robin calls the golden hours, when others are distracting us the least. There is little

 if any outside noise and hustle, everyone is sleeping, and there is not so much thoughts. Robin states that the way we start the day really determines how we live the rest of the day (how to get up early, see in his video ◼ 87).

QR 87

Of course, it's not easy to win the battle against a warm bed, especially in the beginning, but it's not impossible either. If you dare to try, I advise you to start when in your climate days naturally start earlier (it's daylight early and sun outside). It will be easier to get out of bed that way, but if you have the will, nothing will stop you regardless of the seasons. Some find it easier to start radically – to just get up at 5 a.m. tomorrow morning; others choose to set alarm clock 15 minutes earlier than before every week or two, until they reach the desired waking hour. Try it and see what works best for you. Getting up early means going to bed early as well. Each of you knows how many hours of sleep you need, so you should go to bed in the evening accordingly. I know some will say that they are not exactly morning types, but are more inclined to work night shifts. I, too, used to be awake until midnight, but in recent months I have changed my sleeping habits and I am in bed by 22:30 at the latest (in most cases); I wake up at 5 a.m. at summer, and at 7 a.m. at winter. Club 5 a.m. seems to confirm the saying that early bird catches the worm. If you get up two hours earlier each day and go to sleep at the same time, that is a total of 14 hours a week, 56 hours a month, about 672 hours or as much as 28 days a year! Make your own calculations and act.

If your body gets tired during the day, a long afternoon break, usually preceded by a hearty meal (more about that in the last challenge), will often throw you out of balance and take up a lot of your time. Therefore, you can replace it by something called a power nap or a day's sleep/nap up to 30 minutes long (usually 10 to 20 minutes). Some companies have recognized their employees' need for daily breaks (there are some in my country, and especially in Japan and America) and offer them a place to sleep. This allows employees to take a half-an-hour nap at work without feeling guilty, because it enables them to be more efficient, help them function better, reduce irritability and frustration at work. Numerous studies confirm the benefits of such mini rest (which should by no means exceed 30 minutes) as it can refresh us completely. You can also combine your daytime sleep with some guided meditation/hypnosis/affirmations and similar activities, thus enhancing the effect of your rest. If you can't do it at work, you can at least take a deep breath and calm down during a break. If you simply have to sleep, do it at home after work (and if you can't find the right conditions there either, then "steal" as many moments as you can during the day for being in the present moment and for consciously breathing).

Modern humans have a sedentary lifestyle that is characterized by the lack of physical activities. Physical activity is natural to humans but previous generations had been much more active. With the rise of the screens, people started to spend more time in their homes and become less physically active. Thus, medicine today is less focused on fighting infectious diseases; rather it focuses on the painful conditions caused by the advancement of technology and its ubiquity in daily life. We increasingly suffer from neck, shoulder and other pain. I'm addicted to massages and have pretty high standards. I like gentle, light massage, but prefer a stronger grip – to really feel the effects after the massage. There are many types of massages available today, and beside relaxation, they definitely have many health benefits. If you can afford a massage, do it by all means, because today it is no longer reserved for the upper class; rather, it has become an integral part of a healthy living culture.

Nowadays, our backs often suffer because the structure and performance of many jobs has changed, and most people today spend their eight working hours sitting and typing. It is a real attack on our spines and joints (sometimes called the "mouse syndrome", and common condition today is carpal tunnel syndrome as well). Some companies have made progress to facilitate the work for their employees and encourage them to exercise – they set alarms every hour to remind employees to stretch. That way companies try to reduce employees' incapacity for work and possible sick leave, which ultimately reduces business costs. When the alarm sounds, workers should stop looking at the computer, close their eyes for a few seconds, and do simple stretching exercises (especially for neck, wrists, hands and lower spine) during a five-minute break. If your company doesn't set alarms for its employees (which is very likely), set an alarm yourself and do few stretching exercises for five minutes every hour, relax a little, drink a glass of water and breathe deeply.

Mini challenge

Set your own system of breaks during working hours in order to exercise your body.

Speaking of alarms, I want to share with you a method that will surely increase your efficiency, help you establish and maintain focus, and allow you to get the most out of your time (no matter what you do). It is called the time block(ing) method. You may also have heard about the Pomodoro technique (■ 88), where the working time is blocked after 25 minutes, followed by a break of 5 minutes; after four such blocks it is time for a slightly longer break. You need to determine (by trying different variants) what time block suits you best (which depends on the type of activity you are doing) and then you can set an alarm. You can also install one of the apps that will automatically do it

QR 88

for you (I like this because the app puts my phone into silent mode immediately) or just start one of the timers in an additional window on a computer. While in blocked time (the 25 minutes or whatever you have set), the world is unlikely to stop or disappear; however, you will focus solely on what you are doing because the world around you will not exist then. This means that you aren't checking your cell phone at all (which should then be in silent mode). If there are people who panic if you do not answer their call or message immediately, let them know about your new working mode. This shouldn't be a problem as you will get back to them during the break between blocks. Some people make plans for each time block, and it is possible to reserve the time for a daily break, some activity, or whatever. The greatest benefit from the time-block technique can be seen in our working efficiency, as that way we aren't constantly distracted by external influences, which drastically disrupts concentration. It is be better not to do more than one thing at a time, i.e. multitask, because then some of the tasks aren't done properly. It is better to do one thing at a time.

Mini challenge

Try the time-block technique, and compare your efficiency.

The proverb says that a sound mind is in a sound body, but we try (too) little to be healthy. We consider health paramount to happiness, but we do little to preserve it. We spend health to earn money and then we spend money to restore health. Various health tips I have already mentioned throughout the book, but here I will further emphasize the importance of exercise (and nutrition in the next challenge). That helps our body in producing serotonin and dopamine, which can relieve stress and depression. I know that some of you have your hair curl from the very word exercise. I was like that for a long time too, until I finally discovered what works for me. I tried various workouts (from fitness to all sorts of modern Pilates, Zumba etc.), but it was too much for me – my blood pressure would drop, and I would experience dizziness, which demotivated me. Finally, five years ago, I discovered yoga, and soon got rid of a bunch of prejudices I had about yoga (ah, aren't we all really full of prejudices?!). I also realized that I did not know how to stand, sit or breathe properly. Uh, I didn't even know the basics of life.

Additional motivation for me was the information that Steve Jobs had only one book on his tablet – *Autobiography of a Yogi* by Paramhansa Yogananda – and he used to read it at least once a year. You don't have to choose yoga as your challenge, but you have to break free from the comfort zone where there is no exercise, and you have to do something for your body (and your spirit after that). Based on my own experience, I can tell you that every form of physical activity isn't for everybody, therefore you shouldn't give up exercising in general if you didn't like some activity – today you can choose from the range of different methods and physical activities. Even though they say it's best to join some group exercising (especially if you can go with someone who will prevent you from making excuses and skipping classes), internet is full of exercise videos. Are you capable for that kind of self-discipline and continuous home exercise – is another question. For start, don't set your goals too high; five minutes of exercise a day is better that none. And your exercise can be a brisk walk too.

Mini challenge

Find a physical activity you like and dedicate at least one term per week to it (try to find someone to do it with).

It is very useful to train the brain as well, for example by solving crossword puzzles, puzzles, riddles, Sudoku, anagrams, mazes, etc. – in other words, doing whatever that might be called mental training and that could be fun and entertaining. They say our brains are not as old as our bodies (I don't know how true that is, but there are tests that can supposedly ascertain it). One of the useful methods for learning and developing the brain are the mind maps – common tool in schools around the world – because they work similar as the brain and turn learning into fun. We know that in our heads there is a left and right side of this quite unknown organ called the brain, and it is important to strive to activate both sides in every learning activity. Mental maps do just that, so I like to use them in my daily life, and I often ask students to create them (by hand or using one of the many programs).

Something that works very well on both body and mind, something that we cannot live without, and that is free – is our breathing. Breathing is exceptionally important bodily feature because it carries oxygen from the air to our body's cells, and yet we give it a little thought. I have already mentioned breathing several times, but here I want to share information about methods/types of breathing. Although breathing is an automated process, we can consciously influence our breathing rate, thus calming the body. Basically, there are four types of breathing: 1. Abdominal breathing makes the diaphragm moves up and down supplying the body with oxygen in the best possible way, massaging the organs of the abdomen and relaxing the body and mind; 2. Chest breathing expands the chest but does not massage the organs of the abdomen, it consumes more energy than the abdomen breathing and supplies us with less oxygen; 3. Upper or clavicular breathing is a type of rapid and shallow breathing that is achieved by lifting the chest and shoulders and retracting the abdomen (which is the worst type of breathing because it consumes quite a bit energy for low effect); 4. Full lung respiration is achieved by the harmonious work of the diaphragm and the entire chest. You know that in stressful situations our body starts breathing shallowly and quickly, which isn't good for us. Try to lay your hand on your stomach in supine or upright sitting position, and inhale the air through your nose for five seconds, filling your belly (your hand moves); hold your breath for five seconds, and then exhale and push your belly inwards for five seconds. Breathe like that for at least five minutes. This is just one of the various breathing exercises, and you will eventually find the ones that suit you best. Indeed, there are many different breathing techniques today, and they go way back, to the distant past. To help you with this, you can install one of the many smartphone apps that will count your breaths, exhales, pauses, and overall time. I invite you to study this simple, and yet deep knowledge of the use of breath, i.e. proper abdominal breathing, in expelling poisons, filling the body with fresh energy, improving circulation, increasing concentration and power of perception, reducing stress and bringing the body to a state of relaxation and inner peace. Some beliefs claim that each of us has a limited number of breaths in life, that is, the deeper and slower we breathe, the longer we will live. That sentence, I guess more than ever before, calls for action.

Mini challenge

Try the above-mentioned breathing exercise.

Modern humans use only about 30% of their lungs' capacity, that is, we breathe shallowly and thus do not supply the cells of our bodies with sufficient oxygen. I heard this information at a training for certified laughter yoga teachers. Laughter yoga, i.e. the relaxation through laughter, really exists and combines laughter and breathing very well (of course I liked it). Scientific evidence shows that the brain does not distinguish between true or false (simulated) laughter. If you are in a bad mood, but keep a false smile for a while, you will certainly feel at least a little better (and since I believe that a smile is a healing injection of happiness, I wanted to complete the laughter course). Laughter relaxation was designed by Madan Kataira, MD (check his You-

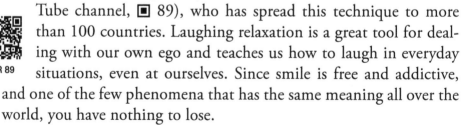

QR 89

Tube channel, ▣ 89), who has spread this technique to more than 100 countries. Laughing relaxation is a great tool for dealing with our own ego and teaches us how to laugh in everyday situations, even at ourselves. Since smile is free and addictive, and one of the few phenomena that has the same meaning all over the world, you have nothing to lose.

It has been scientifically proved that laughter relaxation is beneficial, and here are some of the benefits: instant mood lifting, more laughter, life quality increase, positive attitude towards life, blood pressure balance, reduced stress and interpersonal tension, better communication, empathy development, overall health improvement, reduced depression and anxiety conditions, reduced pain, increased endorphin secretion, increased oxygen uptake, better functioning in working environment, increased self-confidence, increased self-expression ability, numerous muscle groups activation. Kids laugh few hundred times a day, and we adults few dozen (or less). Therefore, it is not surprising that children love and embrace laughter therapy (for example, my son really likes the grounding dance performed at the end of the laughter relaxation lesson, ■ 90). Uh, it's definitely high time for action (especially if you know that one minute of laughing has the same effect as 10 minutes of rowing, for example). Even if you do not opt for this formal relaxation with laughter, you can always choose to watch funny videos or comedies, to read or listen to jokes instead of the imposed TV content.

QR 90

Mini challenge

Implement laughter and smile into your life, laugh at yourself in the mirror as soon as possible. Smile at the people you meet next (whoever they are).

We should certainly take care of our body because it has been given to us, and we have to love it with all its flaws and virtues. That care for our physical body includes caring for our looks as well. You will certainly feel better with neat nails and hair, and with skin that's not all cracked with dryness. You should give proper care to your largest organ, i.e. the skin, just be careful to choose well among numerous products on the market today, as manufacturers put all sorts of stuff in them. Try to give as much advantage as possible to natural cosmetics (preferably those not tested on animals). Be aware that skin is our largest organ and that it is equally important what you put on it as well as what kind of food you eat. Everything you put on your skin becomes, literally, a part of you.

Mini challenge

When buying body cosmetics next time, buy those that are completely natural.

It is also important to feel good about yourself, and we often achieve that through the clothes we wear. Many people nowadays treat sadness, depression and fear by going to the stores, most often those with clothes and shoes (which are the most common in the malls). Just as we tend to clutter our homes with furniture (living spaces also outline our character), many people clutter their wardrobes (with the inevitable morning conclusion that they have nothing to wear). Fast-food trends have spread over into the textile industry, which is now marked by the trend of fast fashion. Thus, textile industry has become one of the largest polluters in the world. This is not surprising if you know that 3/4 of all goods end up in trash cans (and much of it cannot be recycled). As you care for your looks, try not to stack too much clothes in your wardrobes, because this is no guarantee of good looks or a good vibe (and anything you haven't worn for over a year, you probably won't at all). A friend of mine has successfully combined life and fashion coaching into one profession and I admit that I was shocked to find out how much clothes reveal about us and what a real expert can discover about us when he/she peeks into our closet. Changes in dress style can greatly help you implement some new habits, new behaviors, etc. into your life. Clothes can help you to communicate properly with your environment, because while clothing doesn't make a person, it certainly communicates and sends a message.

Mini challenge

Think what your clothes say about you, what message you want it to send, and then make room in your wardrobe (giving the excess clothes to those in need).

In the end, don't let others set the standards of beauty for you. This may sound like a cliché, but true beauty truly comes from within. And that led us to one of the most important part of caring for the body, and challenge no. 12: diet.

ৰ্কী Recommendations to inspire you on your journey of happiness ☺

- [QR 87] How to Wake Up Early, Robin Sharma:
       https://www.youtube.com/watch?v=-xC_DbgpPAc
- [QR 88] Pomodoro Technique:
       https://www.youtube.com/watch?v=mNBmG24djoY
- [QR 89] Madan Kataira:
       https://www.youtube.com/user/madankataria
- [QR 90] Ho Ho Ha Ha Grounding Dance:
       https://www.youtube.com/
       watch?v=DWqmPKy7Atw&t=111s

- The Leader Who Had No Title: A Modern Fable on Real Success, Robin Sharma, 2013.
- The Monk Who Sold His Ferrari, Robin Sharma, 2006.
- Autobiography of a Yogi, Paramhansa Yogananda, 2014.

CHALLENGE 12: CONSUMING ENERGIZING FOOD AND LIVE WATER

Let thy food be thy medicine and thy medicine be thy food.
Hippocrates

We've reached our final challenge, which I have dedicated to extremely important subject: diet. Have you ever asked yourselves "why" in the context of your dietary habits? Why must we eat every day, and several times a day at that? Why must we drink water? I know that most people can get tired of cooking because it takes time, just like creating a varied menu and acquiring necessary ingredients. Moreover, if you want the meal to be healthy and relatively nutritionally rich, you have to put extra effort into the whole process. A friend of mine says that he would love to be able to take a pill every day in order to avoid preparing meals or eating in general (provided he is constantly satiated and healthy). I think we would all agree with him (at least in some life situations). If it weren't so, today there wouldn't be as many fast-food chains around the world, which are going more and more multinational every year and generating increasing revenues. In doing so, they use all sorts of marketing and other tricks and obviously benefit from it all. However, if you asked me, things have gone too far in that field as well. Otherwise, diabetes would not be a top modern disease in many societies.

Popular chef Jamie Oliver has won over people around the world with his unpretentiousness and different approach to cooking. He is a chef, restaurant owner, author of numerous cookbooks and magazines, a frequent guest on radio and television shows. But to me he is also a hero, because for a long time he has been fighting against all odds with his project Food Revolution (■ 91; you can also join the movement and become a revolutionary) and with the Food Foundation. These projects focus on improving food quality in schools and Jamie achieved results in his native UK – he has encouraged the government to change its stance on school nutrition, increase funding, introduce higher quality menus in schools and include food education in the school curricula. Having done that, he tried to achieve the same in the U.S., so the effects of the project quickly spread around the world. Two seasons of award-winning TV shows *Food Revolution* were filmed, and it all began with the show *Jamie's School Dinners*.

QR 91

As a father, Jamie realized how badly children ate in schools, how they couldn't cook at all, and how they soon turned into adults who couldn't cook – which made them dependent on fast-food restaurants and unhealthy convenience food. Data show that there is no country in the world where obesity has not increased in the last 30 years. As many as 1.5 billion adults have been obese worldwide, global obesity has doubled since 1980 (and even tripled in children), 15% of children in the UK under the age of 11 are obese, 42 million children are obese worldwide, 83% of children consume more sugar than the highest recommended adult level… And that's just part of the scary data. The key, therefore, is to teach children where the food comes from, where to buy it or how to grow it and prepare it. Food education is crucial in acquiring the necessary skills and providing the education necessary for life. Jamie has also launched a mid-May global Food Revolution Day campaign, supported by more than 500 cities in more than 60 countries, numerous businesses, schools and celebrities. Check out any show or performance by Jamie Oliver (I recommend the one viewed over 7 million times, ■ 92), and I'm sure it won't leave you indifferent. Isn't it scary that kids didn't know how to name fruits and vegetables? Of course, as parents, we can and should teach them a lot

QR 92

about nutrition (again, most of all by our example and by involving them in the process), but major and radical changes require the help and change of the system (primarily educational).

Why did I start this challenge with Jamie? Because that was my start as well. After several of his videos, I began to search further and widen the circle of my knowledge of food. In fact, this phrase kept ringing in my head (and it still rings): We are what we eat. This is deeply true and powerful, even though people often find it trivial. All my life, I ate quite healthy, always home-cooked food (something with a spoon), mom was careful about the origin of the groceries, we never ate in fast-food restaurants, we had a balanced diet that included everything in small amounts (I ate everything except raw meat and fish). However, I brought my body into full shape by changing my diet. Before I tell you how I did it, I have to invite you to a search. As the point of this book is to help you on your path of happiness, below I will list various sources that will be a great start for your search. So far, I have not made this kind of list of recommendations anywhere in the book, but this is too important to leave out anything. Please take the time and watch at least some of these movies (in fact, I advise and ask you to watch them all – if you endure until the end in some of them). They have changed my view on food and food industries in general (and some of them even on life as a whole). You will have to find these movies by name, as they are often deleted from the links provided.

QR 93

QR 94

QR 95

QR 96

QR 97

QR 98

QR 99

QR 100

- *Our Daily Bread* (■ 93)
- *Counting the Cost – The Price of a Fast-Food Life* (■ 94)
- *Food Inc.* (■ 95)
- *The Future of Food* (■ 96)
- *Earthlings* (■ 97)
- *Food Choices* (■ 98)
- *10 Billion – What's on Your Plate?* (■ 99)
- *Seeds* (■ 100)

I can hardly summarize in a few sentences everything that was said in those movies. The point wasn't to scare you, but to make you aware of how powerful food is to our body, how it is produced today, how the seeds are controlled globally. The point is to make you understand that there is enough food for all of us (it is only a matter of its distribution – while some throw it away, others starve). Think for a moment about the quality of the foods you consume; nowadays in supermarkets almost all products are available all year round, which means we don't purchase seasonal foods and we import a lot of it from all over the world. Why, for example, did garlic in one grocery store near my house come from another continent when it is easily grown in my country? Why do many countries in the world import and export the same amount of food (e.g. milk, eggs)? Who's crazy? Why do apples from UK first go for all sorts of refinements and varnishes to other parts of the world, then return home to Britain and hit the stores? This was brought to us by globalization. China and Japan have long been making artificial eggs, meat, watermelons (pitless and square for easier transportation), rice, and, perhaps the most famous, artificial cabbage (watch how an artificial lettuce is made, at ■ 101). The time has come for us to realize that we are not voting only on official elections, but that each and every one of our purchases is a vote. Demand creates supply, and if we, for example, stop buying product X at location A, they will stop selling it. It's clear as day, but still many people act like they don't understand it. In my opinion, the only solution is to localize economic activities. This is what the aforementioned movie *The Economics of Happiness* talks about – through the concept of localization it contributes to change and awakens people, that is, enables them to understand the power they hold in their hands.

QR 101

Now let's go back to the movies listed. Each of you will choose the movies that you need the most and in the order that suits you the best. Some may comment that not everything that is said in those movies is true; okay, I didn't make them and I can't claim it is, but I know what I see every day around me. Number of sick people is rising, as well as the number of new diseases that haven't existed until recently; more people are allergic to this or that, or intolerant to certain foods; number of strokes and heart attacks, which are affecting an ever younger population, is on the rise as well; more and more people are addicted to drugs (especially antidepressants). The main diseases of modern society are cardiovascular diseases, obesity, diabetes and cancer, and the reason is lifestyle changes (fast pace) and poor eating habits (excessive consumption of "four white deaths": salt, sugar, flour and fat, as well as the consumption of cheap, artificial food that did not exist until recently). These are the facts, and the Chinese proverb says: "The disease comes from the head and from the plate."

This brings us back to the story about energy and the question of why we eat at all. Our fuel is the energy we spend throughout the day (not only through physical but through mental activity as well – thoughts are energy too, remember). Therefore, we eat in order to live and get the energy we need for functioning and metabolic processes in our bodies. So far so good. But how did the energy we get through, say, fruits or vegetables get into those staples at all? Prana or life energy has three main sources: sun, air and earth. And these are the sources that will give energy to our food. Water, however, absorbs the prana from the sun, air and earth with which it comes into contact. Plants absorb prana from the sun, air, earth and water, and humans and animals receive prana

QR 102

from sun, air, earth, water and food (in other words, plants and animals). There are people who live (only or partly) from solar energy, i.e. those who practice sun gazing, the most famous being Hira Ratan Manek (listen to his lecture at ■ 102).

It may seem logical to you, but when I became aware of it and watched all those movies, I completely kicked meat out of my diet (considering that I could live and survive without it, and maybe even be healthier). This is somewhat funny in a way, because throughout my life I had prejudices against those who ate differently, who didn't eat meat or certain products, etc. Talk about the pot calling the kettle black. ☺ As I absorbed new spiritual knowledge, the changes began to happen on their own. I realized that animals also sense everything (everyone who has pets, especially dogs, knows it). We all know that they can feel an earthquake a few days before, that they have incredibly developed intuition, that some of their senses are hundreds of times stronger than ours. In some parts of the world pigs are sacred animals, in others it is cows; some people eat dogs and cats, and to us this is incomprehensible. It all depends on the culture in which we were born. Since everything is energy, even the animals themselves, they feel when something is wrong, they feel that they are about to be killed (that's why they run away and try to save themselves, that's why they let out death cries). Since they are in fear and full of negative emotions, when we eat them, we consume those emotions to, which lowers our vibration. If we had to kill a particular animal before consuming its meat, I think the consumption of meat in the world would be significantly reduced (make sure to check out a short video on this topic at ▣ 103).

QR 103

The situation is even worse when it comes to meat products – all those pinkish salami, canned Spam, pâtés (made from leftovers) and similar products that are packed with additives, preservatives and all sorts of artificial flavor enhancers and color (all those E's). Have you seen in the movies listed above how in some factories, literally, the whole slain animal enters the machine on one end, and a pink mass exits on the other – which then turns into everything manufacturers need and the market is looking for? Ask people who work in such factories what goes into one pâté, for example. Moreover, meat has the longest period of digestion, i.e. breaking down in our bodies. My aha-moment came when I realized that after a good and quality meal, one should feel excellent, refreshed by a new dose of energy (that's why we eat, right?). Instead, we often feel tired, exhausted and drowsy. It's common to eat abundantly (often overeat, especially at lunch) and then experience stomachache and/or feeling of heaviness. We than need to lie down and rest, we don't feel like working anymore, we are sleepy, we need coffee, we don't have concentration, etc. Besides, we have a habit to say to ourselves contentedly that we had a great meal and that we couldn't put another spoon in our mouth. After a meat meal, you will never feel zestful. After all, don't believe me, test it very simply on your own.

Mini challenge

After the next few meals, remember to ask yourself how you feel. Do you have the energy to go running, are you keener to rest, or are you somewhere in between? Do you feel heaviness in your stomach? Analyze yourself for a few days – what you ate and how you felt afterwards.

I also realized that meat, if prepared without spices, was not tasty at all, while fruits and vegetables were. The world consumes a great deal of meat, and instead of meat being a side dish, it is a main dish and everything else is a side dish. Furthermore, there are various diseases that lurk behind the consumption of meat today as it is often of dubious origin, it is constantly being pulled off the shelves, and some meat prices (especially in supermarkets) are so low that one really wonders how it is possible – because it defies all economic and other laws. Now that I cleaned my body, I have heaviness in my stomach all day and I start to yawn the minute I eat some meat. I'm not lying to you, it's true, but people only believe it when they feel it themselves. However, the purpose of this challenge is not to make you stop eating meat, but to enable you to broaden your circle of knowledge and learn something new in order to start answering numerous "why" questions in the context of nutrition and become aware of whether you are in that context in the comfort zone.

My questions led me to the following topic and challenge: raw (vegan) food. At the recommendation of a friend I devoured the book *12 Steps to Raw Foods – How to End Your Dependency on Cooked Food* by Victoria Boutenko. In the book, she describes her journey to a raw diet that saved both her and her husband, as well as their two children, from serious illness. She explains everything in such a simple and straightforward way that not one person who has read the book on my recommendation has regretted it; everyone was fascinated and she got all of them interested to some extent.

Reading one of the books on raw vegan nutrition is the first step, but then you have to start acting. In short, raw food, or more precisely raw vegan food, means that you do not eat anything of animal origin (meat, meat products, milk, cheese, eggs…), so it is a vegan diet with the addition that the staples are not cooked. This means that food should not be exposed to a temperature higher than 105 – 113 F because that way it loses its living, nutritional value, i.e. enzymes are destroyed. People often ask what do you eat then? Lots of things: fruits and vegetables, sprouts, seeds, nuts. At first glance, this all seems very rigorous, but it's not like that at all. People tend to try rawism when they get sick, but I decided to try it while I was healthy because I had nothing to lose and I was curious what the effects would be. I liked that there was no cooking for several hours, everything was done in a few minutes (except for dehydration), there was no greasy dishes (we rarely use a dishwasher because it is easier and faster to just rinse everything immediately). Green smoothie made of fruits and mostly vegetables (in a super blender) is absorbed very quickly, it goes directly into the blood and you feel dashing; the creamy vegetables soup is ready in an instant, just like the various spreads. I make a variety of crackers that are a substitute for bread and a great snack. I dry fruits and vegetables (e.g. apple and kale chips), and I make my own spices. It's a misconception that raw is not tasty; it may seem that way at first glance, because our taste buds have lost their function (i.e. become numb) over time since our food is too sweet, too salty and too spicy. However, after a while, when our bodies and receptors are purified a little, everything is delicious and fine.

After about three weeks of raw diet (during the summer), I felt great. I slept only five hours a day, but I was full of energy, awakened, my mind was brittle. I felt great in my own skin and my body started to shape: my hips were gone. As if the whole body regulated itself bringing it to optimal weight. I had a feeling of some unusual alertness, I was really jumping with joy, I felt like I had double eyes (I could see wider and further – I can hardly explain it in words). Considering that I have always baked delicious and special cakes (all my friends and acquaintances will confirm that), I was especially surprised that in the raw diet, desserts can be made very quickly and be delicious. You will not be able to eat raw cakes in the amount you normally eat because they are full of energy and will satiate you much sooner and differently.

For me, perhaps the best discovery was homemade ice cream, which I guess everyone can and loves to eat: buy ripe bananas, peel them, slice and freeze. And when you feel like eating an ice cream, take the bananas out of the freezer for a minute to soften, place in a blender and mix. Voilà, there is your ice cream. You can add honey, cinnamon, other frozen fruits, almonds – the choice is unlimited. My son already knows how to do this (in fact, he knows a lot about cooking because we include him in everything in the kitchen). The fact that he can have ice cream whenever and as much as he wants makes him very happy (why should I forbid him when it's all just fruit anyway). I also made home-made three-ingredient chocolate. My homemade spread of hazelnuts, cocoa and honey is also a discovery. Generally, almost everything we normally eat can be prepared raw.

It didn't take long before everyone around me noticed that I looked younger, had a lot more energy, laughed more often, that my body transformed, etc. A friend of mine whose son has lactose intolerance convinced me to start organizing raw food workshops, which very quickly became extremely popular. It's one thing when people are told what is good, healthy and delicious; it's completely different when they have the opportunity to try the food and include all the senses. The most common comment I received was: "Oh, this is just like the real one!" I researched and tried new recipes every day, I studied nutrition, and I even dreamed of recipes (literally). All that, combined with my curiosity and scientific mind, led me to a wonderful Mastering Raw Food Nutrition (■ 104) education, run by doctors and spouses Karin and Rick Dina. This program does not deal with recipes, but provides comprehensive knowledge in this specific area of nu-trition, based on scientific research. Karin and Rick really do their best in this yearlong education, with live calls every week and four text-books, together with over 30 years of their personal experience in raw-ism and professional work at various clinics. I warmly recommend you to check out some of the free video content they offer, and those who

QR 104

are more interested, can enroll in their education (be sure to mention who recommended the course to you), because something as comprehensive and backed by experience is hard to find elsewhere.

You don't have to switch to raw diet completely (provided that you want to, it should happen gradually). If you replace only one meal a day with raw food, you have done a lot for your body. Then you just need to listen to your body in order to see what works the best for you (raw food is not an "all or nothing" issue). Raw diet can also serve as a good body cleanser in the short term. For start, it is important to know that such a concept exists. You have to – really have to – watch a movie *The Gerson Miracle* (◼ 105), which I recommend to anyone who resonates with a dietary change. After completing my education, interest for my workshops and consultations grew even more. Over time, I realized that food was the topic from my book that interested people the most, and that it would surely be one of the key companions in my path of happiness. When you help someone to get their type 2 diabetes under control or to get rid of it with small dietary changes, the news spread quickly. Indeed, our bodies are incredibly intelligent machines whose propellant is energy and when we feed them properly, the diseases withdraw. It is not the food that heals us, the body does it itself, but we must provide it with conditions to heal instead of literally poisoning it with the wrong fuel.

QR 105

The experience of working with people in the context of nutrition has shown me that they often aren't ready to make radical changes (remember the comfort zone and how leap into the unknown is often a one-way ticket back to an even deeper comfort zone). That is why after five years I have developed my own dietary concept called 3H Food. It is plant-based, and the staples are mostly uncooked. The aim of the 3H Food concept is to show you that food can and should work for your health, that you don't need hours to prepare healthy and tasty foods and that you don't have to sacrifice and eat tasteless food. The preparation of these meals is quick and easy, and the recipes are equally clear to culinary beginners as well as to experienced cooks. With 3H Food, you will learn more about the foods you consume, about more or less healthy ways to prepare certain food, and you will get to know your body better by making changes and positive steps you are ready for. I have already said that I am not an advocate of extremes, so that is the case in nutrition too. There is something in the sentence my dad always repeats: "Moderation in everything"; just, it is not always easy to find the balance.

3H stands for Happy, Healthy and Hedonic, because I firmly believe that food should be just that: happy, healthy and hedonic. Happy at 3H Food indicates that we should be happy both during the preparation and during the consumption of food, as well as after eating. That is, food can and should help keep our mind, spirit and body happy. Healthy indicates that the food we eat affects the whole body, all organs and our mental state. Food is much more than taste. Hedonic food indicates that we eat not only because of our need for energy and hunger, but also because of our various emotional challenges and imbalances. We want meals that are pleasing to the eye, but above all delicious and satisfying to our taste buds. You can find more about the 3H Food concept, as well as my recipes, tips and educations on my website (◼ 106), and of course on various social networks.

QR 106

Start with raw meals from the simplest; with the help of a regular stick blender you can make delicious fruit and vegetable juice. The juices are the key (whether cold pressed fruit, or green juices from, mostly, vegetables), but you can also eat a variety of salads. In addition, you can make milk, and eat flakes, dried fruits, various crackers, cakes, and much more. When you dig into the story a little, you will become the creator yourself. Fortunately, smoothie preparation has become popular, so in many cities you can buy this healthy meal in a glass, there are more and more places where you can have a variety of fresh juices, etc. Thus, you can start blending fruit and oatmeal with sweetener etc. in any kind of blender. You can also make nut or oat milk (just mix oats and water and then strain it); children usually accept it very well.

Mini challenge

Prepare something raw to drink and try to consume as much fresh fruit and vegetables as possible.

If at one point you decide to go raw to a greater extent, it would be good (though not necessary) to get a premium blender, cold press juicer and dehydrator. My choices are the Vitamix blender, the Hurom juicer and the Excalibour dehydrator. It will cost you a lot, but believe me – these high-end gadgets are worth it. In reality, if you were to throw away your oven, hob and hood (i.e. appliances you bought or probably already have as normal, even though I know people who are on a raw diet and don't have them in their kitchens), you will get to a lot less amount. But we are used to having those appliances in apartments and we buy them as soon as we move in, while blender and dehydrator we consider a luxury.

Considering that in raw diet staples are not cooked, it is very important to be careful with the quality and origin of the food you consume. This can be a challenge because apples, for example, are often sprayed about 20 times (imagine!), but you will research (if you have not already) where organic products can be bought near you. You can shop at one of the local organic markets or through various online stores. It is also important that your food is colorful, that you eat fruits and vegetables of all colors (remember chromotherapy). Some people even get ill on the raw diet because they only eat cabbage all winter long. This is not good for the body, and we need to listen to it and be reasonable.

I advise you to watch following movies too: *Fat, Sick and Nearly Dead* (■ 107), *Simply Raw – Reversing Diabetes in 30 Days* (■ 108). If you need more impetus for change, study the lives of Hunza tribes in Pakistan. They live an average of over a hundred years (some reach 140), not one of them has cancer (you read that right), and their main food is apricot kernels (rich with vitamin B17). Eat what suits you the way it suits you, and if you have any health chal-

QR 107

QR 108

lenges or want to check everything connected to raw diet, go ahead and consume energized foods. However, at least think about everything, get informed, and remember that you are, literally, what you eat.

After repeating that food is energy, that it can (and should) be a cure, we will address water as well – live (spring) water at that, as the name of this challenge indicates. Water is said to be the source/basis of life, an integral part of all living things, and to occupy as much as three quarters of the Earth's surface (or about 70%). Water on Earth is also the only substance naturally found in three states: liquid, gaseous and solid, which enables the water cycles in nature. Data on the amount of drinking water in the world vary in studies, but it seems that there is not much of it, and lately there is more and more talk about potential water shortages and overconsumption. They say that a person can endure much longer without food than without water. Here is one exception that confirms this rule: his name is Victor Truviano, and he is a worldwide phenomenon, the most famous breatharian (a person who willingly lives without food and water, but exclusively on prana – light energy); watch his interview (■ 109). For the rest of us adults who

QR 109

are not so extreme, it is advisable to drink two liters of water (8 glasses) a day (where coffee, tea, soda and juice cannot be a substitute for water). If you are one of the many people who do not drink enough water during the day, you can try one of the various smartphone apps that will remind you to consume water and keep track of your intake. Some say that we should only drink water when we are thirsty; others say that we are already a little dehydrated when we feel thirst; yet others say that when we experience hunger, in 75% of cases we are actually thirsty. ☺ Either way, water is a part of all our organs, it supports physiological and other functions, and the body of an adult contains more than 30 liters of water.

In my opinion, everything you need to know about water, at least initially, and everything you need to tell others around you, especially children – you can find in the movie *Water Has Memory* (■ 110). It deals with the problems of exploitation and manipulation of water, and discusses the unusual properties of this "ordi-

QR 110

nary" fluid. Namely, the film features a famous Japanese scientist, Dr. Masaru Emoto, who has proven that water not only memorizes information, but also respond to different emotions and external stimuli. Water, in other words, is alive, and he proved it by photographing water crystals. He discovered that the most beautiful crystals are made of spring, unpolluted water, but that every other water responds to messages, words or music as well. Water thus creates incredibly regular crystals under the influence of harmonic music. It changes its crystals depending on the words written on a piece of paper and taped to a glass or bottle of water; the most beautiful crystals water creates with the words thank you and I love you (how odd, right; remember that Hawaiian Ho'oponopono technique again), while the ugly words create ugly images. In other words, water feels the vibrations of certain words, which shouldn't be a surprise since everything around us is some form of energy. You can read more about it in Emoto's book *The True Power of Water*.

Mini challenge

Watch the documentary Water Has Memory.

Does this have anything to do with us? It has, big time, because the human body is made of approximately 70% of water. Therefore, if we think positively, and the water can senses it, and if we are the water – then things seem to be connected somehow. I have already mentioned Louise Hay, who is well known to many people in Croatia today because her positive messages are printed on water bottles. Of course, there are always skeptics and those who do not believe in this or that and who refute everything. I can't assert anything with 100% certainty because I don't have the knowledge nor equipment for photographing water crystals. To me it seems both true and possible. On my glass water bottle, I taped a piece of paper with the words "I love you, thank you" on it. If it works, great, if not, I didn't have to buy anything or incur additional costs (just a piece of paper and a little tape). Perhaps my belief that water responds to words is related to the fact that I was baptized with holy water (sanctified through certain words uttered by the priest) in the Catholic Church. Given that most of you very likely also have this sacrament, I suppose you also believe that water is alive, right?

Speaking of water bottles, you saw in the movie how water is exploited to the maximum today and how, paradoxically, water from the tap undergoes much more extensive control than the one that is bottled. The movie called *Tapped* (■ 111) talks about the role of bottled water industry on our health, climate change, pollution and oil dependency. I have not done the analysis, but I can at least advise you to drink as little as possible from plastic packaging and as much as you can from glass bottles (if you cannot or do not want the one from the tap). In particular, avoid leaving water in plastic bottles in warm places (in a car, etc.) because of chemical bisphenol-A (BPA).

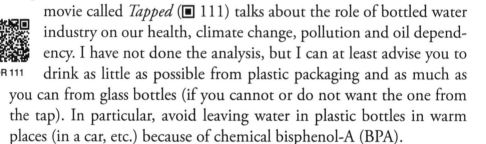
QR 111

Mini challenge

Reduce (or discontinue) the consumption of water (and food as well) from plastic packaging and check the triangular mark with the number in the middle on your plastic packaging (check what it means on ■ 112).

QR 112

Given that solar energy is something you probably all believe in, it would be good to leave the water in the glass bottle exposed to the sun for some time before consuming it. That way you can use the sun as a medicine, produce solar water and cleanse yourself of negative energy. Bioenergists can make living water themselves by dematerializing harmful metals, additives (such as chlorine) and other harmful substances from water. I also use silver water (i.e. colloidal and ionic silver), which I discovered to be a very effective natural antibiotic with wide potential. Besides, I ozone water, and wash all fruits and vegetables in this ozonated water.

If you consume tap water, the market today offers a whole range of devices for water purification and filtration. You should decide for yourself whether you need it or not (sometimes tap water undergoes through more controls than bottled water). Whatever you use, let it really serve you. Besides, you can always, while drinking tap water, think positively and thank the water in order to shape regular crystals (after all, it really costs you nothing but a little mental training). In any case, make sure you drink plenty of water every day, because Iranian medical doctor Fereydoon Batmanghelidj claims that chronic body dehydration is a major cause of many degenerative conditions (such as asthma, allergies, high blood pressure, overweight and certain emotional problems, including depression). He wrote it all down in the book *Your Body's Many Cries for Water*. Instead of expensive drugs, you can try reaching for something much more accessible: water that remembers everything. Furthermore, there are several clinics in the world that provide medically supervised water fasting that help people overcome common ailments such as hypertension, diabetes, autoimmune diseases. In addition, water fasting can help you beat addictions to unhealthy eating habits. However, do not post on water for more than one day without medical supervision.

It is best to start the day with a glass of water as soon as we wake up, as this helps the body to get rid of poisons, improves metabolism, boosts immunity, prevents kidney stones, etc. The body absorbs water as we shower as well; and it is recommended to take hot and cold showers in turn (or you can shower in hot water first, which will calm you down, and then finish with cold water, which will make you more active – I hope you have already done this mini challenge). Water can also help you implement excellent body detox programs. You have probably already heard how important is to make the water alkaline (not acidic) which can be easily achieved by adding lemon (see my website for more ideas). As often as possible, I try to make water with lemon/cucumber and ginger and drink it throughout the day. Whichever of countless options you choose, it is important to drink water slowly (if possible sip by sip), because otherwise it just runs through us. Besides, it should be at room temperature (not nicely cold, perfect for extinguishing the digestive fire). Ultimately, your urine (that is, its color) is the best indicator of your body's hydration (it should be clear and light, not dark). Whether you drink enough water and your body is alkaline or acidic, you can also check using pH indicator strips.

> **Mini challenge**
> *Check the color of your urine and keep your body hydrated.*

At the end of the 12th challenge (and the book), I will briefly address the various nutritional supplements that are very popular nowadays, i.e. the various remedies some people consume excessively (even though nature offers us a cure for everything). I have discovered that, if you eat healthy and diversely, there is no excessive need for supplements (except vitamins B12, D3, and omega-3 fatty acids). It is best to do reliable and detailed laboratory tests (blood and urine) on a regular basis. Consider the transformation of medicine into a market and institutional setting. Aldous Huxley said that medicine is so advanced today that virtually no human is healthy. Think about it, be open-minded and do your best to stay healthy and minimize the need for medication and supplements. Enjoy books, energized food, live water, and all the answers and truths you will come across on your journey of happiness.

⚘ Recommendations to inspire you on your journey of happiness ☺

- [QR 92] Jamie Oliver: Teach Every Child about Food:
        https://www.ted.com/talks/jamie_oliver
- [QR 101] Making Fake Lettuce:
        https://www.youtube.com/watch?v=KluBHFUaK68
- [QR 102] Sun Gazing with Hira Manek:
        https://www.youtube.com/watch?v=D_ERDxxzvQE
- [QR 103] Baby Pig Fresh Pork Sausage Prank:
        https://www.youtube.com/watch?v=TrSL5MlDzNM
- [QR 109] Victor Truviano Interview:
        https://www.youtube.com/watch?v=vWx1r1cMhBI

- [QR 93] Our Daily Bread
    https://www.youtube.com/watch?v=i_VBdCmabVs
- [QR 94] Counting the Cost – The Price of a Fast-Food Life:
    https://www.youtube.com/watch?v=LbHD8nwy-kM
- [QR 95] Food Inc.:
    https://www.youtube.com/watch?v=eHJiNC_7wuw
- [QR 96] The Future of Food:
    https://www.youtube.com/watch?v=M_dninKkRSE
- [QR 97] Earthlings:
    https://www.youtube.com/watch?v=w8B547L5VkQ&has_
    verified=1
- [QR 98] Food Choices:
    https://www.youtube.com/watch?v=wl9S3Wszw0A
- [QR 99] 10 Billion – What's on Your Plate?:
    https://www.youtube.com/watch?v=FQNDQjcHeng
- [QR 100] Seeds:
    https://www.youtube.com/watch?v=xBdeP7sBqQU
- [QR 105] The Gerson Miracle:
    https://www.youtube.com/watch?v=y6l84pQ1Pxk
- [QR 107] Fat, Sick and Nearly Dead:
    https://www.youtube.com/watch?v=8o0pSnp0Xs8
- [QR 108] Simply Raw – Reversing Diabetes in 30 Days:
    https://www.youtube.com/watch?v=2pjkC71exKU
- [QR 110] Water Has Memory:
    https://www.youtube.com/watch?v=FMrQme-DEas
- [QR 111] Tapped:
    https://www.youtube.com/watch?v=dzntuXdE8dY

- [QR 91] Food Revolution, Jamie Oliver:
    https://www.jamieoliver.com/features/food-revolution/
- [QR 104] Mastering Raw Food Nutrition:
    https://rawfoodeducation.com/?page_id=2721
- [QR 106] 3H Food by My Happiness Doctor Anita Freimann:
    https://myhappinessdoctor.com/3h-food/
- [QR 112] Plastics by the Numbers:
    https://learn.eartheasy.com/articles/plastics-by-the-numbers/

- 12 Steps to Raw Foods: How to End Your Dependency on Cooked Food, Victoria Boutenko, 2010.
- Your Body's Many Cries for Water, Fereydoon Batmanghelidj, 2001.
- The True Power of Water – Healing and Discovering Ourselves, Masaru Emoto, 2003.

A MESSAGE
AT THE END
(OF THE BOOK, NOT THE
JOURNEY OF HAPPINESS ☺)

Now you have read all I wanted to tell you about the courage on the path of happiness and the challenges of leaving the comfort zone (abbreviated version, as longer would have 500 pages). The book has more than 100 QR codes, i.e. different sources and opportunities for your growth, so I hope that it will not end up on the shelf. Instead, I hope that you will often read it and search through the recommended content that interests or inspires you at a certain point. There are plenty of sources, you just have to use them. Now take a notebook and write down everything you have highlighted in the book, that is, make notes in order to remember the things you consider most important. With that, you can actually turn each ending into a fresh start. The worst thing you can do is to have all these insights at your disposal and do absolutely nothing (but, you're not one of them, otherwise you wouldn't be reading these last lines now). What you have learned or confirmed in the book, or what you consider important – spread further; share information and/or thoughts with at least one person because this is how we create synergies and a better world together.

> **Mini challenge**
> *After reading the book, once again write down what life, wisdom, happiness, courage, perseverance, love and freedom represent to you, and compare what you wrote earlier. Do your answers differ? In what way and how much?*

Here is how I have finished those sentences:

Life is… the journey on which we live our authentic selves, learn and gain knowledge through the experiences that shape us; opportunity for growth and adventure.

Wisdom is… to suppress the ego, it cannot be bought or borrowed.

Happiness is… to be able to be in the present moment.

Courage is… to relaxedly live the life that I find worth living.

Persistence is… a willingness for unlimited trying and the foundation of success.

Love is… inspiration, joy and peace.

Freedom is… ubiquitous and within us, if we recognize it.

In the end, the point is to create a life outside the comfort zone and grow enough spiritually to be able to easily and with a smile face most of the challenges that life agreeably puts before you, while fulfilling some of your wishes. People around me often tell me how everything I say makes sense, but they can't implement it in their lives because it's not easy and because they have a hundred different BUT's, the most common being they don't have time. Excuses, remember? Just plain excuses. I leave them be, because I have to watch my vibration and give my time to those who deserve it. Besides, everyone is right in their own reality. All of us are right; everyone from their point of view and in their circle of knowledge.

I sincerely wish you plenty of initial courage for walking the path of happiness, which is beyond the comfort zone and where you can witness your personal growth and beauty of life. Remember, even the smallest solved challenge is less of a challenge to solve. Persevere. You can do it. I love you all and I send you peace, love and light.

Your Happiness Doctor

Anita Freimann, PhD

If you think you can do a thing or think you can't do a thing, you're right!
Henry Ford

P.S. Let me know your impressions; I will gladly read them as a feedback motivation.

Lightning Source UK Ltd.
Milton Keynes UK
UKHW020023010720
365831UK00010B/396

9 783347 083639